VICTORIAN WOMEN AND THE ECONOMIES OF TRAVEL, TRANSLATION AND CULTURE, 1830–1870

Both travel and translation involve a type of journey, one with literal and metaphorical dimensions. Judith Johnston brings together these two richly resonant modes of getting from here to there as she explores their impact on culture with respect to the work of Victorian women. Using the metaphor of the published journey, whether it involves actual travel or translation, Johnston focuses particularly on the relationships of various British women with continental Europe. At the same time, she sheds light on the possibility of appropriation and British imperial enhancement that such contact produces. Johnston's book is in part devoted to case studies of women such as Sarah Austin, Mary Busk, Anna Jameson, Charlotte Guest, Jane Sinnett and Mary Howitt who are representative of women travellers, translators and journalists during a period when women became increasingly robust participants in the publishing industry. Whether they wrote about their own travels or translated the foreign language texts of other writers, Johnston shows women establishing themselves as actors in the broad business of culture. In widening our understanding of the ways in which gender and modernity functioned in the early decades of the Victorian age, Johnston's book makes a strong case for a greater appreciation of the contributions nineteenth-century women made to what is termed the knowledge empire.

T0304107

The Nineteenth Century Series
General Editors' Preface

The aim of the series is to reflect, develop and extend the great burgeoning of interest in the nineteenth century that has been an inevitable feature of recent years, as that former epoch has come more sharply into focus as a locus for our understanding not only of the past but of the contours of our modernity. It centres primarily upon major authors and subjects within Romantic and Victorian literature. It also includes studies of other British writers and issues, where these are matters of current debate: for example, biography and autobiography, journalism, periodical literature, travel writing, book production, gender, non-canonical writing. We are dedicated principally to publishing original monographs and symposia; our policy is to embrace a broad scope in chronology, approach and range of concern, and both to recognize and cut innovatively across such parameters as those suggested by the designations 'Romantic' and 'Victorian'. We welcome new ideas and theories, while valuing traditional scholarship. It is hoped that the world which predates yet so forcibly predicts and engages our own will emerge in parts, in the wider sweep, and in the lively streams of disputation and change that are so manifest an aspect of its intellectual, artistic and social landscape.

Vincent Newey
Joanne Shattock
University of Leicester

Victorian Women and the Economies of Travel, Translation and Culture, 1830–1870

JUDITH JOHNSTON

The University of Western Australia and
The University of Sydney, Australia

LONDON AND NEW YORK

First Published 2013 by Ashgate Publisher

Published 2016 by Routledge
2 Park Square, Milton Park, Abingdon, Oxfordshire OX14 4RN
711 Third Avenue, New York, NY 10017, USA

First issued in paperback 2016

Routledge is an imprint of the Taylor & Francis Group, an informa business

British Library Cataloguing in Publication Data
Johnston, Judith, 1947-
   Victorian women and the economies of travel, translation
   and culture, 1830-1870. -- (The nineteenth century)
   1. Women--Great Britain--Intellectual life--19th
   century. 2. Women travelers--History--19th century.
   3. Women translators--Great Britain--History--19th
   century. 4. Women in the book industries and trade--Great
   Britain--History--19th century. 5. Communication in
   learning and scholarship--History--19th century. 6. Great
   Britain--Intellectual life--19th century.
   I. Title II. Series
   001.2'082'09034-dc23

Library of Congress Cataloging-in-Publication Data
Johnston, Judith, 1947-
   Victorian women and the economies of travel, translation and culture, 1830-1870 / by Judith Johnston.
      p. cm. -- (The nineteenth century series)
   Includes bibliographical references and index.
   ISBN 978-1-4094-4823-5 (hardcover) 1. Women travelers-
-Great Britain--History--19th century. 2. Women translators--Great Britain--History--19th century.
3. Women and literature--Great Britain--History--19th century. 4. Women and journalism--Great
Britain--History--19th century. 5. Great Britain--Intellectual life--19th century. I. Title.
   PR756.T72J64 2013
   820.9'355--dc23

2012026159

ISBN 13: 978-1-138-24583-9 (pbk)
ISBN 13: 978-1-4094-4823-5 (hbk)

Contents

This book is dedicated, with all my love, to the Gordon family:
Mereana, Luke, Flynn and Nate.

Preface

This book has been a long time in the making. Generous financial support from a University of Western Australia research grant, in 2004, meant that I could undertake research work in the National Library of Scotland, Edinburgh on the letters of Mary Margaret Busk and Sarah Austin, and two periods of funded study leave, in 2007 and 2011 saw the work finally revised and completed. From 2012 I have been based at my alma mater, the University of Sydney, as an Honorary Associate in the Department of English. I am grateful for the support afforded me in the final stages of production.

Importantly, I want to acknowledge the ongoing support and interest of my friends and colleagues at the University of Western Australia: Kieran Dolin, Tony Hughes-d'Aeth, and Andrew Lynch. Further afield, Professor Srilata Ravi, now at the University of Alberta, listened to my ideas, made suggestions for improvement, and pointed me towards useful critical works that shifted my perspective. My particular gratitude is extended to an anonymous reader from 2009 whose careful and insightful commentary enabled me to revise the entire manuscript in ways that improved it immeasurably. Grateful thanks are due as well for the enthusiastic response of the anonymous reader of the final manuscript. To the members of the Australasian Victorian Studies Association and the British Association for Victorian Studies who listened to various versions of these chapters in their earliest manifestations as conference papers and offered invaluable feedback, please accept my sincere thanks. Bev and Tony Noakes read the first full draft with the care and interest of dear friends. To my colleague Professor Jacqueline Van Gent thanks are due for assistance with translation.

Chapter 5 originally appeared as 'Victorian Appropriations: Lady Charlotte Guest translates *The Mabinogion*' in *Studies in Medievalism. Appropriating the Middle Ages: Scholarship, Politics, Fraud* XI (2001) published by Boydell and Brewer, and Chapter 4 as 'Sarah Austin and the Politics of Translation in the 1830s' in *Victorian Review* 34/1(2008). Both are reprinted here, revised and reworked, by kind permission.

For permission to publish extracts from various manuscript letters I have to thank the Mistress and Fellows, Girton College, Cambridge and the Belloc Estate; Caroline Kelly, University of Nottingham, Manuscripts and Special Collections; Curator Kathryn James, for the Beinecke Rare Book and Manuscript Library; Dr. Gabriele Klunkert, for the Goethe und Schiller Archiv, Weimar, Germany; and David McClay for the Trustees of the National Library of Scotland.

The cover illustration is by John Everett Millais for Part 4 of *Mistress and Maid* by Dinah Mulock Craik which appeared in *Good Words* (London, 1862):

'Soon, … they converged to what was then the nucleus of all railway travelling, the Euston Terminus, and were hustled onto the platform, and jostled helplessly to and fro'.

Image MM005 reproduced by kind permission of J. Thomas, P.T. Killick, A.A. Mandal, and D.J. Skilton, *A Database of Mid-Victorian wood-engraved Illustration* <http://www.dmvi.cf.ac.uk>.

Judith Johnston
March 2012

Introduction

In 1830 the actress, traveller, and later anti-slavery activist, Fanny Kemble, was performing on the Liverpool stage with her family when the first railway line, Manchester to Liverpool, was almost complete and preparations were underway for the grand opening, including trial runs of engines. Kemble was given the opportunity to ride in the cab of the 'Northumbrian' with George Stephenson himself and reported this experience to her close friend Harriet St. Ledger in a letter dated 26 August 1830. Kemble was 21, and recounts her experience in her typically enthusiastic and compelling prose, announcing herself to be 'horribly in love' with Stephenson who she portrays as a cross between a master-magician and a myth-maker. Her excitement is palpable and suggests the degree to which the world is about to change dramatically, as seen through the eyes of a young woman more than willing to embrace modernity and offering, in retrospect, a hymn of praise to the Liverpool merchant investors with 'the adventurous imagination proper to great speculators'. Likening the engine itself to a horse (the analogy is long and sustained, even the coals are 'its oats') she records the actual sensation of the hitherto unknown experience of travelling at speed:

> You can't imagine how strange it seemed to be journeying on thus, without any visible cause of progress other than the magical machine, with its flying white breath and rhythmical, unvarying pace, between these rocky walls, which are already clothed with moss and ferns and grasses; and when I reflected that these great masses of stone had been cut asunder to allow our passage thus far below the surface of the earth, I felt as if no fairy tale was ever half so wonderful as what I saw ... You cannot conceive what that sensation of cutting the air was; the motion is as smooth as possible, too. I could either have read or written ... When I closed my eyes this sensation of flying was quite delightful.[1]

Fanny Kemble notes, almost as an aside, and possibly the first railway traveller ever to do so, that the steady motion of the train permits reading and writing.

Kemble's throwaway remark takes on some significance because it brings into such close proximity the physical journey and the intellectual one. Kemble has translated her thrilling experience to predict with some acuity the way in which modern travel will permit other journeys: journeys of the mind and the imagination. As Georges Van Den Abbeele, in addressing travel as metaphor notes, applying the 'metaphor of travel to thought conjures up the image of an innovative mind that

---

[1]   Frances Anne Kemble, *Records of a Girlhood* (New York, 1879), 278 and 281–3.

explores new ways of looking at things or which opens up new horizons'. Travel, he later adds, is important for Western culture.[2] But Kemble's remark highlights two versions of the intellectual journey. In the one version knowledge is received through reading, in particular via publications produced, as it happens, on steam presses. In the other version knowledges are created, through writing, a process which includes translating. Both offer 'new horizons' to compete with those other new horizons outside the railway carriage window, outside the steamship porthole. Fanny Kemble's train-ride and her translation of that experience highlights for me the degree to which the key terms of this study intersect. I would want to argue that like travel, translation is another form of journey, literally the removal from one place or condition to another. And, like travel, translation has metaphorical as well as literal dimensions. Like travel, translation can produce, in Abbeele's terms, 'new ways of looking at things'.

By focusing on travel and translation and their impact on culture, or transculturation, I want to develop a broader understanding of the way in which gender and modernity functioned in the early decades of the Victorian age to deepen the appreciation of the contribution women made to scholarly and educational advances, the knowledge empire, across the nineteenth century. I am conscious of re-assigning meaning to Mary Louise Pratt's term 'transculturation' here, which was developed to express the meeting of cultures within a 'contact zone' that always assumes a dominant culture and a marginal group, and passages between the two, or 'colonial encounters'.[3] With one notable exception, my contact zone considers the relationships of various British women with continental Europe, through the metaphor of the published journey, be that journey actual travel or translation, and the possibility of appropriation and British imperial enhancement that such contact produces. In much of the British writing encountered here, there is a consistent assumption of dominance, a dominance that is sometimes supported, and sometimes contested in the primary writings in Part II which are the subject of this study.

The concepts *travel* and *translation* have only been brought together in an uneasy nexus in earlier studies.[4] Focusing on the symbiotic relationship between

---

[2]   Georges Van Den Abbeele, *Travel as Metaphor from Montaigne to Rousseau* (Minneapolis, 1992), xiii and xv.

[3]   Mary Louise Pratt, *Imperial Eyes. Travel Writing and Transculturation* (London, 1992), 6–7.

[4]   Earlier studies which have informed my work include, but are not limited to: Ashcroft, Griffiths and Tiffin, *The Empire Writes Back* (1989); Susan Bassnett and André Lefevere (eds), *Translation, History and Culture* (1990); Ali Behdad's *Belated Travelers* (1994); James Clifford's *Routes: Travel and Translation in the late Twentieth Century* (1997); Michael Cronin's *Across the Lines: Travel, Language, Translation* (2000); Roxanne L. Euben's *Journeys to the other Shore. Muslim and Western Travelers in Search of Knowledge* (2006); André Lefevere's *Translation, Rewriting and the Manipulation of Literary Fame* (1992); Sara Mills's *Discourses of Difference. An Analysis of Women's Travel*

the two, and the resulting transculturation, will allow the demonstration of a market economy, the business, of cultural and intellectual exchanges, with an emphasis on those of Britain with Germany in particular, and to a lesser extent with Sweden, France and Italy, and the way in which such exchanges assisted the development of the British nation state, as revealed in a range of literatures and discourses in the period. This nation state consists not only of the four nations which make up the United Kingdom but, as the Centre of the British Empire, also includes the 'legacy of that empire in the United States and the Commonwealth' as David Powell puts it in *Nationhood and Identity.* Powell later adds, 'Not only did the colonies retain the stamp of their early Britishness, but Britain itself was shaped and moulded by the colonial experience'.[5] The focus on Germany in this period comes about because of an increasing interest in German literature and culture from the 1830s on, competing with the hitherto more extensive, but predominantly upper-class, British engagement with French literature and language. Moreover, when it comes to translation, this study, in what might be considered an unusual departure, is far more concerned with the resultant 'rewriting' of a source text, than the issue of faithful equivalence. This issue will be addressed more comprehensively in Chapter I. The concept of 'rewriting' is indebted to André Lefevere's *Translation, Rewriting and the Manipulation of Literary Fame.*

In Chapter 1, 'Travel, Translation and Culture: Unexpected Neighbourhoods', I have engaged with the key terms of this title both historically and as modes of discourse in order to show how the three categories revolve around and penetrate each other to produce interactive dimensions. In using the term 'economies' for the book's title, the designation works in two ways. Firstly, because travel, translation and culture are marketable commodities they reveal wide-ranging fiscal effects at various social levels, from domestic government to national government, from working class to upper class, from the narrow space of home to the broad network called empire. Secondly, because the combination of the three produces marketable goods in the form of the circulation of ideas and information, this becomes in turn the commerce of nations, one with another, through their various intermediaries: traveller and informant, translator and publisher, reviewer and editor, and finally, reader. My assessment of these three economies will be primarily based on women's writing in both books and periodicals, as well as discussions centred on national identity, as categories which are inextricably linked to any investigation

---

Writing and Colonialism (1991); Mary Louise Pratt's *Imperial Eyes. Travel Writing and Transculturation* (1992); Chris Rojek's *Decentering Leisure. Rethinking Leisure Theory* (1995); Chris Rojek and John Urry's *Touring Cultures: Transformations of Travel and Theory* (1997); Edward Said's *Orientalism* (1978) and *Culture and Imperialism* (1993); Sherry Simon's *Gender in Translation. Cultural Identity and the Politics of Transmission* (1996); David Spurr's *The Rhetoric of Empire* (1993) and Lynne Withey's *Grand Tours and Cook's Tours: a History of Leisure Travel 1750–1915* (1997).

[5]   David Powell, *Nationhood and Identity. The British State since 1800* (London, 2002), viii and 16.

which seeks to show how travel, translation and culture come together as a primary product of the Victorian age, linked to those major changes in technology already indicated. I will want to argue too, that the three taken together could be considered to form an organic whole through integration and cross-pollination. By focusing on the decades leading up to the first concerted attempts by women for legal redress with regard to political standing and the establishment of the Langham Place collective, which sought to enable middle-class women to find suitable work and to be fairly remunerated, this study will develop an understanding of the issues with which women of intellect and ability were engaged. The study implies, but does not engage with, how further consideration of these issues will eventually take on new life and form in the later decades leading to the *fin de siècle* and the now-famous New Woman debates of the 1890s.

The vitality of cultural and intellectual exchange is significant in creating 'unexpected neighbourhoods', a phrase that has a broad, even uncanny resonance for my argument. It was used by an anonymous reviewer in the *Quarterly Review* who likened translating practice to 'the effect eloquently attributed by Canning to steam-power – that of "creating unexpected neighbourhoods, and new combinations of social relation"'.[6] Indeed, Mary Howitt in 1843 remarks to her sister that she is 'driving on as by steam with my translation'.[7] The steam-power metaphor brings travel and translation and the resultant culture economy into very close proximity indeed and reinforces Goethe's persuasive description of translation as 'intellectual ... traffic in ideas between peoples'.[8] In thinking about the neighbourhood, my work plays on the proximity of Europe to Great Britain, and the, at times, uneasy acknowledgment of that nearness. Frances Trollope in *Paris and the Parisians in 1835* (1836) summarizes the tension best when she writes of Anglo-French relations:

> The days, thank Heaven! are past when Englishmen believed it patriotic to deny their Gallic neighbours every faculty except those of making a bow and of eating a frog, while they were repaid by all the weighty satire comprised in the two impressive words JOHN BULL. We now know each other better – we have had a long fight, and we shake hands across the water with all the mutual good-will and respect which is generated by a hard struggle, bravely sustained on both sides, and finally terminated by a hearty reconciliation.[9]

---

[6] 'The Improvisatore; or Life in Italy', *Quarterly Review* 75(1844–5): 498; 497–518, a review of Mary Howitt's translation of Hans Christian Andersen's *Improvisatore*. See also Thomas Thomson, 'Henry Bell', *Biographical Dictionary of Eminent Scotsmen* (1870; New York, 1971), I: 119 for a fuller version of Canning's comment.

[7] University of Nottingham Manuscripts and Special Collections, Howitt Collection (ACC 1280), Box 1, Ht/1/1/138/1-2.

[8] Quoted in Antoine Berman, *The Experience of the Foreign. Culture and Translation in Romantic Germany*, trans. S. Heyvaert (Albany, NY, 1992), 55.

[9] Frances Trollope, *Paris and the Parisians in 1835* (2 vols; London, 1836), II: 384–5.

Notably, Trollope's is a positive account, but regardless of this, the product of the unexpected kinship brought about by steam technology is subject to an almost continual adjustment and re-assessment in the development of culture and nationhood in my key timeframe. That development was never the result of a smooth trajectory, rather, as Geoffrey Cubitt puts it, nations are 'always ontologically unstable ... elusive and indeterminate, perpetually open to contest, to elaboration and to imaginative reconstruction'.[10] Nevertheless, travel and translation, through publishing, and its accompanying contestations, elaborations, and imaginative reconstructions, enabled the Victorian age to re-assess its relationships with the Continent, to embrace modernity, and in so doing, changed British society and culture forever.

Despite the dramatic death of William Huskisson MP on the day of the grand opening of the Manchester to Liverpool Railway, despite the protests of Manchester workers who saw machinery as a threat to their livelihoods, despite the expressions of disapprobation regarding upper-class concern for landscape and property, the railway proved to be an unstoppable juggernaut with eager investors ready to forward this wonderful new technology as quickly as possible. The sensation of physical speed which Kemble captures so effectively was replicated in the rapid advance of the railway itself and its impact on the economy of the country and its reputation as a great industrial nation. As Nicholas Faith states so succinctly at the very outset of his *The World the Railways Made*, 'The modern world began with the coming of the railways'.[11]

More importantly, for this project, the advent of the railway is a watershed moment for women, and for women travellers in particular, an excellent reason to choose to make Kemble's experience the starting point for this Introduction. The railway enabled those myriad impecunious middle-class women who had previously lacked the financial resources to travel very far and in safety by coach, to travel independently and in relative safety for the first time. Steamships followed quickly with engineers working on the technology as early as 1835. The noted engineer Isambard Kingdom Brunel's SS *Great Western* left Bristol for New York on 8 April 1838, the first steamship to make the Transatlantic crossing. Brunel was not the only entrepreneurial investor working on steam navigation. Other competitors included the Liverpool-based British and American Steam Navigation Company, and there were already cross-channel ferries plying between Liverpool and Ireland.[12] Mary Shelley, travelling through Germany and Switzerland to Italy called down 'blessings on steam – a traveller's blessing, who loves to roam far and free'.[13] By way of contrast, noted traveller Isabella Bird returning to England

[10] Geoffrey Cubitt, *Imagining Nations* (Manchester, 1998), 3.

[11] Nicholas Faith, *The World the Railways Made* (1990; London, 1994), 1.

[12] Adrian Vaughan, *Isambard Kingdom Brunel. Engineering Knight-Errant* (London, 1991), 95.

[13] Mary Shelley, *Rambles in Germany and Italy in 1840, 1842, and 1843* (1844), repr. in *The Novels and Selected Works of Mary Shelley. Volume 8. Travel Writing,*

from America on board a Cunard steamer in 1854, expresses a more romantic, perhaps even nostalgic, preference for clippers, offering a graphic description of the dirt and noise and the fear of explosion: 'men are always shovelling in coal, or throwing cinders overboard; ... [T]he masts are low and small, and the canvas ... looks as if it had been trailed along Cheapside on a wet day'.[14] The intervening 15 years between the accounts of these two travellers had removed the magic from steam travel and left only the disadvantages of what was clearly, by 1854, a commonplace mode of transport.

The impact of steam technology on travel had similar effects on other industries as well, not least of which was publishing. Steam technology in the early decades of the nineteenth century gave the *Times* newspaper an edge over its competitors in terms of speed and volume,[15] and Frederick Von Raumer, in the translation by Sarah Austin of his book *England in 1835*, reports on the efficacy of the machinery he saw in operation in some detail, suggesting as well the way in which the steam printing-press process contributes to the power of journalism in reaching an ever-expanding readership:

> I went ... to see the steam printing-presses by which the "Penny Magazine", and many other things, is printed. It was a very interesting sight ... Twenty presses, moved by steam, worked with such unwearied rapidity, that a thousand sheets were printed in an hour; *i.e.* in ten hours, by the twenty presses, 200,000 copies ... If we compare the snail's process of transcribing with this communication and communicability of thought, idealism and realism – those reconciled antagonists – seem to have acquired such force as no human being could have imagined ... A steam printing-press like this would strike terror into an army of censors ... Two hundred thousand sheets read by some millions of people may become the source of such infinite blessings, or such infinite calamities to mankind, combining to diffuse really "useful knowledge", would exercise a far more powerful tutelary influence in the state, than the whole body of those negations, censors and censorial boards.[16]

This advanced technology, along with improved schooling, contributed to the spread of literacy, of ideas, with the accompanying political implications. This phenomenon in turn gave women expanded opportunities to participate in an information and entertainment publishing industry which could afford them financial independence. Von Raumer's publication is a case in point; the first

---

ed. Jeanne Moskal (London, 1996), 104.

[14]   Isabella Bird, *The Englishwoman in America* (1856; Köln, 2000), 369.

[15]   E.E. Kellett, 'The Press', *Early Victorian England, 1830–1865*, ed. G.M. Young (2 vols; London, 1934), II: 17.

[16]   Frederick Von Raumer, *England in 1835: Being a Series of Letters written to Friends in Germany, during a Residence in London and Excursions into the Provinces*, trans. Sarah Austin (3 vols; London, 1836), I: 191–2.

two volumes were translated by Sarah Austin who was undertaking such work to supplement the family income.

The astonishing transformation of the publishing industry was one of the more interesting direct outcomes the advent of the railway produced, and as noted was also to be a factor in the development of mass literacy, along with better educative opportunities for artisan and working class people, and increased urbanization (to which the railway was also a contributing factor). Jeffrey Richards, discussing John Ruskin's long campaign against the railways, offers quotations from Ruskin's various publications in which travelling members of the public are taken to task because they never look at the scenery through which they pass but are instead reading French novels, the newspapers, the *Graphic*. As Richards comments, 'a measurable upsurge in the sales of books and periodicals accompanied the almost manic expansion of the railways in the 1850s' adding that 'reading matter was essential'.[17] Bookstalls were established on railway stations, monopolized by W.H. Smith who had acquired most of the concessions by 1863,[18] and publishers were designing books specifically for rail travel. Despite Ruskin's class-bound prognostications, the news was not, in fact, all bad. Richards notes that W.H. Smith monitored the kind of book sold at his stalls and a range of publishers produced solid reading matter designed specifically for train journeys. The *Spectator* in 1851, in a note headed 'Traveller's Library', remarks in parenthesis:

["The Traveller's Library" is a speculation by Messrs. Longman, to provide a new class of reading for a new class of readers, whom the conquests of science over time and space have called into being. "He who runs may read" is the animating purpose of the typographical part of this serial; the size handy, the type handsome and legible, the books brief – the very thing for what they are intended, for "reading while travelling" whether by water or rail.

They have a larger feature than this competition with *Punch*, newspapers, periodicals, "shilling libraries", or whatever else people buy to while away the time as they whisk along. "The Traveller's Library" is not only copyright of works of high class, but often copyright not otherwise procurable except by a large outlay …][19]

The comment on practicalities, print and size and length, precedes the long note on the content, suggesting that the physical dimensions of the book are now of particular importance to the potential consumer. E.E. Kellett, reviewing the development of the press in early Victorian England, in an essay published in 1934, remarks that 'alike in format and in content thousands of books have adapted

---

[17] Jeffrey Richards, 'The Role of the Railways', *Ruskin and Environment. The Storm-Cloud of the Nineteenth Century*, ed. Michael Wheeler (Manchester, 1995), 136–7.

[18] Richards, 137. See also Kellett, II: 42, who dates Smith's monopoly from 1848.

[19] 'The Traveller's Library', *Spectator* 24(28 June 1851), 618.

themselves to the supposed needs of railway travellers. A whole genre, perhaps, has grown up for the short suburban journey, and another to ease the tedium of a long one'.[20] Laurel Brake confirms that publishers 'bought into this [quickening] rhythm ... through creation of their own series of volumes ... organised variously around topics (such as travel, biographies)' and it is noteworthy that she names 'travel' first.[21]

The practice of producing volumes specifically for rail travel did give authors a broader coverage, in producing further reviews of their publications, and in reaching a far wider readership than the traditional two- or three-volume work. For instance, as part of Longman's 'Traveller's Library' speculation, Anna Jameson's three-volume *Winter Studies and Summer Rambles in Canada* (1838) was shortened, reprinted, and given a catchier title, marketed as *Sketches in Canada and Rambles among the Redmen* (1852). The word 'Sketches' in the new title, along with the alliterative *Rambles among the Redmen*, suggests a more ephemeral, lighter tone. The serious, contemplative sections of the original work, signalled by the words 'Winter Studies', Jameson's discussions of Goethe, of German philosophy, and other esoteric material, were all removed. The reviewer for 'Brief Notices' in the *Eclectic Review* observes that her book is 'admirably adapted to "The Traveller's Library", and will be found most amusing and instructive, whether in the railway-carriage or in the more quiet seclusion of home'.[22] This comment reveals with exactitude the nexus of journey, reading and armchair travel.

The publishing industry, with the combination of improved technology and the rapid spread of education and increased readerships to form a new and ever-burgeoning market, therefore saw another boom possibly almost equal to that of the railways themselves. Books on Geography, Travel, History and Biography made up 17.3 per cent of the market in the 1814–1846 period, exceeded only by books on religion (20.3 per cent).[23] The expansion of publishing allowed those same educated women, who were suddenly able to travel more easily and readily than ever before, to find opportunities to become financially independent and even to locate professional careers as writers, translators, journalists, critics, editors: the engineers of culture and cultural exchange. Jane Sinnett, long-time critic and translator, claimed for criticism a very particular office, in 'discovering, by analysis and observation, in what true excellence consists' and in forming public taste.[24] Her successor on the *Westminster Review*, George Eliot, would have readily endorsed such a comment. Naturally enough it was not just women who were economically

---

[20]   Kellett, II: 42, fn2.

[21]   Laurel Brake, *Print in Transition, 1850–1910. Studies in Media and Book History* (Basingstoke, 2001), 11–13.

[22]   'Brief Notices', *Eclectic Review* NS4 (1852): 375.

[23]   Simon Eliot, 'Some Trends in British Book Production 1800–1919', in *Literature in the Marketplace. Nineteenth-Century British Publishing & Reading Practices*, ed. John O. Jordan and Robert L. Patten (Cambridge, 1995), 37.

[24]   Jane Sinnett, 'Schiller', *Dublin Review* 11(1841): 503; 477–505.

advantaged by these technological changes, but it is their engagement with them in the earliest decades of Victoria's reign, and what emerges from that engagement in terms of culture, as a marketable commodity, a business in which women engaged, that my work explores. It is these economies of travel, translation and culture, as they imbricate on each other, and their intersections with social and political ideologies, that make this precise period such a profitable one to explore.

Politically the British world was changing as well. It seems almost an inevitable given, that the opening of the railway should come just two years before the first Reform Bill of 1832. The coincidence produces a timeline to modernity which George Eliot uses to magnificent effect in her retrospective novel *Middlemarch* (1871–2) to signal the various ways in which the politically and socially re-forming world of her protagonists, who are representative middle-class figures, is changing, almost a period of metamorphosis, in which the certitudes and attitudes of the time come under a scrutiny that is intense and far-reaching. Part of that intense scrutiny can be located in the travelogues and translations of the period itself, as well as their related reviews and essays, which are the subjects of my critique.

Metaphorically, reform, especially political reform, is another and major journey which creates its own poetic, in particular with regard to nationhood and national identity. It is therefore not surprising to see the anonymous author of 'French Libels on the English' critiquing the American envoy Richard Rush's *Narrative of a Residence at the Court of London* (1833) by suggesting that Rush 'was, at last, reluctantly convinced that Great Britain has no parallel – that she stands alone a colossal miracle among nations, an inexplicable wonder even to those most conversant with her history'. There is extraordinary confidence in this partisan statement, with its epic, even Homeric, propensities, and it is made because the author is opposing two travellers' views of Britain in the review, that of Rush, and another by the Frenchman Charles Lemercher de Longpré, Baron d'Haussez, titled *Great Britain in 1833* (1833). Our reviewer complains of the latter, in comparison to Rush, that 'continental authors, and especially those of France, so often fail when they attempt to describe Great Britain', and this extraordinary failure comes about despite the author's ingenuous claim that Britain 'invites the scrutinising inquiry of all'.[25] In the following chapters reference will be made to other publications by continental authors on their investigative journeys into Britain, and in particular the degree to which these, both in translation and in review, are deeply politicized, not necessarily only by the authors themselves, but also by the translators and reviewers.

Travel, translation and culture can provoke, promote, or contest a range of ideologies as they surface in the nineteenth-century writing critiqued here. Theoretical approaches to them do offer a broad spectrum: critique can be undertaken through gender, through discourse, through transculturation,

[25] 'French Libels on the English', *New Monthly Magazine* 39(1833): 402 and 403; 401–10.

representation, performance, imperialism, marginality, landscape, theories of place, the list could go on, including metaphoric interpretations. In other words, there is no one all-embracing theory which might be applied to these categories per se, rather scholarly exploration of the concepts is polyvalent – indeed has as many byways as the journey itself. The polyvalent approach lends such studies a richly intense discursiveness. Naturally enough, because the focus is on women writers, gender and gendered discourse will be foregrounded, as will concepts like 'Englishness', the mapping of place, ideologies of class and race, dislocation, and its opposite, theories of home and the everyday. Discussion will be based on a range of primary material, published travels, as well as essays and reviews taken from a variety of periodicals publishing in the 1830–1870 period, supported by engagement with relevant modern literary criticisms and explorations centred on my three key categories. In Part II of this work, the individual women with whom I engage offer journeys, sometimes as travellers, sometimes as translators, metaphoric or actual, which will demonstrate the variations my argument permits. Nevertheless, they provide only a small representative sample of a far broader group whose separate endeavours would add exponentially to this work. Obvious omissions are those canonical women writers George Eliot and Harriet Martineau, both of whom embarked on philosophical journeys via translation, Eliot with her translations of David Friedrich Strauss's *Das Leben Jesu* [*The Life of Jesus, Critically Examined*] published in 1846 and Ludwig Feuerbach's *Das Wesen des Christenthums* [*The Essence of Christianity*] published in 1854; and Martineau with her influential condensed translation of Auguste Comte's *Philosophie Positive* in 1852–3. This topic proved too large to be undertaken here, not least because of the intellectual and cultural impacts of their work across subsequent decades.[26] While less well-known today, the women whose work has been the focus of this study contributed in interesting and varied ways to the development of British intellectual life and cross-cultural understanding: they produced for their readers 'unexpected neighbourhoods' promulgated both through their original publications as well as subsequent reviews.

In Chapter 2, 'Sarah Austin and the Politics of Translation', Austin's response to Prince Pückler-Muskau's threat to replace her because she censored his *Briefe eines Verstorbenen* [literally, *Letters from a Deadman* but translated more sedately as *Tour in England, Ireland, and France, in the years 1828 and 1829* (1832)] demonstrates the extent to which her translation was aimed deliberately at a designated or target readership:

---

[26]   The most recent, comprehensive study of Eliot and Martineau and their translations of Continental philosophy, can be found in *Translation, Authorship and the Victorian Professional Woman* by Lesa Scholl (2011).

I have been a guardian angel to your book, and you abuse me ... I shall be trop charmée to be rid of you and to see you delivered over, with the aid of your *faithful translator*, to all the rage, scorn and vituperation of the whole press of England.[27]

In this chapter I explore the possibility that Sarah Austin's 'unfaithfulness' to Pückler-Muskau's text, cleaning it up to conform with the moral and domestic ideology of 1830s England, is not the only way to engage with her work. Rather, this is a case of cross-cultural exchange appearing at a very precise moment in English cultural formation, a moment when reform was in the air, and Austin was vehemently pro-Reform. Her Whig politics, coupled to the new and burgeoning sense of Englishness which was taking hold, inevitably affected the register she would choose in her translating practice and the attention she would pay to the German Prince's comments on both English national identity and national politics. Austin's translation of Fredrick von Raumer's *England in 1835* (1836) will also be considered briefly because of its bearing on the subsequent discussion in Chapter 3.

Mary Margaret Busk, writer, translator and traveller, is the subject of Chapter 3, 'Mary Busk and the Business of Culture'. Rather than merely appropriating European culture for English consumption, Busk qualified the ideas from the continent that her work imported into England, to affirm England's superior standing in the world. This chapter explores her early journey and the way in which she shaped her periodical contributions discursively to the business of cultural exchange. Busk was proficient in German, French, Spanish and Italian and was indeed a prolific contributor to periodicals of the 1830s. Busk gave her readers the opportunity to experience the foreign, even if that experience was nevertheless predicated upon her very strong sense of a superior Englishness at a moment when the British Empire was at its most powerful. Busk's Tory politics will create an interesting contrast to the foregoing chapter in which Austin's Whig politics predominate. Busk produced a number of full-length review articles for both *Blackwood's* and the *Foreign Quarterly* (although not necessarily of the lengthy, substantial kind which appeared in the major review quarterlies) and it is on these that I will focus, concentrating both on the 1832–1838 period, and on her discussions of continental literatures that interconnect France or Germany, with England. In other words, my analyses will allow investigation of the complex and dynamic processes that occur when travel and translation intersect with the business of cross-cultural exchange.

Chapter 4 is titled 'Anna Jameson's Sentimental Journey Elsewhere'. In the winter of 1836–7 the writer and critic Anna Jameson, found herself in Toronto, Canada where she had travelled to reunite with her uncongenial husband, a reunion based on the practical needs of both: his to demonstrate, for the purposes of promotion, a functional marriage; hers to obtain a formal separation and some

---

[27] Quoted in Lotte and Joseph Hamburger, *Contemplating Adultery. The Secret Life of a Victorian Woman* (New York, 1991), 104–105.

financial maintenance. She expresses her feelings of desolation and loneliness in her published travels, *Winter Studies and Summer Rambles in Canada* (1838) abandoning the generally bold, brisk tone of the British lady traveller in the first part of the narrative at least.

In this chapter I argue that while her references in her travelogue to 'home' are often to England, it is not to this 'home' that Jameson journeys constantly in her mind during the long Canadian winter, of which the first third of *Winter Studies and Summer Rambles in Canada* is comprised. 'Home' is somewhere altogether elsewhere and unexpected, not Canada, not England, but Germany. John Leonard writes of 'the exasperations and romance of Elsewhere' and captures Jameson's situation nicely with these precise terms.[28] Elsewhere, which is Germany, is not unproblematic for Jameson but nevertheless is the site of a deeply-seated romance with that country on a number of grounds. First, her feelings for Ottilie von Goethe, daughter-in-law of Germany's supreme man of letters, as expressed in a letter dated 30 November 1833: 'Leaving Germany was leaving *you*, you, round whom some of the deepest feelings of which my nature is capable, had imperceptibly twined themselves'.[29] Second is her cordial reception and ready *entrée* into the highest literary circles in Germany. Third, is her sense of independence, generated by the ease with which travelling in Germany could be accomplished.

The exasperations consist in her struggles to learn the language, and to make herself *au fait* with the writings of the most noted of the German literary intelligentsia, and the demands and recriminations generated by Ottilie von Goethe who, as Needler perhaps unkindly puts it, inflicted 'the recurrent whims of her naïvely emotional temperament' on the long-suffering Jameson (Needler, vii). Nevertheless Anna Jameson's sentimental journey to Elsewhere extends the travel writing genre to accord with Rita Monticelli's description that it is constructed 'through a process of translations and inter-textual movements'.[30] To this end Jameson demonstrates the significance of British awareness of European literatures and philosophies in a colonial setting and the impact of that transatlanticization on publishing in the British State.

Charlotte Guest's medieval Welsh translations offer a very different perspective to the previous chapters and this work is the notable exception I remarked on page 2, a contact zone outside European culture, and moreover one that addresses the metropolis and the periphery in distinctly colonial terms. Chapter 5, 'Charlotte Guest, Wales, and Cultural Appropriation' addresses a hitherto unexplored aspect

[28]   John Leonard, *Lonesome Rangers. Homeless Minds, Promised Lands, Fugitive Cultures* (New York, 2002), xv.

[29]   Anna Jameson, *Letters of Anna Jameson to Ottilie von Goethe*, ed. G.H. Needler (London, 1939), 17. All subsequent references are to this edition and will use the abbreviation 'Needler'.

[30]   Rita Monticelli, 'In Praise of Art and Literature. Intertextuality, Translations and Migrations of Knowledge in Anna Jameson's Travel Writings', *Prose Studies. History, Theory, Criticism* 27/3(2005): 300; 299–312.

of colonialism that is very close to home indeed. Translation into English in the Victorian age as part of an imperialist enterprise takes on various shapes because translation gives access not only to prevailing ideas and philosophies, but also to myths, tales, legends and songs; another form of cultural colonization. Such appropriations enable the breaking down of resistance by locking the colonized into a particular mode: quaint, noble savage, child-like. The colonized culture is brought to a standstill, held by the printed English in a time-frame from which it never escapes. This chapter explores a colonial enterprise very close to home: the translation of medieval Welsh into English. Women had a particular part to play in colonization via translation: the female translator is like the female colonist, she participates almost as an equal partner in the undertaking. Translation might be likened to colonial botanizing, the practice of naming and transcribing enables acquisition. Therefore, Charlotte Guest's translation of the Welsh *Mabinogion*, for instance, a title which she bestowed due to a mis-translation of 'mabinogi', is part of an imperialist project, an enterprise celebrated in contemporary reviews for its patriotism but simultaneously denigrated as a literature 'which has found such grace in ladies' eyes'.[31] Guest's project was undertaken just as the concept of a united kingdom [a nation state] was becoming more fully developed. In revising this work I would want to argue that Wales, despite being 'more fully assimilated into the British state' as David Powell claims, nevertheless was perceived as having a 'semi-colonial status' to use Powell's words regarding Ireland.[32]

The focus of Chapter 6, 'Jane Sinnett and the German Traveller' explores how English translator, Jane Sinnett, seems eager to offer the reading public alternative perspectives from those of British travellers, with an emphasis on mainly German travel books. She notes in her 'Translator's Preface' to Eváriste Huc's *The Chinese Empire* (1855): 'In matters of opinion it cannot be expected that the views of the author should always agree with those of English Protestants; he has of course looked at things with his own eyes, and not with ours'.[33] Impartiality emerges as the key characteristic which recommends a particular author to Sinnett, thereby offering the British reading public travel literature which promises a different point of view, a re-orientation of the, by then, standard British response to exotic travel destinations and colonial outposts.

Ida Pfeiffer, author of *A Lady's Voyage round the World*, was the only woman traveller whose work Sinnett ever translated and she celebrates her subject not as an emancipated woman, but in more unsettling vein as a woman free of 'indolence, and vanity, and fear'.[34] Sinnett was the first to translate Pfeiffer's world journey,

---

[31]   'Notices', *Monthly Review* 153(1840): 610.

[32]   Powell, 6.

[33]   Jane Sinnett, 'Translator's Preface', *The Chinese Empire: Forming a Sequel to the Work Entitled 'Recollections of a Journey through Tartary and Thibet'* by Eváriste Huc, trans. Jane Sinnett (London, 1855), vii.

[34]   Jane Sinnett, 'Translator's Preface', *A Lady's Voyage round the World; a Selected*

but other editions quickly followed from other unnamed translators. Plain and middle-aged, Ida Pfeiffer's matter-of-fact approach to the hazards and dangers of her undertaking, her calm acceptance of whatever might befall her, expressed with what Sinnett terms 'housewifely sobriety' made this particular translation project an attractive one (iv). One instance of Pfeiffer's sobriety is the issue of water wells while travelling through India:

> Pleasant as it is, on many accounts, to meet with these wells, it is, however, very disagreeable to see the men going down into the water, washing themselves, and pouring it over them, and to consider that this is the water one has to drink. But the necessities of thirst "have no law", and so I went and filled my pitcher with the rest.[35]

Ida Pfeiffer travelled through British colonies, and the territories of other nations with whom the British were in dispute, offering, I argue, her impressions in a straightforward prose unconstrained by Victorian gender ideology and untrammelled by the national pride which restrained her British counterparts. As Sinnett writes of Pfeiffer's *Voyage* in her 'Translator's Preface':

> Its chief attraction will most likely be found in the personal narrative, and in the singular character of the authoress; who, though apparently far removed by circumstances from the romantic or adventurous, yet passes through the most surprising scenes, and encounters the most imminent perils, with a calm and unconscious heroism that can hardly fail to command admiration (iii).

The final case-study, Chapter 7, 'Emancipatory Politics: Mary Howitt translates Fredrika Bremer' demonstrates how travel and translation, both separately, and when combined, produce different frames of reference through which alien cultures can be interpreted or perhaps distorted, impacting in particular on long-held ideologies of gender and race. The Swedish author Fredrika Bremer travelled to England and then on to the United States and Cuba in the summer of 1849. Her private letters to her sister describing her American journey were first published in English as *Homes of the New World* (1853) (translated from manuscripts of the letters themselves by Mary Howitt) for the British and American markets, before being published in Swedish as *Hemmen i den nya Verlden* (1853) for her Swedish readership. English, and England, however, is Bremer's lingua franca, the medium through which she obtains information, and the medium through which her journey is first presented to a reading public.

Translation from the German of Ida Pfeiffer (London, 1852), iii–iv. All subsequent references to this preface are to this edition.

[35] Ida Pfeiffer, *A Lady's Voyage Round the World: a Selected Translation from the German of Ida Pfeiffer*, trans. Jane Sinnett (1851; London, 1988), 141. All subsequent references are to this edition unless otherwise stated.

Bremer anticipated the journey as a translation of her female and of her European self. She desired to travel, she said, 'in order that the new human being in me, in thoughts, in will, may develop its wings more freely, come to a consciousness which it cannot win under the old conditions at home'.[36] Ironically however, this quest for freedom from Old Europe's gender ideology comes into diametric collision with the key political debate of the day in the United States: slavery. The issue of race continually complicates Bremer's quest for a new and freer self. While generally slavery had, in Europe, become an uncomplicated metaphor for the condition of women, for Bremer her American experience translates into an empowering sojourn: slavery becomes a pervasive actuality in the confrontation with which she perversely discovers release from her own fettered condition.

Bremer undertook a range of other journeys, producing the staidly conservative counter narrative to *Homes of the New World*, a work originally titled *Life in the Old World; or, Two Years in Switzerland and Italy* first published in Philadelpha in 1860, in which the focus is on religion, but also more importantly *Travels in the Holy Land* (1862) and *Greece and the Greeks. The Narrative of a Winter Residence and Summer Travel in Greece and its Islands* (1863) both of which contain considerable reflection on the bid for political freedom in Italy and Greece. Mary Howitt had translated Bremer's novels from the 1840s and would, for the most part, render all of her travel narratives into English.

---

[36] Signe Alice Rooth, *Seeress of the Northland. Fredrika Bremer's American Journey 1849–1851* (Philadelphia, 1955), 5–6.

PART I:
Historical and Theoretical Background

Chapter 1
Travel, Translation and Culture: Unexpected Neighbourhoods

The term 'journey' seems deceptively simple but it contains a plurality of meaning. It is rich in nuances: metaphorical implications, imaginative possibilities, romance, knowledge acquisition, and redolent with anticipation. As a term, the journey is linked semantically to 'journal' and 'journalism'. This book is about a range of journeys undertaken that are always implied in the key terms of my title: travel, translation and culture. The outcome of such journeys, as noted in the 'Introduction', is that traveller, translator and reader find themselves arriving in 'unexpected neighbourhoods'. Canning suggested that steam power would create 'unexpected neighbourhoods and new combinations of social relation'. However, while the reviewer who quoted Canning's words applied this statement to the function of translation alone, I want to extend its impact yet again by applying it across my three key terms. Physical and intellectual journeys take the traveller, the translator, and the reader who journeys through the pages of a book into new regions that broaden perspective and understanding and contribute to knowledge. Travellers read the topography they traverse and inscribe their readings into travel books. Translators provide maps that offer pathways to new ideas, philosophies, and ways of seeing. Readers take up those books and become companions on the various journeys undertaken.

Indeed readers are often specifically invited by authors to accompany them. Emily Lowe assumes, in *Unprotected Females in Norway* (1857) that her readers may be prepared 'to follow us bodily, sharing our hardships and our pleasures' but acknowledges that others will 'merely follow us in imagination, and from a comfortable fireside chair'.[1] In a most unusual journey, *Investigation; or, Travels in the Boudoir*, Caroline Halsted directs her young heroine Agnes, and by implication her readers, to undertake a foreign tour within the confines of her own bedroom by investigating the goods with which it is furnished, noting in the 'Preface' 'that a mere transient survey of the most attractive scenes, will leave little useful impression on minds not previously prepared to comprehend the nature of the things beheld'. The work's didactic thrust is discovered in her assertion that new discoveries in art and science will 'produce, at the end of a few years, a fresh mass of information important in itself, and desirable to be gained

---

[1] Emily Lowe, *Unprotected Females in Norway; or, the Pleasantest Way of Travelling there, passing through Denmark and Sweden* (London, 1857), 2.

by the young, as enabling them to keep pace with the times in which they live'.[2] Fredrika Bremer, whose translated travels to America are the subject of the last of the case studies in Part II, lost both mother and sister between journeys, relatives who were the recipients of the letters which became her travel book, *The Homes of the New World* (1853). In the Preface to *Two Years in Switzerland and Italy* (1861) titled 'To My Reader', Bremer asks, plaintively, 'To whom should I now write? ... My first inquiring glance found – empty space; but my second showed me thee, my R.' Her reader is thus invited into a very close relationship with the author, taking on the role of relative and confidante. Bremer delivers an encomium praising this reader as kind and encouraging, as the source of her inspiration 'to write and to learn, and to travel'. She warns that the journey will be long and labels her chapters 'Stations', 'to indicate certain divisions of our travelling-life. I say *our* – because, are we not all of us travelling through life?'.[3]

Knowledge acquisition, and education more generally, is always a motivating force in the publishing work of women. Modern languages often formed a part of a young woman's education. Skill in one or more (generally European) languages could, I suggest, be included with piano playing and painting, as a middle-class girl's 'cultural capital', as Margaret Beetham puts it.[4] It is at this point culturally that translation necessarily becomes a vital factor. Some women, to gain a footing in the publishing industry, translated the journeys of Europeans, particularly those who travelled through Britain and subsequently published their impressions. Their translation activities put these women at the forefront of this very modern business of cultural exchange. Beetham has noted of women defining themselves as readers that this produces a 'different kind of economy than the market, namely the circulation of meanings, ideas and identities'.[5] In the mandarin quarterlies, the *Quarterly* and the *Edinburgh Review*, as well as any number of monthly journals in the 1830–1870 period, review essays based on published travel narratives, both journeys by British travellers and explorers, and the translated travels of Europeans, predominate. Thus women became increasingly participant in what might be considered a forefront publishing industry during these years. They wrote about their own travels or they translated the foreign language texts of other writers, texts that also often included travel books, activity suggestive of their participatory roles in the broad business of culture. Sherry Simon makes the point too, in *Gender and Translation. Cultural Identity and the Politics of Transmission*, that for women, translating provided an opportunity to discover a public voice and

---

[2]   Caroline Halsted, *Investigation; or, Travels in the Boudoir* (London, 1846), ix and ix–x.

[3]   Fredrika Bremer, *Two Years in Switzerland and Italy*, trans. Mary Howitt (2 vols; London, 1861), vi and viii. Also titled *Life in the Old World; or, Two Years in Switzerland and Italy*.

[4]   Margaret Beetham, 'Women and the Consumption of Print', in *Women and Literature in Britain, 1800–1900*, ed. Joanne Shattock (Cambridge, 2001), 70.

[5]   Beetham, 63.

enabled them to express certain political positions in democratic terms.[6] This is particularly so of the women whose work is the focus of the case studies in Part II.

Simon uses the phrase 'literary exchange' to describe the impact of translation as connected to a sense of nation and national democratic life. Charlotte Guest's translation of the medieval Welsh 'Mabinogion', discussed in Chapter 5, is an interesting example of the way in which 'exchange' can be overturned as 'appropriation'. My work, however, considers the probability that *exchange* may not be the only outcome. While the subsequent chapters in Part II will explore the possible interchanges which travel and translation brings about, nevertheless, I also want to consider the extent to which translation might prove to be not limited to reciprocity but rather, more likely to produce intellectual impacts through forms of appropriation in which the source language and author disappears altogether, and meanings and ideas become authorized as integral to the target culture's own sense of identity and nationhood, as Venuti argues.[7] When the translator is a woman, gendered dismissal probably aids such invisibility. Margaret Oliphant said of Sarah Austin that she 'did not pretend to be an original woman, notwithstanding some able articles in the *Edinburgh Review*, chiefly on foreign subjects, but she was a translator of singular ability and success'.[8] Oliphant implies that the practice of translation precludes a woman from producing original work while at the same time she endorses what she interprets as Austin's proper feminine choices to act as handmaiden to the original writings of others because to do so accords with the gender ideology Oliphant herself was so careful to support, even if she did not practise it.

James Duncan and Derek Gregory suggest there 'is a sense in which all travel writing, as a process of inscription and appropriation, spins webs of colonizing power'.[9] I would want to extend this to include the translation of travel writing as a part of that process. While conscious that this is a concept around which there has been considerable debate, ideas nevertheless warrant interrogation and the best way to undertake this is to think laterally, against the grain even, and as flexibly as the very semantics of the terms *travel* and *translation* may allow. The *Shorter OED* offers among other meanings for the word *travel*, that it is 'to journey, through (a country, a district, or a space); to traverse (a road); to follow (a course or path);

6 Sherry Simon, *Gender in Translation. Cultural Identity and the Politics of Transmission* (London, 1996), 2.

7 Lawrence Venuti, 'Translation as cultural politics: regimes of domestication in English', *Textual Practice* 7/2(1993): 212–13; 208–23. See also *The Translator's Invisibility. A History of Translation* (1995; London, 2008), 64–5. Chapters 2 and 3, while based on this earlier work, have been revised and expanded without abandoning the original premise.

8 Quoted in Carol T. Christ, '"The Hero as Man of Letters": Masculinity and Victorian Nonfiction Prose', in *Victorian Sages & Cultural Discourse. Renegotiating Gender and Power*, ed. Thaïs Morgan (London, 1990), 25.

9 James Duncan and Derek Gregory (eds), 'Introduction', *Writes of Passage. Reading Travel Writing* (London, 1999), 3.

or to be transmitted'. For the word *translation*, the dictionary offers the following meanings: 'the process of turning from one language into another, and its product; a version in a different language; the rendering of something in another medium or form; transference; or transformation, alteration, change or renovation'. All of these meanings infer some kind of encounter, and when travel and translation are brought together, we can locate what Michael Cronin has termed 'the translation encounter'. As he rightly argues, any range of synonyms (like those I have listed above) is not intended to trivialize translation practices but to highlight the way in which the mediation which translation generates should not be restrictive but open to a range of enquiries, demonstrating translation's 'interpretive reach and relevance'.[10] The traveller encounters the strange and the new which is interpreted according to his or her own cultural register, only to have that transformation undergo a further 'translation encounter' in being rendered into another language and culture altogether, so that the original journey is retraced through language.

J. Hillis Miller claims that any words 'in any language ... may be translated ... to a different context and be appropriated there for new uses'.[11] While his is a discussion about the travelling of literary theory across borders which makes a particular case for literary studies and theory, I am thinking of the even more permeable borders I am claiming for travel and translation. With regard then to such 'new uses', it is necessary to ask if the appropriation of ideas and cultural material via translation and travel writing in particular, might not resemble a form of colonization with similar economic and cultural impacts? Although on the surface both recorded and translated travelogues can seem non-violent and non-aggressive (as opposed to acts of invasion associated with colonialism) they may only seem so because the narrative style permits the translator and the woman travel writer to disappear almost completely from sight through the adoption of an objective, reporting voice where both traveller and translator speak always from a liminal position. Certainly non-violence accords with the gender ideology of the period regarding women's role in society. Nevertheless, the resultant transformations have been wrested from source cultures and are, therefore, put to 'new uses'. Venuti remarks on the violence caused by translation as 'partly inevitable', as part of the process, but also as 'partly potential' in the production and reception.[12] With these issues in mind I want to address the social, cultural and intellectual impacts of such productions on their targeted anglolexic British readerships as evidenced

---

[10]   Michael Cronin, *Across the Lines. Travel, Language, Translation* (Cork, 2000), 17–18.

[11]   J. Hillis Miller, 'Border Crossings, Translating Theory: Ruth', in *The Translatability of Cultures. Figurations of the Space Between,* ed. Sanford Budick and Wolfgang Iser (Standford, Ca, 1996), 208.

[12]   Venuti 'Translation as cultural politics', 209, or *The Translator's Invisibility,* 15.

in British reviews of publications and in personal commentary on the part of the travellers and translators who are the subjects of Part II.[13]

The anglolexic Briton is connected to a further strand in my work to which the advent of the railway also contributed: national pride and identity, sometimes referred to as 'Englishness', but intersected always by ideologies of class, gender and race. As the railway tracks connected towns, cities, and countries, and as people availed themselves of this new, cheaper form of transport to travel, so the need for improved communication and understanding also developed. While it is amusing today to read some of the advice offered in Murray's Redbooks, the advice highlights the degree to which misunderstandings occurred and the reason why Murray advised the traveller to 'learn something about the language and customs of the country'.[14] The sixteenth edition of the *Handbook for Travellers in Switzerland* warns that:

> The passport should be carried on the person, as it will be wanted, if at all, at some unexpected moment. Travellers should not resent too impetuously any want of manners on the part of subordinate officials, with whom they may come into contact. The offer of a cigar will often have more effect than the most spirited remonstrance in bringing to a speedy close a difficulty arising from misapprehension of their character.[15]

The necessarily increased interactions between Britain and the Continent tended to reinforce, in high relief as it were, Britain's often fraught relationships with France, Germany, and Italy in particular. And at the same time the need for translation became ever more insistent. Mona Wilson celebrates the historical fact of the railway and its impact on travel but also observes that the boom 'was a great labour-absorber', and in an enthusiastic aside notes that the 'navvy became a national type: ... his working powers were an object of admiration to foreigners and of pride to English travellers'.[16] This statement helps to highlight that sense of English superiority as a source of developing and ongoing tension, which exists even now, between the United Kingdom and Europe. Back in 1843, however, William Makepeace Thackeray addressed perhaps the most historically virulent of those tensions, that between Britain and France, in 'French Romancers on

---

[13]   The term 'anglolexic' I first noted in J.L. Nelson's review of Geary's *The Myth of Nations*, *London Review of Books* 25/11(2003): 23, and means an audience which is English-speaking with limited knowledge of other languages. I have to thank Prof. Anne Pauwels for this explanation.

[14]   Lynne Withey, *Grand Tours and Cook's Tours* (New York, 1997), 71.

[15]   *Handbook for Travellers in Switzerland*, 16th edn (1837; London, 1879), xii–xiii. Notably this advice is clearly aimed at male travellers and fails to acknowledge women travelling alone.

[16]   Mona Wilson, 'Travel and Holidays', *Early Victorian England, 1830–1865*, ed. G.M. Young (2 vols; London, 1934), II: 295.

England', a review of Frédéric Soulié's *Le Bananier* [*The Banana Tree*] which, Thackeray asserts, has been 'manufactured' less for literary and more for political purposes 'to show the beauties of slavery in the French colonies, and the infernal intrigues of the English there'.[17] The novel is set in Guadeloupe. Thackeray, who adopts an urbanely rational tone, translates judiciously from Soulié's novel to show that in French eyes, the English are 'kings of commerce', of 'the coal-mine' and the 'rail-road', while the French are 'kings of the fine arts, of literature, of every thing which elevates the soul' (230). He points to various solecisms on Soulié's part including an assertion that the French don't need to know English to appreciate English literature. Throughout the review Thackeray reminds his readers of Bonaparte's famous jibe that England is a nation of shopkeepers, but is prescient when we see where these many reminders lead, to the idea that 'coarse commerce' (246) will break down patriotic and nationalistic borders – as if he already had the European Common Market in sight. This happy outcome will be achieved by a 'gross merchant despotism' which 'spreads daily ... foot by foot, all over Europe' (245). He refers of course to the railway:

> It has been carried over to France by Englishmen. It has crept from Rouen to the gates of Paris; from Rouen it is striding towards the sea at Southampton; from Paris it is rushing to the Belgian frontier and the channel. It is an English present. *Timete Danaos*: there is danger in the gift. (246)

Thackeray jokes that the railway is a gift from England to the Continent but warns, with his Latin tag, that it will prove a form of Trojan horse. The danger lies in the abandonment of animosity between individual nations. The railroad will remove frontiers, and Thackeray is not referring solely to physical borders, but to those other barriers to understanding, 'ancient usages, interests, prejudices' (246) all of which he predicts will change and disappear. The French will then see 'that the ironmonger is not thinking about humiliating France, but only of the best means of selling his kettles and fenders' (246) and reassures them that with such close proximity the English will 'for ever be absorbed in the flood of French Civilization' (246).

I noted numbers of essays and reviews which explored this type of mutual anxiety and suspicion regarding what Margaret Beetham terms 'cultural "invasion"'.[18] As early as 1824 John Stuart Mill, in the first number of the radical *Westminster Review*, had accused the *Edinburgh* of carefully nourishing and fostering 'the prejudices which prevail in this country against the French'.[19] Later journalism would often take a less openly trenchant position than the *Edinburgh's*

---

[17]   William Makepeace Thackeray, 'French Romancers on England', *Foreign Quarterly Review* 32(1843): 227; 226–46. All subsequent references are to this article.

[18]   Beetham, 65.

[19]   John Stuart Mill, 'Periodical Literature. Edinburgh Review', *Westminster Review* 1(1824): 521; 505–41.

journalists, choosing either terms of humorous resignation as Thackeray's article demonstrates, or preferring a calm assessment of prevailing attitudes. 'French Criticism of English Writers', for instance, with due acknowledgement of the Napoleonic wars which so separated the two nations, asserts that through Madame de Staël's exile into England 'Byron and Scott poured over the Channel in a tide, that soon reached the farthest limits of Europe. French critics indeed at first withstood the invasion,' but finally, '[T]heir triumph was won in the most legitimate of ways; by translations'. Moreover, it is claimed that the French reading public indulgently consumed such translations 'long before the critic interferes to tell the *why* for or against'.[20] The old type of review which Mill so roundly condemns, when it does occur in this period, seems so extreme as to appear almost irrational. For instance, John Steinmetz, in 'Modern French Romance', accuses French writers of openly championing vice as a commercial enterprise which '[E]ven England has not escaped ... and if a purer sense of national dignity forbids translations, yet those are not wanting who need not such assistance'.[21] It seems that the English propagators of this 'moral cholera' (354) to use another of Steinmetz's vituperative phrases, are socialists who derive all of their principles from French novels. Such reviews almost always refer at some stage to George Sand, a name synonymous in the public mind, of course, with immorality. The issue of politicized and nationalistic reception of European publications is addressed in more detail in Chapter 3 which explores the journalistic journeys of Mary Margaret Busk.

The periodical press as a generality never espouses a common voice or position. In this regard, it is striking to compare Thackeray's mocking approach designed to amuse his English readers, to that of Sarah Austin, writing just three years later in *Bentley's Miscellany.* She complains that the English know nothing of the Italian people, despite so many travel books on Italy, books which offer a standard and expected cultural perspective that ignores contemporary Italian society. She considers this to be less surprising given 'how little we know of that powerful and eminent nation, with which we are at so many points in daily and hourly contact.' She is referring to France. And the ignorance of which she complains is 'of that simple, and laborious, and frugal peasantry which cultivates, and in great measure possesses, the broad fields of fertile France – of the thrifty and united households of her small *bourgeoisie*'.[22] Austin's comments privilege the everyday (and everyday culture) over cultural encounters that are literary and historical, rather than social. That is not to say that Austin discards literature and history in her thinking and in her work, far from it, as Chapter 3 in Part II will show. Rather, she is making a special case for the need for more complete knowledge to enhance mutual understanding and so offers her readers a translation from a

---

[20] 'French Criticism of English Writers', *Foreign Quarterly Review* 30(1842): 2–3 and 8; 1–12.

[21] John Steinmetz, 'Modern French Romance', *Dublin Review* 9(1840): 354; 353–96.

[22] Sarah Austin, 'Travels and Travellers in Italy', *Bentley's Miscellany* 20(1846): 244 and 245; 244–52.

German author's work on Italy even as she remarks resignedly: 'His suggestions, however, are not very likely to be listened to ... they suppose the necessity of *knowing* something. Who would submit to the trouble of study, or to the *gène* [sic] of conscience, when flippancy and presumption, set off by a smart style, will satisfy the public?' There is of course the irony, of which Austin is aware, that Italy was at that time under Austrian control. Austin remarks it is paradoxical 'that the reparation of her wrongs ... will come from Germany' and 'the very tongue of her masters' will prove 'the medium of a fair, and candid, and indulgent statement of her real character'.[23] Austin's translation practice is an attempt to educate and transform, even as she complains that English arrogance, intolerance and injustice on the part of writers and readers will prevent the cultural impact she desires.

Nationalism, or Englishness, as an ideology is, as the foregoing shows, an issue debated frequently in the British press in the first decades of Victoria's reign and is tied closely to concepts of culture across the nineteenth century. The 'Prospectus' for the *British and Foreign Review*, by its founder T.W. Beaumont, offers an excellent example of the issues being debated at the time, arguing that the English need to overcome their indifference to the state of other nations and that their journal will bring to public attention 'the close connexion which exists between the progress of social and intellectual improvement in England and in other countries'. Beaumont's 'Prospectus' declares England's insularity to be at an end, pointing out that the 'power of steam has thrown a bridge over the channel, which separates her from the continent – a bridge which no storm can scatter. Her liberty can no longer exist alone'.[24] This 'Prospectus' is followed by a much lengthier 'Introduction' which suggests in marketing and economic terms the ways in which Britain can profit from interchanges with the continent, especially in the form of new knowledges while at the same time British superiority is still being asserted:

> We do not forget the peculiar advantage to be derived to this country, by a concentration within it of European knowledge. Already London is the metropolis of the commercial world. The materials are provided, the opportunity is afforded, and the fault will be in the present generation, if they do not avail themselves of those materials, to render it the centre of knowledge, the capital of scientific discovery, and of political improvement.[25]

Despite my insistence regarding the interconnection, and at times interdependence, of my key terms 'travel' and 'translation', it seemed to me useful to separate them

23   Austin, 'Travels and Travellers in Italy', 245 and 244.
24   T.W. Beaumont, 'Prospectus', *British and Foreign Review* 1(1835): 1 and 3; 1–4. See also D.R. Fisher, 'Thomas Wentworth Beaumont', *Oxford Dictionary of National Biography* (Oxford, 2004), 4: 676–7. All subsequent references will use the abbreviation ODNB.
25   Christopher Bird, 'Introduction', *British and Foreign Review* 1(1835): 5; 5–16.

semantically in what follows to enable some detailed investigation as to how these two terms will operate within the case studies in Part II, by explaining their relevance and impact in the nineteenth century, and in particular in those early decades of Queen Victoria's reign. Further consideration of gender ideology will inevitably be included, as will those other ideologies of class, and Englishness, colonialism and empire. The following discussion will also offer some consideration as to how these key terms have been critically analyzed and investigated in more recent times.

I. Travel Writing

Travel writing proves to be a dominant form in the nineteenth century, from the publication of the journals of navigators and explorers, to emigrant accounts of colonization, to individual journeys of a range of men and women. A glance at the contents pages of the myriad periodicals and magazines of the nineteenth century will reveal that reviews of travel, exploration and tourism, and theories about travel writing generally, outnumber other kinds of writing, even fiction, particularly in the 1830–1870 period. Ina Ferris argues, and offers convincing evidence, that the *Edinburgh Review* at least had always taken the travel genre seriously, quoting Henry Brougham's statement in 1804 'that books of travel deserve a greater degree of attention, in proportion to their merits, than other works'.[26] The expansion of the British empire and the rapid changes to forms of transportation which made travel and tourism so much easier in the Victorian age provided both men and women with the opportunity to travel in relative ease and they did so in far greater numbers than ever before. Indeed by 1873 R.J. King, reviewing popular travel guides for the *Edinburgh Review*, notes that the 'enormous extension of Continental travel is one of the great features of the last ten years. During the autumn months the whole of Europe seems to be in a state of perpetual motion'.[27] The rapid escalation of journeys to the Continent naturally gave rise to interest in and demand for reading material in translation in which the histories, philosophies, poetry, drama and literature generally, of Germany, France and Italy in particular, might be accessed by travellers. Moreover, the fact that King is actually reviewing travel guides signals the degree to which travel writing too, in all its various manifestations, from guidebook to adventure tale, from essays to short stories, becomes so closely associated with that other most prolific industry of the Victorian age, publishing, in particular its two main branches, book publishing, and the periodical press. The periodical press itself, through review essays which always included lengthy quotation from the works being considered,

---

[26]   Ina Ferris, 'Mobile Words: Romantic Travel Writing and Print Anxiety', *Modern Language Quarterly* 60/4(1999): 451; 451–68.

[27]   R.J. King, 'Travellers and Handbooks', *Edinburgh Review* 138(1873): 497; 483–510.

through position essays on colonization, emigration, and travel, and through short stories and occasional pieces by noted travel writers, helped to foster and expand the book publishing industry almost incestuously, as many of the most influential periodicals and their reviewers were linked to specific publishers.

Although the conservative press in the 1830–1870 period still favoured male writers, the lives of British women began to change radically within this same timeframe. Reception in the press is one method of gauging the impact of this change and, because women wrote about their own travels or translated the journeys of others, as a way into publishing, the press's connection to the economies of travel, translation and culture is profound. As well, although the press was disproportionately gendered male, women's travel publishing was nevertheless starting to be noticed alongside that of men more consistently at this time, in part because these particular women were offering their audiences works that were presumably not fictional. Fiction, or romance-writing, still, in the 1830s at least, was a gendered commodity associated primarily with women and therefore of less import than supposedly non-fiction works on travel, history, economy and so on, although it should be noted that the enormous popularity of Walter Scott's historical romances was making inroads into that gendered perception, the category 'history' giving his work that necessarily more serious masculine quality.

A further change takes place with the advent of travel fiction, in the form of adventure narratives, a genre which rapidly became the province of men. Isabella Bird, reflecting on what she sees from the train window as she journeys across the American prairies in 1854 makes occasional references to her own novel reading, in particular to James Fenimore Cooper's epic series of the American West, usually labelled the Leatherstocking tales (1823–41), and Thomas Mayne Reid's numerous popular romances of the American West. Titles like *The Rifle Rangers* (1850); *The Scalp Hunters* (1851); and *The Boy Hunters* (1852) indicate the genre unmistakably. Bird remarks 'Cooper influences our youthful imaginations by telling us of the prairies – Mayne Reid makes us long to cross them; botanists tell us of their flowers, sportsmen of their buffaloes – but without seeing them few people can form a correct idea of what they are really like'.[28] Bird suggests here a range of genres into which travel writing can be subsumed, but offers her own record, confirmed by the act of seeing for herself, as ultimately the 'correct' version. British women travellers often present their work in this way, as a journey undertaken to verify the accounts of others, a form of witnessing, and supposedly objective reportage, undertaken from the sidelines as it were, but with a keen scrutiny nevertheless. Nona Bellairs in *Going Abroad; or, Glimpses of Art and Character in France and Italy* (1857) asserts in her conclusion that she has 'tried to describe simply what I saw and heard, without prejudice, seeking with diligent eyes for the good, as well as the evil; for the true amidst the untrue;

[28]   Isabella Bird, *Englishwoman in America*, 117–18. See also John Sutherland, *The Longman Companion to Victorian Fiction* (Harlow, 1988), 527–8.

the germ of life, hidden so often under the rubbish', comments clearly, however, provoked by her anxiety regarding Roman Catholicism in both countries and possibly undermined by the modest term 'glimpses' in her title.[29] Just as critics have noted a tendency in Isabella Bird to reinvent herself which constitutes in part a 'fictionalising process' as Susan Bassnett puts it, so too other travellers must to some extent invent a persona which inevitably produces a tension between such a process and the traveller's claims of 'veracity'.[30]

While women's travel writing was being reviewed seriously in this period, this is not to say that all reviewing of travel-writing generally was positive, or when by a woman, did not receive a gendered response. The anonymous author of 'German Tourists', reviewing nine titles on Germany, Belgium and Holland, for the *Westminster Review*, offers us two very good examples of both these provisos. She or he complains, in distinctly marketplace terms, of the sheer number of books published on the one approximate region:

> But driven as they are in droves to the market, by the impatience of authors
> and the avarice of publishers, they become huddled together like cattle in a
> fair, to the grievous injury of their own effect. Any country which possesses the
> smallest temporary political interest, is now instantly overspread with a swarm
> of English tourists ... whose chief impulse seems to be, not ... who shall best
> describe, but ... who can fastest write. The London booksellers are on the alert
> to whip up each trite and trivial production, the subject is overdone, the market
> overstocked ...[31]

Notably this reviewer is also making a very negative distinction between the genus *traveller* and that of *tourist*, and all the writers under review are clearly designated as belonging to the inferior sub-genus, *tourist*. Moreover, Ina Ferris demonstrates that anxiety about the 'crass commercialism' associated with published travels was being expressed in the periodical press from the start of the century.[32] Terms like 'swarm', generally used of the insect world, recur without fail when the hapless tourist comes into view. H.F. Chorley makes an identical complaint regarding the 'swarm of insignificant beings who now travel because they would write'. A more extreme example, demonstrating the longevity of this prejudice, can be found in Enzensberger, when he quotes Gerhard Nebel (1950): 'The swarms of these gigantic bacteria, called tourists, have coated the most distinct substances with a uniformly glistening Thomas-Cook slime, making it impossible to distinguish

---

[29]   Nona Bellairs, *Going Abroad; or, Glimpses of Art and Character in France and Italy* (London, 1857), 283.

[30]   Susan Bassnett, 'Travel Writing and Gender', *The Cambridge Companion to Travel Writing*, ed. Peter Hulme and Tim Youngs (Cambridge, 2002), 235.

[31]   'German Tourists', *Westminster Review* 22(1835): 511–12; 510–20. All subsequent references are to this article.

[32]   Ferris, 460.

Cairo from Honolulu, Taormina from Colombo ...'[33] As Enzensberger confirms, little has been 'so thoroughly mocked and so diligently criticized as tourism' and he argues, rightly, that such critique is either merely reactionary in stemming from a sense of privilege (in the case of his cited traveller Nebel) or a psychological response to the disappointment that the gains or values advertised by tourism itself, of adventure in an untouched or pristine locale, turn out to be deceptive.[34] Tourism, in nearly all its facets, is heavily linked to commercial practices.

In both Victorian and modern studies, 'travel' and its significant other, 'tourism', have been carefully separated semantically, where 'travel' is accorded first-class status, but 'tourism' denigrated to a much lower level, reflecting the social class divisions which often distinguish commentary on the two orders. The process of differentiation between the two is thus carried out predominantly along class lines, but racial or national identity can also be a factor. Not just in modern times, but in the Victorian age itself, the tourist came in for considerable abuse, as the previous discussion and quotation from the author of 'German Tourists' shows, a practice which persists, despite the fact, as John Urry points out, that tourism as an industry has 'economic significance'.[35] Travel, on the other hand, is always accorded a particular dignity as being descriptive of journeys which are of a comparatively original kind, such as avoiding the so-called 'beaten track', but without the same venturing into the geographically unknown that one would expect in an account designated 'exploration'. The journey can also be dignified with the epithet 'travel' if undertaken in unusual transport (on the back of an elephant; in a camel train; rafting down a river) or, in the case of women travellers, entails a region into which no woman has ever before ventured. As H.F. Chorley so acutely remarks in his article 'Lady Travellers':

> As we rise higher in the scale of poetical endowment, or originality of character, we shall find one of the sisterhood venturing alone across the Desert to India, another aspiring to scale Mont Blanc, a third in male attire gymnastically making her way downward from story to story (sic) of an Austrian mine, a fourth with sketch-book and umbrella, "camping out" by the great lakes of America.[36]

This last is an obvious reference to Anna Jameson's seven-day canoe voyage, from Mackinaw to Sault Saint Marie, in Canada, the only woman with 21 men, who carefully constructs herself in class terms as lady-like and feminine to avoid censure and suspicion of impropriety because of the circumstances under which

---

[33]   H.F. Chorley, 'Lady Travellers', *British and Foreign Quarterly* 13(1842): 491; 486–508 and Hans Magnus Enzensberger, 'A Theory of Tourism' (Trans. Gerd Gemünden and Kenn Johnson), *New German Critique* 65(1996): 120; 113–35.

[34]   Enzensberger, 120 and 121.

[35]   John Urry, *The Tourist Gaze. Leisure and Travel in Contemporary Societies* (London, 1990), 5.

[36]   Chorley, 'Lady Travellers', 487.

the journey is undertaken. Chorley, who worked primarily for the *Athenaeum* (1833–1868) as a reviewer, and had travelled frequently on the Continent, had reviewed Jameson's book for the *British and Foreign Review*.[37]

As already discussed, much has been written and explored addressing the distinctions between travel and tourism since the mid twentieth century from Hans Magnus Enzensberger in 1958 on. Enzensberger's overview is comprehensive, from his recognition that 'technological progress ... allowed capitalism to expand the network of traffic necessary for this homogenization of space' to the list of travellers whose writings created an imaginative tourist scape whose 'pristine landscape and untouched history have remained the models of tourism'.[38] Whether, as he concludes, tourism reveals an acceptance that the concept of freedom is now a 'mass deceit' demands further investigation.[39] For Victorian women 'freedom' as such is always going to be a debatable term. If they took with them their own class and national ideologies as restraints on that freedom, nevertheless, middle-class women in the early decades of the Victorian age did achieve greater freedoms than had ever been known before. Today their freedom might seem to be of a deceptive kind. In their own day, however, comparisons with a generation earlier, and with their less mobile sisters, must have given certain middle-class women a sense of liberty to be themselves, to be independent, to go out into the world and report on what they saw. No woman traveller demonstrates this more compellingly than Ida Pfeiffer, whose journey round the world will be addressed in Chapter 6.

However, this said, in the case of the author of 'German Tourists', touristic swarming is more to do with the fact that all nine titles under review might be considered as belonging to the same cultural register, that is they are all undifferentiated tourist accounts of an identical region, despite any gendered differences in what is observed and commented on, and in writing style. They are deficient in terms of the circulation of ideas. Three of the nine titles under review are by women, Anna Jameson's *Visits and Sketches at Home and Abroad* (1833), Frances Trollope's *Belgium and Western Germany* (1834) and one anonymous author whose sex is clearly known to the reviewer. Her book, *Slight Reminiscences of the Rhine, Switzerland, and a corner of Italy* (1834) is revealed by the British Library Catalogue to be by Mary Boddington, one of the many women writers who never make it into the standard reference books. Only two of the *Westminster's* original nine authors are considered in a *Quarterly Review* on the same topic.[40] The latter two are awarded precedence 'in point of merit' but the critical terms used of their travel narratives are distinctly gendered female: 'grace', 'delicacy', 'genuine taste', 'unassuming' (512 and 514) are words that would not normally

---

[37] See Judith Johnston, *Anna Jameson: Victorian, Feminist, Woman of Letters* (Aldershot, 1997), 112–15. See also Robert Bledsoe's entry on Chorley, ODNB 11: 514–15.

[38] Enzensberger, 124 and 125.

[39] Enzensberger, 135.

[40] See 'Belgium and Western Germany by Mrs. Trollope and Sir A. B. Faulkner', *Quarterly Review* 52(1834): 203–33.

be applied to men's writing, unless disparagement was the intention. Noted Tory and monarchist, Frances Trollope, who had caused a sensation with her caustic first travel book, *Domestic Manners of the Americans* (1832), attracting widespread opprobrium in both Britain and America, is, naturally enough in a radical journal like the *Westminster*, given an extended but negative notice, in which she is castigated as a 'traveller for the Absolutist firm', as 'vulgar', and as absurd (514 and 516). The male authors do not fare much better, the anonymous *Simeon [South]'s Letters to his Kinfolks* is 'a melancholy proof of degeneracy in our living literature' (512). Three of these authors, Jameson, Trollope and Simeon [South], were also reviewed by Christian Isobel Johnstone in the equally radical *Tait's Edinburgh Magazine* but on the whole her review proves to be no gendered counterbalance to the *Westminster*'s objections, because Johnstone always reviews equitably, regardless of the author's sex, rarely if ever employing gender-specific terms in her critiques. To this end Jameson receives only limited notice, and the review is once again dominated by Frances Trollope whose work is, however, praised as more 'business-like' than Jameson's and 'more authentic' than that of Simeon.[41] The term 'business-like' can only be defined here through Johnstone's further comment that Trollope's book contains 'no affectation ... whether of poetic enthusiasm, rapturous admiration, or of any thing else' although she mourns the fact that there 'is no scolding in it; no caricature, no satire, no malice' as in *Domestic Manners*. As to authenticity, the very title of the South book, it seems, implies 'invention, fiction, and disguise'.[42]

Percy G. Adams coined what he termed 'the truth-lie dichotomy', in particular as it applied to the literary productions of the medieval period, and subsequent centuries, in which the category 'travel' could include imaginary voyages, or fiction might be dressed as a travel narrative (Daniel Defoe's *Robinson Crusoe* (1719) and Jonathan Swift's *Gulliver's Travels* (1726) come immediately to mind).[43] By the nineteenth century more sophisticated readers expected that an actual journey had indeed taken place. For this reason, the modifier 'authentic', like 'real' and 'true' is, in the nineteenth century, a marvellously uncomplicated term that required no qualification. In the nineteenth century all three modifiers attach themselves readily to travel writing because, as with the categories *History* and *Biography*, the readers back then always assumed that an actual journey had taken place and that the events recorded were actual events. Today these three terms will give pause. There is a ready understanding that all such writing is a construction, be it intersected by various ideologies, discursively managed to produce a particular effect or to avoid over-stepping ideological boundaries, or coloured by the politics of the author.

---

[41]   Christian Isobel Johnstone, 'Travels in Germany; By Mrs. Trollope, Mrs. Jameson, and Simeon South, Esq.' *Tait's Edinburgh Magazine* 1(1834): 553; 552–67.

[42]   Johnstone, 'Travels in Germany', 553.

[43]   Percy G. Adams, *Travel Literature and the Evolution of the Novel* (Lexington, KY, 1983). See Chapter 4.

In the Victorian age such easy generic crossovers disappear, in part because, as Ina Ferris compellingly argues, the *Edinburgh Review* helped to stabilize what had been only a 'generic possibility' and to establish travel as a 'knowledge genre': 'travels', she argues, 'served their middle-class readers as signs of both social status and intellectual capital'.[44] Nor was the *Edinburgh* alone in privileging travel literature. A random check of the *Quarterly Review* provides evidence of a similar precedence given to works on travel and exploration. Apart from the usual travel narratives, Great Britain's colonial empire naturally yielded many essays and reviews addressing publications focusing on the nation's various colonies. Thus, publications which come under the rubric 'Travel' might be subsumed into yet another set of various sub-genres including emigrant advice literature, exploration, and colonial policy, all of which accommodate themselves to Ferris's 'knowledge genre', along with those previously suggested by Bird.

Gillian Beer points out, in addressing science and literature, that genres 'establish their own conditions which alter the significance of ideas expressed within them', adding a further proviso that readerships are not only made up of individuals, 'but of individuals reading within a genre', that is, the reader comes to the text with particular expectations and anticipations which the apprehended genre has inspired.[45] The issue regarding the standing of travel writing as a genre, the fact-versus-fiction debate, becomes even more complicated if the travel narrative incorporates fictional material. Some women travel writers made early errors of judgment, Anna Jameson for instance, mixed two genres by creating a novelistic sentimental dying heroine as narrator who is confusingly also a very active and enthusiastic pre-Victorian traveller, in her first published work, *Diary of an Ennuyée* (1826).[46] Similarly, Janet Robertson's *Lights and Shades on a Traveller's Path* (1851) is a fractured narrative shifting between fact and fiction. She writes 'Truly I lived at that time in two worlds at once; one way my own – a painful enough world, God knows! – and the other was the region of romance'.[47] The resultant fracture offers the reader an informative example of how unproductive the mixture of two genres, what Ferris describes as 'sentimental travel',[48] with Victorian guidebook sturdiness, can prove. Frances Trollope did not make the same mistake. For a number of her published travel narratives she produced accompanying, but separate, fictional variants.[49] Fredrika Bremer, in *Two Years in Switzerland and Italy* (1861) includes, from the fourteenth chapter on, an extraordinarily tedious

---

44   Ferris, 452 and 453.

45   Gillian Beer, *Open Fields: Science in Cultural Encounter* (Oxford, 1996), 186.

46   For a further discussion, see Johnston, 'Fracturing Perspectives of Italy in Anna Jameson's *Diary of an Ennuyée*', *Women's Writing* 11(2004): 11–24.

47   Janet Robertson, *Lights and Shades on a Traveller's Path; or, Scenes in Foreign Lands* (London, 1851), 8.

48   Ferris, 455.

49   For instance, *Domestic Manners of the Americans* (1832) and *The Refugee in America: a Novel* (1832); *Vienna and the Austrians* (1838) and *A Romance of Vienna* (1838).

love story between two people she meets on her travels, a digression which she attempts in the 'Preface' to account for both ways, as containing 'a great deal of truth' to which has been added 'a few grains of fiction, besides weaving up two of the romances into merely one'.[50] The *Spectator* reviewer at first disarms the reader by terming the tale itself 'graceful and touching', but then sternly rounds on Bremer regarding her confession that the tale has in part been fictionalized: 'Such tampering with fact, in a work professing to report realities, we cannot but regard as an impertinence'. Furthermore, if the tale was a true one, 'we should still object to the novelist policy of making literary capital out of the sacred communications of friendship'.[51] The *Athenaeum*, more simply, condemns outright the fictional aberration as unlikely to appeal to modern readers: 'nothing can be more thoroughly out of taste than the heart-romances of her fellow-travellers'.[52] Journalist Jane Sinnett, reviewing Bremer's *The Mid-Night Sun; a Pilgrimage* for the *Westminster Review* ten years earlier, also expresses concern at the mixture of fiction and travel-writing, remarking that the reader will have to take on trust that Bremer actually made the journey as described and expressing regret that 'instead of a very flimsy and insipid *nouvellette*, she did not give us a simple account of her "Summer Journey"'.[53] For Bremer, as primarily a novelist who only turned to travel writing late in her career, resorting to a fiction in her travel book on Switzerland and Italy, which engrosses over 100 pages of the second volume, may have been a device to help fill the required two volumes (two- and three-volume works were in demand as most profitable for the lending libraries). Her journey in Switzerland and Italy seems, after the excitements of her travels in America, pedestrian at best. Riveting slavery politics, and the impact of that dynamic on Bremer personally, the primary subject of Chapter 7, is lost on this continental journey, and replaced with long forays into comparative religious practices which, for the most part, is an outdated investigation into Roman Catholicism.

Ina Ferris has argued that 'early romantic reviews tried hard to relocate the knowledge genres from contestatory public space into rule-governed scientific space'.[54] Adapting this comment to the post-Romantic or Victorian period, it might be argued that some women writers appear to have been working to shift the knowledge genres yet again, as with Bremer's discussions on slavery in *Homes of the New World*, and her less original religious discussions in *Two Years in Switzerland and Italy*, removing them from contestatory public space into non-contestatory domestic space. Politically the move is an interesting one, where the discourse is marked by a temperate, moderate tone, and a drive towards

---

    50   Bremer, *Two Years in Switzerland and Italy*, vii.

    51   'Two Years in Switzerland and Italy', *Spectator* 33(22 December 1860), 1222; 1221–2.

    52   'Two Years in Switzerland and Italy', *Athenaeum* No. 1728(8 December 1860), 785; 785–6.

    53   Jane Sinnett, 'Foreign Literature', *Westminster Review* 52(1850): 231; 227–31.

    54   Ferris, 464.

open-minded investigation. In this, and in other ways, women travel writers did establish their own gendered conditions which inevitably impacted on the travel genre. Not all women's writing, naturally enough, reveals such characteristics to the marked degree located in Bremer's travel writing.

As evidenced by the presence of Christian Isobel Johnstone as editor and chief writer for *Tait's Edinburgh Magazine*, women were not only producing travel books, and translating travel books, they were also writing reviews, especially for the newer monthly journals and the significant weeklies like the *Athenaeum* and the *Spectator*, and the more radical quarterlies. Politically, then, women participated in the marketing of European social and cultural practices to a British readership which allowed comparisons to be made with British practices, by both author and reader, with a concomitant sharpening of awareness of national identity that takes firm hold at this time. For women such participation in the marketplace created by travel often came at the risk of being held up to ridicule. Anthony Trollope's short story published in *Cassell's Illustrated Family Paper*, 'An Unprotected Female at the Pyramids' (1860), for instance, represents Miss Dawkins as battening on to family groups with the hope that she will have some of her expenses defrayed and gain masculine protection, while paying lip service to her own independent spirit as a forceful representative of women's rights.[55] The term 'unprotected female', with quotation marks, is used often by Isabella Bird in *The Englishwoman in America* (1856) and may have become something of a wry joke in the 1850s. Emily Lowe uses the term in the titles of two books, *Unprotected Females in Norway* (1857) and *Unprotected Females in Sicily* (1859), and in the former advises that it 'is astonishing, if ladies look perfectly helpless and innocent, how people fall into the trap, and exert to serve them. "Unprotecteds" cannot do better than keep firm to the old combination of the qualities of the serpent and the dove' (20).[56] The anonymous author of 'A Few Words on Tours and Tourists', published a year later, surely had Trollope's short story in mind when he or she responded, but in notably sympathetic terms: 'we may think that the adventures of some unprotected females were hardly such as to be proud of ... but on the whole we may well rejoice to see such numbers [of women] use a rational freedom'.[57] This strikingly more moderate tone occurs in an article generally celebrating the advent of the railway as enabling women to travel unaccompanied and thus fostering female independence, and as the agent breaking down 'all conventional etiquette on the subject'. Moreover, the author adds, so many people travel that a woman travelling alone does not appear unusual.[58] This article appears to signal a comparatively recent change in

---

[55] Anthony Trollope, 'An Unprotected Female at the Pyramids', *The Complete Short Stories. Volume Three: Tourists and Colonials*, ed. Betty Breyer (London, 1991). See also Johnston, 'The Pyramids of Egypt: Monuments to Victorian Desire', *Australasian Victorian Studies Journal* 7(2001): 71–88.

[56] Lowe, 20.

[57] 'A Few Words on Tours and Tourists', *Fraser's Magazine* 63(1861): 352; 340–55.

[58] 'A Few Words', 352.

attitude. Isabella Bird, in 1856, comments on travelling alone by train in America, that there is only one class, or as she puts it, 'the mingling of all ranks', and that the male passengers always treat her with civility, adding 'We must be well aware that in many parts of England it would be difficult for a lady to travel unattended in a second-class, impossible in a third-class carriage'.[59] Politically, the author of 'A Few Words on Tours and Tourists' focuses only on gender ideology and has not factored class ideology into the equation, possibly simply because, as an ideology, it would be taken as understood in the circumstances.

The growth in tourism saw an accompanying growth in the guidebook industry which, as a separate topic in itself, has attracted considerable interest and analysis across the centuries. James Buzard, in his contribution to the *Cambridge Companion to Travel Writing*, offers a brief potted history of the tourist guidebook as having been invented simultaneously by Karl and Fritz Baedeker in Germany in 1835 and John Murray III in Britain in 1836.[60] Both Baedeker and Murray belonged to family publishing houses and with an eye to the gap in the market saw the need for such guides with the sudden expansion of tourism. Buzard rightly indicates that both publishers created the 'generic distinction' that characterizes travel guides still. The guidebook is 'impersonal, objective', features which separate it from the more 'highly personal, impressionistic book of "travel writing"'. Separating the two kinds of travel writing, Buzard points out, meant that 'personal travelogues' could dispense with the 'guidebook burden'.[61] Buzard, in *The Beaten Track*, points out that Mariana Starke's travel books 'were an important precedent' for the Murray guidebooks.[62] Lynne Withey, however, takes this further, describing her as probably the first 'professional guidebook writer'.[63] According to Withey, Starke's *Letters from Italy* ran to nine editions in the 1800–1839 period, the earlier editions being personal travelogues burdened with guidebook information, to use Buzard's terms. In 1820 Starke produced a revised edition for John Murray titled *Travels on the Continent: Written for the Use and Particular Information of Travellers*, which offered the best routes between various towns, and advice on where to stay and what to see. This became the model for the more formal guidebook series which John Murray III developed, which were always called *A Handbook for Travellers* with the relevant country, or set of countries added, and which were always bound in red, a distinctive badge that is often commented

---

[59]   Isabella Bird, 83.

[60]   R.J. King, back in 1873, claimed the handbook for travellers as 'essentially an English invention' (483).

[61]   James Buzard, 'The Grand Tour and after (1660–1840)', *Cambridge Companion to Travel Writing*, ed. *Peter Hulme and Tim Youngs* (Cambridge, 2002), 48–9. See also Buzard's *The Beaten Track. European Tourism, Literature, and the Ways to 'Culture' 1800–1918*.

[62]   James Buzard, *The Beaten Track. European Tourism, Literature, and the Ways to 'Culture' 1800–1918* (Oxford, 1993), 68.

[63]   Withey, 69.

on in novels, in reviews, in essays. Withey also notes that the Murray handbooks standardized their format (and claims that Baedeker copied that format) with an introductory chapter which included a 'capsule history', 'practical information on transportation, currency, passport and customs requirements, inns, and major sights' and advice on behaviour. This was followed by suggested itineraries and detailed chapters on the various regions. Baedeker, to increase his market, turned to translations of his guidebooks as early as 1846, producing French and English editions. Because the home market was enormous, Murray handbooks were only ever published in English.[64]

As a separate and distinctive generic form, the guidebook quickly began to impact on the reception of other kinds of travel publishing. One of the earliest examples I located is a review by Nicholas Wiseman of Charles Dickens's *American Notes for General Circulation* and Frances Trollope's *A Visit to Italy*, both published in 1842. Wiseman headed his review 'Superficial Travelling' and he returns a number of times to the guidebook model in condemning the travel narratives of both novelists. One of his main complaints is that a travel book should offer 'information', that it is 'not a fiction, but truth'. Both writers are condemned as belonging 'to one very common class of travellers ... who skim over the surface of the land, who see it out of carriage windows, and visit its sights by the guide-book' and later, in attacking Trollope's recorded adventures, remarks with something of a sneer:

> This sort of "romance of travel" is very much cut up by one's knowing that every year, A. and B. and C. have gone just over the same ground, or the same water, or the same snow, and yet have met nothing particular in the way of adventure, but have had a mere ordinary guide-book journey; little thinking how much might have been made of a puff of wind ... in dishing up their tour, had they been so disposed, for the public.[65]

Such pejorative comparisons to guidebooks do establish a pattern in travel writing reviews that will continue throughout the century in which the failure to strike out an independent itinerary reduces the writer to the status of mere tourist. The *Dublin Review* was Roman Catholic in affiliation, part of the moderate Catholic revival in England and Nicholas Wiseman, Rector of the English College at Rome (1828–1840) became its proprietor with the Irish Nationalist, Daniel O'Connell. Wiseman, with C.W. Russell, decided on editorial policy. Both Dickens and Trollope had offended in their travelogues with ill-considered remarks reflecting

---

[64]   Withey, 71–3.

[65]   Nicholas Wiseman, 'Superficial Travelling – Dickens – Trollope', *Dublin Review* 14(1843): 257 and 260; 255–68.

negatively on the history and practices of the Roman Catholic church, which may in part explain Wiseman's hostile tone.[66]

The critic R.H. Cheney reviewed the American George Hillard's *Six Months in Italy* (1853) for the *Quarterly*. Cheney offers his readers first a brief account of other travellers' excursions into Italy as possible models, suggesting that for some the tour may be so subjective as to be defined as autobiographical, citing Laurence Sterne's *A Sentimental Journey* (1768), or so objective as to be only useful as a guide, remarking 'Marianne Starke's miscellaneous list of prices, sights, and inns – where the washerwoman and the Coliseum figure side by side'.[67] He mentions Goethe's tour as a life narrative, famed Gothic writer William Beckford's as a source of various personal sensations, and reminds the reader about Jameson's unhappy choice of a framework for her *Diary of an Ennuyée* (1826). This overview of so many travel books on Italy concludes with a quotation from Frances Trollope's *A Visit to Italy* (1842) in which she complains that 'Italy is an exhausted subject' (355). Cheney's approach is erudite and clever, followed by the final blow, that guidebooks have made such accounts redundant. 'Mr. Hillard', he says, 'is full of gratitude to Mr. Murray's Handbooks, and with reason' and then offers fulsome praise for them as not merely guide books but 'quite as necessary to the scholar who stays at home, as to the tourist on his travels' (355). His panegyric reads suspiciously like a puff, given that John Murray published the *Quarterly Review*. Nevertheless the critic then turns to Hillard's book only to digress through the remainder of the review into various exegeses on tourism itself, on the failure of most travellers to comment on the social, moral and political condition of the country, on Italian art, on Italian antiquities, on Roman history prompted by comments in Hillard's book. Phrases like the 'credulous novice' (356), 'superficial tourists' (357), 'preconceived opinions' (358) and 'the bewildered novice' (362) are sufficiently repeated to condemn Hillard's authority as an informed traveller. The author's own disclaimers, his 'modest regrets at his imperfect preparation' (364) are cited also at regular intervals to effectively, if indirectly, create a negative impact.

Travel writers themselves quickly became conscious of not allowing their books or essays to take on the characteristics of a 'Murray' or a 'Baedeker'. Isabella Bird, exploring Montreal in Canada remarks 'some very fine public buildings and banks; but as I am not writing a guidebook, I will not dilate upon their merits'.[68] In his essay 'Across the Channel', J.H. Burton, goes so far as to warn his readers that if they are travellers who study 'Murray', as 'guide, philosopher, and friend', who only go where the handbook directs them, only see what they are taught to see, 'in fact, follow him with blind implicit obedience in thought, word and

---

[66]   Walter E. Houghton et al. (eds), 'Dublin Review Introduction', *The Wellesley Index to Victorian Periodicals 1824–1900*, 5 vols (Toronto and London, 1987), II: 13–19.

[67]   R.H. Cheney, 'Italian Tours and Tourists', *Quarterly Review* 103(1858): 348; 346–90. All subsequent references are to this article.

[68]   Isabella Bird, 208.

deed, as a sort of tourist's scripture – to such a person I have nothing to say'.[69] Burton positions himself as someone ahead of other travellers, that his visit to the Continent will be undertaken 'before the general rush of tourists' (15), but the only real difference in approach rests in the fact that he had visited the Continent 20 years earlier and his present travels merely contrive points of comparison: then and now. Despite that initial warning, he produces an overlong disquisition on tourism and guidebooks generally, admitting 'it would be signal ingratitude ... to say a word in disparagement of Mr. Murray's red books', and advocates using 'the redbook as a servant or assistant, not a master' (16–17).

Guidebooks, as some of these contemporary critiques show, produced very mixed responses. They had the potential to ease travel, and to assist the novice traveller, but also had the counter-distinction of so dominating an itinerary that other equally interesting points, sights, ideas, might be missed along the way. The guidebook became ubiquitous, like the tourist, and therefore could receive the same kind of disparagement as the 'common tourist' (18) to use Burton's term. Some Victorian critics, R.J. King for instance, praised the guidebook, Murray's in particular, as having 'influenced modern tastes, and even modern learning', converting the traveller into an 'intelligent and interested sight-seer' (498). As an antiquary King was a significant contributor to the series of Handbooks published by John Murray on the various English counties beginning with Kent and Sussex in 1859 which reveals some self-serving in his praise of the Murray handbooks. Anonymity permitted this type of compromised journalism.[70] King later conflates traveller and reader in remarking of Murray's Rome handbook that the 'traveller through the Roman volume will rise from it with a more accurate knowledge of the city ... It is a worthy aid to the study of ... one of the great centres of the world's history' (502). It is this conflation of traveller and reader, which I consider next in investigating translation as another form of journey.

II. Translation

The process and practice of translation is complex and as Edwin Gentzler explains in the opening pages of *Contemporary Translation Theories* 'even translation "proper" entails multiple linguistic, literary, and cultural aspects'.[71] André Lefevere and Susan Bassnett in the Introduction to *Translation, History and Culture* (1990) argue the need 'to move from "text" as a putative "translation unit", to culture –

---

[69]   J.H. Burton, 'Across the Channel', *Blackwood's Edinburgh Magazine* 92(1862): 15; 15–39. All subsequent references are to this article. See also Michael Fry, 'John Hill Burton', ODNB 9: 27–8.

[70]   See also W.P. Courtney, rev. Ian Maxted, 'Richard John King', ODNB 31: 667–8.

[71]   Edwin Gentzler, *Contemporary Translation Theories* (London, 1993), 1.

a momentous step'.[72] The general consensus emerging from the development of translation studies through the 1990s appears to be that approaches dominated by linguistics create scientific models, according to Lawrence Venuti, that ignore 'the fact that translation, like any cultural practice, entails the creative reproduction of values', a clear reference to the work of Nida and Chomsky in the 1960s as discussed by Gentzler in detail in his Chapter 4.[73] James Clifford moves the debate along by arguing that cultural action, 'the making and remaking of identities, takes place in the contact zones, along the policed and transgressive intercultural frontiers of nations, peoples, locales'. He equates 'translation' with 'encounters', an interpretation which specifically informs my own work.[74] As Carmine G. Di Biase so compellingly sums up Clifford's approach, by '"translation" Clifford means what happens when two cultures come together'.[75] Di Biase goes on to argue, by comparing Clifford and Venuti, a position that usefully proves more than appropriate for my own work, that if:

> by "travel", therefore, one intends cultural encounters and the resulting transformations that take place on both sides, then travel is indeed translation extended beyond the linguistic limits.[76]

Anthony Pym in *Exploring Translation Theories* (2010) also argues of Clifford's thinking that the 'way translations (in the narrow or broad sense) represent cultures through travel and for travellers is a huge area that remains virtually untapped'.[77] This book goes some way perhaps to remedying this situation.

In the nineteenth century skilled translators who may well have imagined their work as 'faithful' would inevitably have introduced aspects of the source culture at least into their process and practice. Carlyle, as early as 1831, recognizes how essential this is in his review of William Taylor's *Historic Survey of German Poetry* (1830) when he asks 'what is the culture of the German mind ...?' and points out that such a question, among others he poses, 'appears not to have presented itself

---

[72]   André Lefevere and Susan Bassnett, 'Introduction: Proust's Grandmother and the Thousand and One Nights: the "Cultural Turn" in Translation Studies', *Translation, History and Culture*, ed. Susan Bassnett and André Lefevere (London, 1990), 4.

[73]   Lawrence Venuti, *The Scandals of Translation. Towards an Ethics of Difference* (London, 1998), 1.

[74]   James Clifford, *Routes. Travel and Translation in the late Twentieth Century* (London, 1997), 7 and 11.

[75]   Carmine G. Di Biase, 'Introduction', *Travel and Translation in the Early Modern Period* (New York, 2006), 24.

[76]   Di Biase, 25.

[77]   Anthony Pym, *Exploring Translation Theories* (New York, 2010), 154.

to the Author's thought'.[78] He later applauds what he terms Taylor's 'fidelity' but faithful translation does not compensate for the lack of cultural context and this is the far more pronounced issue in Carlyle's critique. Thus does Carlyle understand the issue of cultural encounter and translation that moves beyond the linguistic borders. The women whose translating work I explore in the case studies in Part II did, for the most part, consider themselves to be addressing an audience unfamiliar with the language being translated, enabling them to take that reader on a journey impossible without the translation. There is an assumption that many readers will be anglolexic and also that comparison with the foreign text will not prove necessary or will simply not be possible. The work of these women functions in similar ways to that of the women who interpreted science, botany and mathematics for either female or child readerships, or for self-educating working-class men, pedagogical publications designed to interpret, inform and educate.

Ina Ferris observes that the 'critical attention paid to travel writing ... helped attach early-nineteenth-century national discourse in Britain to a cosmopolitan European culture'.[79] This critical attention, gathering momentum in the 1830–1870 period, coincided with the increased production of travel-writing, and of translations of travel-writing, among other translated works, by women, and advanced the connection of British writing to European culture which Ferris notes and which I trust the previous discussion on travel writing has revealed. Women in this period often chose to tread a careful discursive line as Sara Mills discusses in *Discourses of Difference*, explicating the 'multiplicity of constraints' which impacted on women's travel writing which included: 'gender, class, purpose of their journey, textual conventions, audience'.[80] For women, these same constraints operated in their translation work and their journalism as well. Despite such constraints, women writers were able to challenge ideological assumptions, to promote them, to refute them, to create them and contravene them, and in so doing varied the generic conditions. Female travel, and its various products, travel-writing, guidebooks, translation, was for them emancipatory, as too were those other different arm-chair journeys in which women participated, in particular the reviewing of travel-writing and translation, journeys, in part perhaps, assisted by the enforced anonymity of journalism in particular. There is also a third traveller involved in the print processing of any of these journeys, and that traveller is the reader.

Translation is always a highly fraught and much disputed category. For instance, back in 1841 Jane Sinnett argued, in reviewing translations of Schiller, that 'mere matter-of-fact books', which she designates 'mercantile', do not lose by

[78] Thomas Carlyle, 'Historic Survey of German Poetry', repr. *Critical and Miscellaneous Essays*, vol. II (1831; London: 1901), 170. See also Johnston, *Anna Jameson*, chapter five.

[79] Ferris, 464.

[80] Sara Mills, *Discourses of Difference. An Analysis of Women's Travel Writing and Colonialism* (London, 1991), 21.

translation, and I would assume that travel books would fall under this category. On the other hand, more complex publications by those she terms 'distinguished writers' require the reader to acquire the language involved, likening the process to the 'gradual approach to a distant country' where 'every object we meet with on the road informs us of some new particular concerning it'. She maintains the journey metaphor reinforcing its effectiveness in adding that 'in forming an acquaintance with a foreign author by means of a translation, we are, as it were, dropped by a balloon into the strange city, and walk about puzzled and bewildered as in a dream'. Sinnett's analysis assumes, to begin with, that translation takes the reader into 'unexpected neighbourhoods', and moreover is concerned that a translation without context will create confusion, leaving the reader bewildered, whereas a translation which domesticates the work to its target readership will create a more comfortably familiar terrain. As a case in point, the works of Schiller, she argues, need to be connected to his life, and his philosophical writings 'may be suddenly illuminated by reference to poems', adding 'his lyrical productions contain in microcosmic diminution his whole system of philosophy'.[81]

Lawrence Venuti, in his compelling study, *The Scandals of Translation*, offers thought-provoking statistics regarding translation and pedagogy, pointing out that since World War II, English remains 'the most translated language worldwide' which establishes a 'hegemony over foreign countries that is not simply political and economic ... but cultural as well'.[82] While his particular discussion is focused on the teaching of texts translated into English, or as he terms it, the 'pedagogy of literature', some of his insights in this and his other various publications are pertinent to travel and translation in the Victorian age. For instance, he argues that the teaching of translated texts, in failing to factor in the issues surrounding translation, such as the possibility that the foreign text will be inscribed with British or American cultural values, means that English becomes 'the transparent vehicle of universal truth' which has two significant impacts: a 'linguistic chauvinism' and a 'cultural nationalism'. This, he says, quoting Guillory, permits 'the easy appropriation of texts in foreign languages'.[83] This appropriative action is of some significance back in Victorian Britain where *appropriation* is a term of intensified meaning in an imperial nation. Chapter 5, on Charlotte Guest's Welsh translations, is a case of appropriation where Guest is an English 'incomer', part of a 'powerful foreign ruling caste' as Mario Basini puts it.[84] However, the translated Victorian travel texts featured in my work are a different matter. I read these as forms of territory, across which the reader journeys, and as palimpsests because overlaid with an English form which is targeted politically and culturally at readers of English and in which the historical moment, even the dominant culture, of the original, can be lost. 'The only true motive for putting poetry into a fresh

---

81   Jane Sinnett, 'Schiller', 478 and 479.
82   Venuti, *The Scandals of Translation*, 88.
83   Venuti, *The Scandals of Translation*, 92–3.
84   Mario Basini, *Real Merthyr* (Bridgend, Wales, 2008), 35 and 34.

language', wrote Dante Gabriel Rossetti in the late 1850s, 'must be to endow a fresh nation ... with one more possession of beauty', a point made much earlier by Madame de Staël whose views on translating I will address later.[85] Rossetti's term 'endow' suggests a voluntary offering and helps to modify 'possession' into a less aggressive term. By the same token, the outcome, appropriation, remains.

As Venuti argues, such translation subordinates the original to the target language by inscribing the target language's 'domestic cultural values'.[86] In other words, respect for cultural difference is lost, but at the same time an appropriated culture is gained. In his 1993 article 'Translation as Cultural Politics' Venuti makes this point even more firmly, first in terms of loss and gain, and then with regard to the nineteenth century, arguing that 'a translation method of eliding the linguistic and cultural difference of the foreign text was firmly entrenched as a canon in English-language translation' and pointing out that 'the translator domesticates the foreign text, causing its difference to vanish by making it intelligible in an English-language culture that values easy readability, transparent discourse, and the illusion of authorial presence'.[87]

Georges Van Den Abbeele argues an almost identical position for travel, the 'danger of loss' poised against 'the possibility of gain', the latter providing the incentive for travel in the first place and gains being listed as including 'riches, power, experience, wisdom'. He formulates that motives for travel can be both economic and ideological, suggesting that 'tourists accumulate "cultural experiences" that then increase their social value within their home communities'.[88] The kind of accumulation described by Van Den Abbeele can be as readily applied to the impact of translations into English, which Venuti's meticulous research evidences. The travel and translation described here, tourism, and what might be termed naturalized translation, are all forms of domestic journey in which 'reading' the site or the page is a cultural experience but one which might be termed second-hand rather than first.

Loss and gain are, of course, economic terms and translation, more than most forms of writing, appears to attract economic metaphors. Goethe, in addressing the role of the translator in *Schriften zur Literatur* [*Writings on Literature*] in 1824, views such work as a form of mediation between nations. At the same time, translation practice becomes a market place 'where all nations offer their wares', a form of interchange. The translator is thus a mediator operating under market conditions, much like a tour guide, and translation is an enterprise 'in the general commerce of the world'.[89] Madame de Staël, in her essay *De l'esprit*

[85]   Quoted in André Lefevere (ed.), *Translation/History/Culture. A Sourcebook* (London, 1992), 67.

[86]   Venuti, *The Scandals of Translation*, 95.

[87]   Venuti, 'Translation as cultural politics', 212–13. See also Venuti, *The Translator's Invisibility*, 64 and 65.

[88]   Abbeele, xvii.

[89]   Quoted in Lefevere, ed. *Translation/History/Culture*, 24–5.

des traductions [*On the Principle of Translation*], according to Sherry Simon, also uses 'metaphors of commerce and exchange' in discussing the practice of translation, metaphors which reveal 'the framework of political and economic liberalism which she sees as sustaining the work of literature'.[90]

The role of women in translation is mostly assessed in direct discussions of gender. Sherry Simon makes a convincing case for the function of translation as a form which has allowed women 'to enter the world of letters, to promote political causes and to engage in stimulating writing relationships'.[91] The case studies in Part II particularly, demonstrate these outcomes. From the 1990s on, the role of women translators as cultural mediators over the centuries, in western literature at least, has slowly been more fully addressed but can still be marked by silence. In Lefevere's *Translation/History/Culture. A Sourcebook* (1992), for instance, there are some 60 commentaries on translation, only two of which are by women. This is in part explained by the fact that the collection covers some 20 centuries, and women are mostly omitted from publishing records until the sixteenth century at least.

Lawrence Venuti, as already noted, has written comprehensively on the invisibility of the translator, a situation that is intensified in the nineteenth century if the translator is a woman, in part because of the convention in the Victorian age, and earlier, that women should avoid attracting public notice. For this reason, women translators in particular often published their work anonymously. George Eliot's first published work, her translation of David Friedrich Strauss's controversial *Das Leben Jesu* [*The Life of Jesus*], was published anonymously in three volumes in 1846. But, as Simon points out, the work of women translators often reveals 'their intervention in cultural and intellectual movements of their times, and ... the ways in which they themselves construe their gendered identities as relevant'.[92] Eliot offers an excellent example of a woman caught up both in the radical politics of her day and in her awareness of the conjunction between identity and relevance. In both cases she is transgressive but determined to have a significant public voice in which her sex is not the issue. While Eliot's journalism was also anonymous, the Strauss translation is the last book Eliot published anonymously, preferring instead her own name, Mary Ann Evans, for her translation of Feuerbach's *Das Wesen des Christenthums* [translated as *The Essence of Christianity*] published in 1854, the only time her given name ever appeared on any of her publications, her chosen male pseudonym being reserved for her later fiction and poetry. Eliot's is, I admit, an extreme example, given her subsequent fame and her place in the canon of English literature, but the women whose work I focus on nevertheless produced cultural interventions endorsing a range of political and social positions via travel and translation. One journey most women translators never undertake is a return

[90]   Sherry Simon, 63. See Germaine de Staël. 'De L'Esprit des Traductions', *Oeuvres Complètes de Mme La Baronne de Staël* (1816; Paris, 1821), 17: 387.
[91]   Simon, 39.
[92]   Simon, 42.

to the classical past. Classical translation is, writes Simon, the 'outstanding line of demarcation' separating male and female translators. In the nineteenth century middle- and upper-class women were, for the most part, taught modern European languages if sufficiently fortunate to have a comprehensive education. Their male counterparts were taught the classics.

The gendered system of education in the period accounts, in part, for the number of women engaged in translating modern languages. Critic Elizabeth Rigby in 'Lady Travellers' remarks to her *Quarterly* readership, in comparing the travel writing of men and women: 'If the gentleman knows more of ancient history and ancient languages, the lady knows more of human nature and modern languages'.[93] At the same time it is important to acknowledge that some men of letters did know modern languages too, Thomas Carlyle is an obvious example, as is Matthew Arnold. However, as James Anthony Froude recalled, in his reminiscences of university days at Oxford in the 1840s, 'Oxford knew nothing of Goethe, knew nothing of modern languages or modern literature outside England'.[94] What Oxford did know, however, as did Cambridge, were the so-called classical languages: Ancient Greek and Latin. Classical learning, within the British education system, is neatly summed up by an American journalist reviewing a pretentious Latinate publication for the *North American Review* in 1842:

> A very exact verbal knowledge of Greek and Latin, and especially of the laws
> of metrical composition, has been considered indispensable to the education of
> an English gentleman. Hence we have seen eminent professional men filling up
> the intervals of their daily occupations by writing Latin and Greek verses, or
> translating into those tongues favorite passages from English authors ... At the
> schools, boys are most laboriously trained in this discipline; prizes and honors
> are obtained by it at the University; and the high places of the church are brilliant
> objects in the scholar's perspective, the steps to which are trochees, spondees,
> and anapaests. Classical learning is thus preeminently esteemed in England.

On first reading this passage I suspected a certain dry, sly humour on the part of the anonymous author. But he or she goes on to state the benefits of a classical education. In sum, classical studies 'are unquestionably the best means to train the manly mind to habits of accuracy and of patient labor'.[95] The concept of Manliness was developed as a distinct requirement for a colonizing nation, and the training essential for future colonial administrators.

---

[93]   Elizabeth Rigby, 'Lady Travellers', *Quarterly Review* 76(1845): 99; 98–137.

[94]   Quoted in Rosemary Ashton, *142 Strand. A Radical Address in Victorian London* (London, 2006), 66.

[95]   'Classical Learning in England', *North American Review* 54(1842): 269–70 and 273–4; 269–82. The work under review is by Henry Drury, styling himself Henricus Drury, *A.M. Cantabrigiae,* 1841.

G.C. Swayne, however, in 'The Art of Travel', a review of Francis Galton's book of the same title and Albert Smith's *The English Hotel Nuisance*, provides a counter-voice to the general acceptance of the superiority of a classical education and rails against the British system of education which favours study of classical languages over the modern, signalling what seems to be a lively debate in the timeframe:

> While all over the Continent modern languages are made a matter of primary importance as an element of education, the directors of our English schools still treat them with great disrespect, in comparison with the ancient; and not only do this, but keep the mass of scholars so hard at work at writing nonsense verses, that they have little time or energy left for anything else. Yet there is, perhaps, no European better situated for learning the modern languages than an inhabitant of Great Britain.[96]

Swayne also ranks the languages which should be learned, naming French, German and Italian as 'first in importance' because of the closeness they bear to English.[97] His position seems to suggest a sense in which an education confined to the classics locks scholars into the past rather than preparing them for the modern present and the new and changing future. Research suggests that Swayne's position was not the standard one and his argument, today, seems prescient. James Hannay, a decade later, asserts that 'Plutarch is quite as enjoyable in English as in Greek'.[98]

The situation regarding the dominance of classical languages had slowly begun to change from 1854, however, with the appointment of Max Müller as Taylorian Professor of Modern European Languages, although his focus was on language development, an interest later reflected when, in 1868, Oxford abolished the Taylorian chair and created in its stead a Chair of Comparative Philology.[99] Despite these changes, however, knowledge of Ancient Greek remained a requirement for admission to Oxford and Cambridge until after World War I, naturally impacting on curriculum in the secondary public schools. Turner suggests that knowledge of Greek also advantaged those sitting for Home Civil Service, Indian Civil Service, and Royal Military Academy examinations, making knowledge of the classics apparently mandatory for those seeking a career in politics, in the public service or within the Church of England.[100] The first women undergraduates at Girton College, Cambridge University, were expected to follow the same curriculum as

---

[96]   G.C. Swayne, 'The Art of Travel', Blackwood's *Edinburgh Magazine* 79(1856): 601; 593–608.

[97]   Swayne, 601.

[98]   James Hannay, 'The Classics in Translations', *Cornhill Magazine* 16(1867): 111; 109–28.

[99]   R.C.C. Fynes, 'Max Müller', *ODNB* 39: 706–11.

[100]   Frank M. Turner, *The Greek Heritage in Victorian Britain* (New Haven and London, 1981), 5.

the male students although most lacked sufficient education in mathematics and the classics.[101] Throughout the Victorian age, therefore, Greek and Latin appear to have remained the mainstay of language study predominantly for men, albeit men of a particular privileged class and financial standing. By contrast, essayist, journalist and translator, Abraham Hayward, from a more modest background, had been educated in the modern languages, French and German, and epitomized what Philip Harling terms a 'self-made man of letters'. Hayward translated and published Goethe's *Faust* in 1833 which helped to establish his reputation, and a career in journalism.[102]

In the nineteenth century, women were for the most part written out of the classical education debate. Look at Matthew Arnold, writing in 1861 about translating Homer. In just a short extract Arnold assumes that the reader will be male, the translator will be male, that scholars of Greek language and literature will be male.[103] In the 'Preface' to his *Poems* (1853) Arnold says of classical scholars that they are 'more truly than others under the empire of facts, and more independent of the language current among those with whom they live'.[104] In part this appears to have been a response to a critic (coincidentally endorsing Swayne's later position) writing in the *Spectator*, 2 April 1853, who asserted that poets 'must leave the exhausted past' and focus on the present.[105] The prevailing ideological attitude was that women were not sufficiently able, intellectually or physically, to study and learn Greek and Latin, despite real evidence to the contrary. Gender ideology was not the only barrier. The study of classical languages was also tied to class. I would argue that this practice (noticeable in the mandarin quarterlies in particular) was also a deliberate means of creating a barrier against both women, and men from lower social orders, entering the fray, especially with regard to journalism and to publishing more generally. Acquiring classical languages was to gain access to a particular power. Charles Stuart Parker, whose essay 'On the History of Classical Education' appears in F.W. Farrar's *Essays on a Liberal Education* (1868), addresses what he terms 'liberal education for women' noting that 'the sacred precincts of the classics' had been tabooed against women, with the result that girls knew more about modern languages and literature, and sometimes more about science, than their brothers'. Similarly, Richard Monkton Milnes (Lord Houghton) observed that such French and German as boys possessed was probably picked up from a sister's governess. Notably, most of the essays in

---

[101]   Janet Howarth, ed. 'Editor's Introduction', *The Higher Education of Women by Emily Davies* (1866; London, 1988), xliii.

[102]   Philip Harling, 'Abraham Hayward', *ODNB* 26: 82; 82–4.

[103]   Quoted in Lefevere, *Translation/History/Culture*, 68–9. See also Richard Jenkyns, *The Victorians and Ancient Greece* (Oxford, 1980), chapter 9.

[104]   Quoted in Jenkyns, 65–6.

[105]   Quoted in Matthew Arnold, 'Preface to Poems (1853)', *Poetry and Criticism of Matthew Arnold* (Boston, 1961), 205.

Farrar's collection do not mention the education of girls at all.[106] In *Rambles in Germany and Italy*, Mary Shelley recalls the amazement of one of her son Percy's Cambridge undergraduate friends on her facility with Italian:

> "You *do* speak Italian!" exclaimed one of my companions in accents of surprise and pleasure; – so many difficulties in the future disappeared under this conviction. I certainly did speak Italian: it had been strange if I did not; ... mine was a peculiarly useful Italian; from having lived long in the country, all its household terms were familiar to me.[107]

The young man's reaction indicates the degree to which their travels had been hampered until this moment because no-one in the group spoke German, and French and English were of no avail along the route they had chosen through Germany and down into Switzerland to Italy. There is a sense in this exchange of a new level of respect accorded to young Percy Shelley's mother.

Conclusion

In terms of culture, travel and translation was absorbed into the coffers of the British Empire. The knowledge industry operated at any number of levels, across topics, across classes, across gender. Women played a more prominent part in this industry than is generally allowed. Barbara Gates in *Kindred Nature. Women Embrace the Living World* exposes the importance of women's roles as educators in providing non-specialist readerships access to ideas and information generated from a variety of disciplines. Women, as travellers and translators, and as writers, always struggled against dismissive labelling of their work as amateur or merely popular. While Gates's focus is on science and nature study, my own work locates within women's travel writings and translations particularly, challenges to the meaning of home, to national politics, to gender politics, with sharp comparisons which explicitly reveal direct engagement with the world around them. Even when these women journey along routes which others have travelled extensively before them, each brings to the familiar journey an idiosyncratic gaze. This is especially so when the traveller and translator are in tandem, seeking to engage a third for the journey, the reader. In the case of women writers, that reader, it is often implied, is another woman who will sympathize with the gendered constraints that dictate a book's content.

---

[106]   See Charles Stuart Parker, 'On the History of Classical Education' and Richard Monkton Milnes, Lord Houghton, 'On the Present Social Results of Classical Education', in *Essays on a Liberal Education*, ed. F.W. Farrar (London, 1868), 78 and 370.

[107]   Shelley, 104.

For women, importantly, the domestic and the everyday, what Susan Bassnett describes as 'other kinds of narrative',[108] come into focus from the 1830s on with a clarity never before seen. Laurie Langbauer, in *Novels of Everyday Life*, makes the important point that the everyday is 'the very medium of culture', and can represent a gender politics which means contestation in 'the struggle to be heard rather than silenced'.[109] Travel and translation were both publishing avenues which gave women a voice. They deployed often extraordinary sites and sights into a discourse of the everyday which ensured the maintenance of personal respectability while at the same time enabling the sly contestation of prevailing ideologies and a determined countering of the politics of home. Bassnett rightly points out the danger in too readily essentializing women travel writers into a category in which broad assumptions are made about a common style designated feminine – and I would add there is a similar danger in assessing the work of women translators. Women travellers often did, however, document the everyday as they encountered it wherever they travelled, because the everyday, the domestic realm, was ideologically their particular space. For the woman travelling, however, that space no longer confined her because she was elsewhere, free to observe and to comment on the everyday lives of others, and free to make specific political and ideological connections across borders, across the channel. In precisely the same way, the woman translating, whose work was often published anonymously (George Eliot is an excellent example) could also engage in that journey with considerable freedom.

This other kind of narrative, the everyday, can be located almost immediately in the titles themselves of travel accounts by women, Anna Jameson's *Visits and Sketches at Home and Abroad* (1834) and Fredrika Bremer's *The Homes of the New World* (1853) are instances, Jameson's substantive noun *Visits*, and Bremer's *Homes*, indicating a more intimate and domestic format, suggestive of the everyday. Similarly, titles using the words 'Journal' or 'Diary' or 'Letters', are further examples, for instance, *A Residence on the Shores of the Baltic. Described in a Series of Letters* (1841) by Elizabeth Rigby. The illusion of unproblematic narrative and personal anecdote contained in such titles demonstrates the way in which women were able to negotiate gender ideology and the actual narrative often reveals a heavily politicized everyday in which gendered restrictions back home are brought into relief, to be constructed, amended, contested, according to the politics of the writer and the locus on which the travel narrative is centered. Jameson offers an excellent example in a general discussion comparing English and German women which is discursively managed. Framed as a dialogue between a woman and a man, Alda and Medon, there are many statements supposedly designed to illustrate 'the moral and social position of the women in Germany' for her English readers but at the same time, she opportunistically

---

108   Bassnett, 'Travel Writing and Gender', 225.
109   Laurie Langbauer, *Novels of Everyday Life: The Series in English Fiction, 1850–1930* (Ithaca, NY, 1999), 15 and 18.

explores more generally the relationships between men and women in patently political terms that have everything to do with the British 'Woman Question' and little to do with Germany.[110] At one stage chivalry is condemned as an affectation which, she says, women would gladly exchange 'for more real honour, more real protection, more equal rights', a statement almost immediately undermined by a disclaimer: 'I am no vulgar, vehement arguer about the "rights of woman"' (I:174), a typical Jamesonian ploy allowing her to state what she wishes to say, but then to assert (falsely) that no polemic is intended.[111] Similarly, Marianne Finch in *An Englishwoman's Experience in America* (1853) offers in chapter 12 an 'Account of the Woman's Movement' in America and takes the opportunity to remind her English readers that 'anti-woman's-rights men seem to forget that the highest office in the British government is filled by a woman! ... [S]uch being the case, it seems great inconsistency ... to deprive any English woman of her political existence on account of *her sex*'.[112] Elizabeth Rigby in 'Lady Travellers' discountenances such political practices as these, complaining of women travellers who 'take all the trouble of travelling abroad merely to express those private opinions upon affairs in general which they could as well have given utterance to at home', not realizing the degree to which encountering another culture might well trigger a reaction to conditions 'at home' which had not previously occurred to the traveller.[113]

In his review of travel guides, R.J. King observes with some acumen, 'a volume which at once carries you away to Thebes or to Athens, to Cintra or to Archangel ... converts you for the time into an actual traveller'.[114] Through the pages of the press, then, in all its various forms, journeys of cultural significance experienced and recorded by women took place. Such journeys included the dissemination of European culture into English homes, but also the transformation of the European gaze at what is sometimes termed Europe's 'others', where European is always the superior category, although this now seems a distinctly dubious formulation. Sara Mills, drawing on Peter Hulme's argument, shows that for some travellers, confrontation with different cultures makes them question their own culture's claim to superiority.[115] Anna Jameson, engaging with the First Nations people in Canada, illustrates such a confrontation to a nicety and neatly genders her response:

> Really I do not see that an Indian warrior, flourishing his tomahawk, and smeared with his enemy's blood, is so very much a greater savage than the pipe-clayed, padded, embroidered personage, who, without cause or motive, has sold himself to slay or be slain: one scalps his enemy, the other rips him open with a sabre ...

[110]   Anna Jameson, *Visits and Sketches at Home and Abroad* (London, 1835), I: 12.
[111]   Jameson, *Visits and Sketches*, I: 174.
[112]   Marianne Finch, *An Englishwoman's Experience in America* (London, 1853), 226.
[113]   Rigby, 101.
[114]   King, 504.
[115]   Sara Mills, *Discourse* (London, 1997), 117.

and to me, femininely speaking, there is not a needle point's difference between the one and the other.[116]

In terms of British contact with other places, other cultures, other languages, however, precedence in my timeframe is given to European literature and culture, and it is on these specific interactions that I will for the most part focus, arguing that these continental interconnections not only had an impact on British culture but contributed in part to the power of the British Empire from this period with the expansion of knowledge and information. As Gail Turley Houston has noted, the Victorian age, 'prefigured modern concerns about who creates, controls, and distributes a culture's knowledge systems and oversees inter- and intra-cultural exchanges'. Houston expresses this in terms of the nation as a pre-eminently capitalist one in a period when various modern careers were becoming professionalized, thereby shifting, one assumes, from dilettante amateur status to one of economic viability.[117] At the outset of *Touring Cultures*, the editors Chris Rojek and John Urry note it 'is now clear that people tour cultures; and that cultures and objects themselves travel'.[118] Whether people tour or travel, certain national characteristics come under scrutiny. The vaunted insularity of the English as tourists and travellers provided material for an ongoing debate. In the writing of the period on which this work is focused, and beyond, the word 'English' is commonly used to denote most inhabitants of the United Kingdom. I will shift between the terms 'English' and 'British' as seems most appropriate to the context.

Mona Wilson, writing in the post-Victorian 1930s, offers a classic example of the ways in which the class ideologies and anxieties of the Victorian age continued well into the twentieth century when she turns to the tourism debate while simultaneously addressing the notion of cultural exchange. She considers the impact of cheap travel, encapsulated by the activities of the tourism impresario Thomas Cook, which enabled working class people to holiday abroad, by quoting Charles Lever who complains in an article for *Blackwood's*, in unremittingly offensive language, of 'the cities of Italy deluged with droves of these creatures', terms which can be immediately connected back to 'swarm', discussed earlier. Wilson herself, barely less impolitic, describes Cook's tours as a 'scamper for the multitude', adding much more interestingly, however, that the 'internationalism of culture perished with the ascendancy of the class that maintained it: increasing mobility served rather to intensify the insularity of the islanders'. Lever apparently told his Italian friends that the British tourists were 'convicts rejected by the Australian colonies' and that Cook had been contracted by the British government

---

[116]   Anna Jameson, *Winter Studies and Summer Rambles in Canada* (1838; Toronto, 1990), 459–60. All subsequent references are to this edition.

[117]   Gail Turley Houston, *Royalties. The Queen and Victorian Writers* (Charlottesville and London, 1999), 6.

[118]   Chris Rojek and John Urry (eds), *Touring Cultures. Transformations of Travel and Theory* (London, 1997), 1.

to 'dump a few in every city in Italy'.[119] Wilson's use of the terms 'insularity' and 'islander' is striking, as is her claim that cultural exchange perished. Her argument is clearly a class-based one, implying that no amount of travel will undo inherent prejudices and ideologies.

As previously noted, British insularity and with it the chance of being misunderstood and misjudged by their Continental neighbours, was a common anxiety across the nineteenth century. In 'The English on the Continent' (1843) it is argued that the English are 'water-locked' and fail to take advantage of their travelling experiences, which theoretically should, through 'observation and intercourse' open them up to new ideas, and 'human knowledge and sympathy'.[120] Thackeray, in 'The Kickleburys on the Rhine' (1850) complains 'We carry our nation everywhere with us; and are in our island, wherever we go'.[121] Both these examples might be classified as salutary journalism, a style unexceptional in an age when didacticism was common, when the educated middle classes wrote instructively for the benefit of 'the million' as the journalists William and Mary Howitt termed their putative working-class readership, and manuals on proper conduct (especially for women) abounded, while treatises on muscular Christianity and self-help were aimed at the male reader. Tales for children and servants, especially, were more usually homiletic in style than entertaining. All of this educative process might more broadly be subsumed under the label 'Culture'.

E.E. Kellett, in his comprehensive historical essay on the British Press, covering the years 1830–1865, describes one of its functions as 'an engine of moral improvement'.[122] British consciousness of a wide world and their own extensive role in it, in terms of imperialism and colonialism at this time, also contributed to this kind of national soul-searching. The author of 'The English on the Continent' makes this connection in no uncertain terms, asserting that colonization and empire are all very well but ultimately they produce 'no change in the inner life of the individual':

> It is one thing to ship off our superfluous population to distant lands, to plant the Union Jack on some savage rock, and crack a bottle with a huzza! to the health of Old England; and another to maintain intimate relations and constant interchange with nations as civilized as ourselves.[123]

This author's opposing terms, 'savage' and 'civilized', form a pointed corollary to the anxieties expressed about the degree to which the nation can consider itself

---

[119]   Wilson, Mona, II: 312.

[120]   'The English on the Continent', *Foreign Quarterly Review* 32(1843): 92–3; 90–106.

[121]   William Makepeace Thackeray, 'The Kickleburys on the Rhine', *Christmas Books, Rebecca and Rowena and Later Minor Papers, 1849–1861* (1850; London, n.d.), X: 256.

[122]   Kellett, 'The Press', II: 42.

[123]   'English on the Continent', 93.

to be enlightened and the degree to which it must be on sound terms of cultural exchange with the like-minded Continental nations across the channel.

Knowledge of others as interchange remained, however, a predominantly print form in the early decades of Victorian England, and that can be problematic. In *Journeys to the Other Shore*, Roxanne L. Euben comments on the philosopher James Mill's defence of insularity, in his preface to *The History of British India* (1817), as a means of attaining objectivity. Mill wrote 'Whatever is worth seeing or hearing in India, can be expressed in writing'.[124] Later Euben returns to her discussion of Mill to raise two very compelling points. First, that if 'travel occasions comparisons that, in turn, initiate an often … transformative mediation between what is unfamiliar and familiar', how sufficient or extensive does that travel have to be? And secondly, what if '"seeing with one's own eyes" produces its own kinds of distortions of what is unfamiliar and its own closures to critical reflection'? Both these questions readily produce in my mind examples that illustrate these issues precisely. For instance, those nine publications severely critiqued by the author of 'German Tourists' address the first question because they are found wanting in both sufficiency and extensiveness. With regard to the second question, the over-wrought, highly sexualized accounts of women of the Middle East in so many travel books by men, produce a distorted picture despite the numerous corrections made available through the access women travellers had to harem culture, in particular. Euben rightly points also to the unpredictable element that can be the result of 'personal, cultural, historical, and institutional' interaction. While I find this argument convincing, and agree that the knowledges located are fluid, it is the writing down that does indeed fix, map, possess and control them.[125]

My work seeks to make a crucial intervention here to counter both the impression given by Wilson's 1930s argument regarding culture, and that general anxiety regarding English insularity so often expressed in the nineteenth century itself, to argue instead that despite so many contrary signs, 'internationalism of culture' as Wilson puts it, did not perish as she claims, but was assimilated through writing, publishing and reading into British intellectual thought and practice, which at one level, admittedly, reinforced the British Empire's sense of power and superiority and did indeed encourage an insular pride. At the same time, however, new ideas did remain fluid in my timeframe, and gained currency, generating new tolerances and understandings, along with a readiness to listen and to understand other points of view. This may have much to do with the period itself because there was such significant engagement and critique with the many publications recording travels, tours and journeys.

Madame de Staël, an important literary figure for British women in the early decades of the nineteenth century, theorized, according to Sherry Simon, translation as a necessary component of literary exchange in precisely these terms.

---

[124]   Quoted in Roxanne L. Euben, *Journeys to the Other Shore. Muslim and Western Travelers in Search of Knowledge* (Princeton and Oxford, 2006), 20.

[125]   Euben, 188–9.

Simon states that the thrust of de Staël's essay, *De l'esprit des traductions* (written in 1816 and published in 1821) resides in its celebration of translation as a service to literature in transporting 'from one language to another the masterpieces of the human spirit'.[126] De Staël argues that translations of great foreign texts will bring about a 'renewal of literary form' in the target culture and, Simon adds, de Staël's vocabulary 'is grounded in the principles of liberalism which encourage the free circulation of ideas and forms. Literary exchange, she suggests, is just as necessary to the life of society as it is to literature: it rejuvenates and enriches the national spirit'.[127] Despite a focus on the 'production and circulation of literature' as Simon puts it, in what seems prescient analysis, de Staël, so early in the nineteenth century, manages to intimate an economy of exchange with the possibility, I would argue, for critics today to expand beyond her more narrow definition of 'literature' to embrace various genres on a plethora of topics. Goethe recognized the economy of exchange in de Staël's work when he said that her study of Germany, *De l'Allemagne*, 'which owed its rise to social conversations, is to be regarded as a mighty engine which at once made a wide breach in that Chinese wall of antiquated prejudices, which divided us from France'.[128]

Women travellers, in the first decades of Victoria's reign, were more likely than men to report on their contact with the domestic, everyday lives of other people in other places, even as they simultaneously addressed the prevailing politics of a place (as Bremer does to such life-changing effect in her account of confronting the domestic, everyday lives of American slaves, addressed in Chapter 7). Women translators were also more likely to choose texts to translate that reflected on everyday life or which they deemed politically interventionist (sometimes the two are interchangeable) in ways which accorded with their own political sensibilities. These considerations dictated choice of text to translate for instance. Women understood both the connection between the private and public spheres, and that the functioning of the private sphere in foreign context would be of interest to their female readerships, both issues which Elizabeth Rigby comments on at length in her 1845 article 'Lady Travellers', remarking that 'every country with any pretensions to civilization has a twofold aspect, addressed to two different modes of perception, and seldom visible simultaneously to both. Every country has a home life as well as a public life, and the first quite necessary to interpret the last'.[129]

John Urry argues that even in a more modern context, tourists seek experiences that are different to their own everyday lives, and that they locate in the actual domestic lives of others 'a reality' which is more authentic than their own

---

[126]   Quoted in Simon, 63.

[127]   Simon, 63 and 64.

[128]   Quoted in Jameson, *Visits and Sketches*, I: 59. The information is contained in a note Sarah Austin provided.

[129]   Rigby, 99.

ordinary, humdrum lives back home.[130] But this can be taken further. The women who publish, either translations or their own travels, suddenly see the reality of their own lives against the foreign domestic backdrop. The reaction is often more radical in traditionally exotic locations, or when confronted with the lifestyles of other races, nevertheless, as the example above from Jameson shows, the foreign domestic backdrop can operate as an excuse to confront the reader with specific issues of the day relating to the home culture. Women, both in travelling and translating, could more readily penetrate private domestic spheres and gain a more comprehensive view of home life in other countries. Women, in publishing, and through reviews of their work, could similarly reach a domestic readership. Either way, they could enter a private inner circle where the standard guidebook, for instance, keeps the tourist and the reader strictly on the public path and offers, as Rigby puts it, 'mere roadside information'.[131]

The varied impacts of travel writings and translations on the British reading public, against which readers could test themselves and their sense of nationhood include the reviews of such transformed texts (or rewritings as André Lefevere puts it),[132] as located in periodicals and newspapers, and anecdotally, in letters and diaries. The enormous range in the kinds of travel translations available, from Prince Pückler-Muskau's forays into Britain as translated by Sarah Austin to Fredrika Bremer's journeys in the Old World and the New, translated by Mary Howitt, made my choice and selection of texts, which will dilate on the concepts on which this work is based, both difficult and challenging. The key is choosing texts which were widely accessible to a large readership, as evidenced by a strong publication history (more than one edition) and a relevant and broad reception history. Through a close analysis of such texts it is possible to explore the probable effect on England's intellectual empire and its imperial agenda of cultural ascendancy, as such texts manifest in a variety of topic areas and a variety of source languages. Focusing on women translators participating in and promoting the new leisured practice of reading, enables consideration of the degree to which reception and effect is gendered. In the case studies that follow, all of the writers selected were travellers and translators, and their publications produced journeys which do indeed reveal 'unexpected neighbourhoods'.

---

[130]   Urry, 8.

[131]   Rigby, 104.

[132]   André Lefevere, *Translation, Rewriting, and the Manipulation of Literary Fame* (London, 1992), 7.

PART II:
Case Studies

Chapter 2
Sarah Austin
and the Politics of Translation

Sarah Austin was an early Victorian translator of note, working to supplement her lawyer husband John Austin's income and, after his death, editing and publishing his famous treatise on Jurisprudence. As she drily remarked to a friend in 1841, 'I am the man of business in *our firm*'.[1] She belonged to that Unitarian circle of intellectual thinkers, writers and philosophers which included Jeremy Bentham, John Stuart Mill, the Grotes and the Carlyles, and she was related to the Martineaus. Her nephew was Henry Reeve, later influential and long-term editor of the Whig quarterly, the *Edinburgh Review*, from 1855 to 1895. Austin's translations from the German in the decade 1831–1841 were significant in introducing German intellectual thinking and writing into England.[2] Austin had located what we would term today a 'niche' market in which she offered to the British reading public a range of texts translated, or to use André Lefevere's term 'rewritten', from the German. Lefevere defines this term very broadly as follows and my own use, as applied to Austin's translation, is similarly flexible but with ideology and manipulation an important factor:

> Whether they produce translations, literary histories or their more compact spin-offs, reference works, anthologies, criticism or editions, rewriters adapt, manipulate the originals they work with to some extent, usually to make them fit in with the dominant, or one of the dominant ideological and poetological currents of their time.[3]

As I have noted elsewhere, Austin, Carlyle and Coleridge spearheaded an industry which introduced German intellectual thought into England.[4] One contemporary commentator notes in a review of *Fragments from German Prose Writers*

---

[1]   Quoted in Lotte and Joseph Hamburger, *Troubled Lives: John and Sarah Austin* (Toronto, 1985), 66. Austin's emphasis.

[2]   In 1830 she had published 'Specimens of German Genius' in 5 parts in *New Monthly Magazine* 28(1830): 311–17; 444–50; 519–26; and 29(1830): 34–42 and 180–89. See also Christoph E. Schweitzer, 'Sarah Austin's Assessment of Goethe's Character and Works and of Weimar' in *A Reassessment of Weimar Classicism*, ed. Gerhart Hoffmeister (Lampeter, 1996), 145–56, for a comprehensive discussion of this topic.

[3]   Lefevere, *Translation, Rewriting, and the Manipulation of Literary Fame*, 8.

[4]   See Johnston, *Anna Jameson*, chapter five.

(1841) that Austin 'has done more, perhaps, than any living writer, to bring the German mind into contact with the English'.[5] Carlyle too was impressed with her *Characteristics of Goethe* (1833), as his emphases indicate: 'You can *actually translate Goethe*, which, (quietly, I reckon) is what hardly three people in England can',[6] and Herman Merivale, writing for the *Edinburgh Review*, expresses his 'admiration of the truly extraordinary manner in which she has rendered ... – metaphysical reasonings, poetical declamation, and social dialogue – into correct, nervous, vernacular English'.[7] Like her contemporaries, Austin's engagement with literature and translation characterized the practice of a generation of thinkers whose early work would come to inform the intellectual thrust of the Victorian age. This is especially so with regard to the literary output of women and it is notable the degree to which Austin's ability was admired, the publisher Lardner assuring Sismondi she is 'our best living translator'.[8]

Across the decade Austin offered to an English readership, both general and scholarly, an assortment of German literature: Hermann Pückler-Muskau's *Tour in England, Ireland and France, in the Years 1828 and 1829* (1832); *Characteristics of Goethe* (1833) from the German of Johann Falk and Friedrich von Müller among others; Friedrich von Raumer's *England in 1835* (1836); Leopold von Ranke's *The Ecclesiastical and Political History of the Popes of Rome* (1840) and *Fragments from German Prose Writers* (1841). While Austin also translated works from the French by Victor Cousin, *Report on the State of Public Instruction in Prussia* (1834), among others, French was far more established in Britain as the second language of the educated middle classes. Austin's own correspondence reveals the degree to which this was so in her particular case, extensively interlarded as it is with French words and phrases (as are her translations). The personal correspondence of other British women of the same period and of comparable intellectual and social standing (Elizabeth Barrett Browning, Harriet Martineau and Anna Jameson for instance) suggests, however, that Austin's over-use of French forms and idioms was idiosyncratic.

As previously noted and the reviews of the magisterial *Quarterly* and *Edinburgh Review* amply demonstrate, travel accounts were a dominant literary form in the early decades of the nineteenth century. Translation and travel writing also has a symbiotic relationship. The following from a review of Antoine Berman's *The Experience of the Foreign* summarizes precisely my point, '[T]ranslation is clearly but radically defined ... as the model for all forms of transmission between cultures ... since it is Berman's belief that cultures only develop a sense of identity by testing themselves against what is foreign and testing the Other

---

[5]   'Austin's German Prose Writers', *North American Review* 54(1842): 504; 504–506.

[6]   Quoted in Hamburger, *Troubled Lives*, 70. Carlyle's emphasis.

[7]   Herman Merivale, 'Mrs. Austin's *Characteristics of Goethe*', 57(1833): 372; 371–403.

[8]   Quoted in Hamburger, *Troubled Lives*, 71.

against themselves'.[9] For these reasons, I find it significant that Austin translated accounts by two German writers and scholars of their excursions into England. This foregrounds for me two factors which may have influenced Austin's choice of texts to offer the reading public. The first is strategic. Nothing sells so well to a reading public as accounts of their own nation by visiting dignitaries and as the Hamburgers note, she 'worked primarily for money'.[10] As Charles Buller asserts in his review of *Briefe eines Verstorbenen* [*Letters from a Dead Man*], Pückler-Muskau's German original, the 'English public has always displayed what we consider a laudable curiosity to know the opinions respecting their country and themselves, entertained by intelligent foreign travellers'.[11] In the 1830s, England is emerging as a significant political entity and the nation is caught up in a process of self-analysis. The second issue is that Austin is intellectually engaged in the debates about the political condition of England in the 1830s as the following comment in a letter to Jane Carlyle, written on Christmas Day, 1832, confirms. She remarks that she excites 'horror among my Radical friends for not believing that all revolution comes from certain organic forms of government, and ... am that monster made up "of all *we* Whigs hate", a radical *and* an absolutist'.[12] The circle in which she moved was immersed in the politics of the day and every possible political stance would have been canvassed, discussed, dissected. The obvious tension between those two positions, radical and absolutist, highlights the complexity of the debates and Austin's sense of humour.

Austin's decision to translate and market, as her first major publication, Prince Hermann Von Pückler-Muskau's supposedly anonymous and very risqué *Tour in England, Ireland, and France, in the years 1828 and 1829*, as she conservatively titled her translation, may well have been influenced in part because the text is so readable and an easy introduction to German literary style for the 'non-professional reader', to use Lefevere's term.[13] This chapter will accordingly focus for the most part on the Pückler-Muskau translation. Austin's decision may also, of course, have been influenced by the notoriety of Pückler's German publication which would have ensured her translation significant pre-publicity and equally significant earnings. Journalist and critic Charles Buller comments on the 'vehement abuse' to which the Prince's work is subjected and 'a consistent disposition for detecting licentiousness in every allusion to a female'.[14] In the event Austin published her

---

[9] Angela Esterhammer, review of Antoine Berman's *The Experience of the Foreign: Culture and Translation in Romantic Germany*, trans. S. Heyvaert, *Wordsworth Circle* 27(1996): 233; 232–4.

[10] Hamburger, *Troubled Lives*, 74.

[11] Charles Buller, 'Letters of a German Prince', *Foreign Quarterly Review* 9(1832): 290; 290–312.

[12] National Library of Scotland, Edinburgh. Sarah Austin to Jane Welsh Carlyle, Manuscript 1774, f. 32. Austin's emphases. The transcription is mine.

[13] Lefevere, *Translation, Rewriting, and the Manipulation of Literary Fame*, 7.

[14] Buller, 308 and 310.

translation of the first two volumes in London in 1832, followed shortly after by two more volumes covering the years 1826 and 1827. On publication, the press had a field day with the prince's name, the *Westminster Review* declaring 'what a name for a fairy tale' and the less kind distorting his name to 'Prince Pickling Mustard' or 'Prince Prettyman'.[15] At the same time, the Prince's *Tour* could be said to have made Austin's name and whether the decision to translate his *Tour* was fortuitous or simply shrewd judgment it is difficult to tell. At last count, however, her translation was reviewed in at least 15 separate periodicals and newspapers in 1832 alone.

In 1830, after publication of the first two volumes of *Briefe eines Verstorbenen* in Germany, the publisher John Murray II appears to have asked for Austin's opinion about publishing a translation of this then-anonymous German book which was such a very recent best-selling sensation in Europe.[16] Her response to Murray in a letter dated 25 December 1830 shows a business-like and capable approach to his request, assuring him that 'they would answer translating'; that 'nine people out of ten would say that they *cannot escape* being translated' and then offering the reasons why such a translation would succeed, including the Prince's acuteness regarding English and Irish manners; his picturesque descriptions; his conversations with public figures like Lady Morgan, Beau Brummel, the Archbishop of Dublin; and the vivacity of his account of Ireland. These are the qualities she believes will 'make the book popular in England'. She describes the work to Murray as designed for a 'light-reading public' as a relief from Reform politics which was dominating the publishing industry at that time. There is no hint that Murray himself would find the Prince's position on some of these listed attributes politically unsound. For Austin herself, however, the work's greatest charm, so she tells Murray, lies in 'the peculiar and interesting mind of the author'. Austin then announces to Murray that she plans to begin translating straight away and is certain of finding another publisher if he declines it.[17] As Austin became more enthusiastic for the project so this Tory publisher of the *Quarterly Review* became more cautious. On 22 March 1831 Austin again contacts Murray urging him not to delay:

---

[15]   E.M. Butler, 'Introduction', *A Regency Visitor. The English Tour of Prince Pückler-Muskau Described in his Letters 1826–1828*, trans. Sarah Austin, ed., E.M. Butler (London, 1957), 17 and Janet Ross, *Three Generations of English Women. Memoirs and Correspondence of Susannah Taylor, Sarah Austin, and Lady Duff Gordon* (London, 1893), 85.

[16]   All four volumes of *Briefe eines Verstorbenen* were published in Stuttgart 1830–31. The first two volumes were published in Munich in 1830.

[17]   National Library of Scotland, John Murray Archive, MS. 40031 dated 25 December 1830. Emphases Austin's.

To prevent therefore all doubt and all mistake I write to say that if you wish to publish it I shall be happy to treat with you – But that as delay would be sure to be fatal to my project – (for if I do not, somebody else will translate it) I shall take your silence not as consent, but the very reverse. If I do not hear from you definitely before Saturday next I shall take for granted that the scheme does not please you and shall consider myself at liberty to offer the MS elsewhere.[18]

It is in this letter she reveals that the author is 'the late Prince Puckler-Mowsku', at this stage apparently still believing the implication of the original German title that these are indeed the edited letters of a dead man. Finally Murray declined the project and Austin turned to publishers Effingham Wilson instead.

What Austin does not mention specifically in her letter of 25 December 1830 to Murray are possible reasons why one would not publish the Prince's volumes, in particular the racy, erotic anecdotes, the assignations and flirtations with married women and other material of a licentious kind, as well as the very decided critical statements on English manners and customs. Austin does, however, point out to Murray, again in her letter of Christmas Day 1830, that the 'vast number of personal anecdotes, conversations, etc.' is decidedly not *'public property'* and should be omitted. She adds, rather naively, that 'it is quite certain that they were never meant to be published'. She reminds Murray that the author is 'a Prince – an eccentric man – a German – and a man who travelled to see men and things and not to make a book'. But clearly the rumour mill about the work was already operating (although the *Athenaeum* reviewer of the German edition does not mention this aspect) and it seems to me that some of Austin's terms in this particular letter to Murray are loaded. Words like 'peculiar' and 'eccentric' are linked to what she describes as Pückler's 'strong sense of the ludicrous'.

The twentieth-century critiques of Austin's translation have focused for the most part on the politics of sexuality, exploring her censorship of Pückler-Muskau's work. Lotte and Joseph Hamburger in *Contemplating Adultery* have given a very full description of the kind of material censored by Austin in her rewriting of Pückler's *Tour*. She removed his 'fanciful introduction, ... portions of the personal satire, political harangues, and economic arguments she thought faulty' as well as accounts of erotic dreams; accounts of prostitutes; a bathhouse massage; a visit to a courtesan; crude doggerel; and anecdotes which they describe as 'in bad taste'. Indeed the Hamburgers assert that she 'mercilessly transformed the bohemian prince ... into an approximation of an English gentleman whose adventures could be read aloud in a Victorian drawing room', an estimate I would argue that is over-stated.[19] For instance, while Austin may have removed his direct

---

[18]   National Library of Scotland, John Murray Archive, MS. 40031 dated 22 March 1831.

[19]   Hamburger, *Contemplating Adultery*, 102 and 103.

encounters with prostitutes, his more general observations of such women 'with whom London swarms', she certainly included.[20]

As I have noted above, however, there is another form of political discourse which emerges from the Prince's tour, an exploration of the way in which class and parliamentary politics are interconnected. The Prince attacked the British aristocracy and the Tory class position and this material Austin did not censor. For instance, he observes:

> The happiest and most respectable class in England is, without all doubt, the middle class, whose political activity is confined to the improvement of their own immediate province ... People of this unfashionable class ... are wholly devoid of the arrogant airs so disgusting in their superiors ... They love their country passionately, but without any view to personal interest – without hope of sinecures, or intrigue for place. They are often ridiculous, but always deserving of respect, and their national egotism is restricted within more reasonable bounds than that of their superiors. (194)

As if to confirm this, *Foreign Quarterly* reviewer Charles Buller remarks that Pückler's book has become 'an interesting object of attack and defence for all the reviews, magazines, and newspapers, until it has become nearly an additional field for the eternal combat of aristocratic and democratic politicians'.[21] My brief, therefore, is with Austin's 'rewriting', her transformation of this work into English both as a marketable commodity, but also for its possible impact on the issue of radical parliamentary reform in spite of her designation of the work as 'light reading'. Austin's translation produced a rewriting based mostly on a shift in emphasis. She achieved this outcome by censoring some of the more licentious detail and accommodating the work culturally to an English readership. The result was that the politics of the work came more sharply into view. In the end she published a text in English which functioned culturally, and more specifically politically, in the England of her day. The Prince's impressions of England in the years 1826–1828, those vital pre-reform years, enabled Austin to forward her own radical and pro-reform politics, and were a vital corollary to the political debates which were so much a part of her intellectual milieu, although Susanne Stark has argued that the Prince himself was not politically consistent, admiring for instance, the wealth of English landholders.[22] These are the years leading up to the first Reform Bill of 1832 arguably the political beginning at least of the age designated 'Victorian'.

---

[20]   Prince Hermann Pückler-Muskau, *A Regency Visitor. The English Tour of Prince Pückler-Muskau Described in his Letters 1826–1828*, trans. Sarah Austin; ed. E.M. Butler (London, 1957), 83. Unless otherwise stated, all subsequent references are to this edition.

[21]   Buller, 308.

[22]   Susanne Stark, *Behind Inverted Commas. Translation and Anglo-German Cultural Relations in the Nineteenth Century* (Clevedon, OH, 1999), 161–2.

Prince Pückler-Muskau, the author and subject of Austin's translation, is described by E.M. Butler in over-wrought terms as 'Rogue, rover and rake', as 'markedly eccentric, handsome, dashing and brave', a traveller, a writer and a landscape-gardener. To rescue his impoverished estates he had to find a wealthy wife and was, says Butler, 'a husband to dream of, with his high station in life, his star quality and his all-conquering charm'.[23] The Prince found a wealthy wife and promptly expended all of her money on upgrading his estate, which, according to the Hamburgers, became a 'sensation, a fantasia, the creation of a romantic imagination and inspired landscaping'.[24] With the money evaporated the Prince planned with his wife to set out on travels forthwith to seek another wealthy spouse and then to divorce amicably (a plan never carried out but which might well account for his admiration for wealthy English landholders). His adventures were duly set down in *Briefe eines Verstorbenen* (literally, 'Letters from a Deadman'), as were his sexual intrigues and various indiscretions. No less a literary figure than Goethe, reviewing the book in the *Berliner Jahrbücher für wissenschaftliche Kritik* [*Berlin Annual for Scientific Criticism*], a review translated by Austin and appended to her 'Preface,' cheerfully dismisses the Prince's peccadilloes: 'That he excites the attention of women is natural enough – he attracts and is attracted; but his experience of the world enables him to terminate any little *affaires du coeur* without violence or indecorum'.[25]

More interesting, however, are the derogatory comments which Goethe goes on to make about the English, comments excited by his reading of what he terms Pückler's unexaggerated narrative which captures English peculiarity of manners and habits. It is significant, I think, that Sarah Austin so carefully incorporated almost the entire review by Goethe into her 'Translator's Preface', not simply because it was by Goethe, who she admired, and who was not at that time well known in England, but possibly to reinforce a politicized purpose, targeting her English readership, because she felt his comments on them would make provocative reading. Goethe writes, with some malice perhaps, of 'that insular life':

> based in boundless wealth and civil freedom, in universal monotony and manifold diversity; formal and capricious, active and torpid, energetic and dull, comfortable and tedious, the envy and the derision of the world. (Vol. 1.2, xi–xii)

The inclusion of Goethe's comments suggest that Sarah Austin had a specific interest in European assessment of the English and that her representation of the

---

23 Butler, 'Introduction', *Regency Visitor*, 10.

24 Hamburger, *Contemplating Adultery*, 96–7.

25 Quoted in Sarah Austin, 'Translator's Preface', *Tour in England, Ireland, and France, in the Years 1828 and 1829; with remarks on the Manners and Customs of the Inhabitants, and Anecdotes of Distinguished Public Characters. In a Series of Letters*. By a German Prince, 2 vols (1.2 and 3.4) (London, 1832), x–xii. All subsequent references to this preface are from this edition.

Prince's book was not confined to conforming merely with the moral and domestic ideology of 1830s England. What is more, she was placing a sample of Goethe's writing before her readership and it is not surprising to note that her next major translation was *Characteristics of Goethe* (1833).

The resulting transformation of Pückler's book was not, therefore, as it is so often categorized, simply an inevitable case of domestication for the home audience, a practice Lawrence Venuti explores and explicates in his *The Scandals of Translation*.[26] Rather, what we have here is a case of cross-cultural exchange appearing at a very precise moment in English cultural formation, a moment when a new and burgeoning sense of pride in Englishness and what it meant to be English was taking hold within the middle classes particularly. This sense of cultural worth would and did have an inevitable impact on the movement towards political reform. A review in the *Athenaeum* of the Prince's original German volumes, *Briefe eines Verstorbenen*, actually begins by suggesting that the Prince's imperfect knowledge of English social laws and institutions have caused him to under-rate a 'noble national character' and that his publication reveals 'a petty, and indeed puerile, jealousy of England, and everything English'.[27] The review indicates a very natural national sensitivity in a period when England's political scene was changing rapidly, and reform was the by-word of the day. Austin appears to make no attempt to ameliorate such insensitive comments.

Austin herself is very conscious of the immediacy and relevance of this subject matter at the time. In the 'Translator's Preface' to Volume 3.4, she states that she has regarded the Prince's recording of people and incidents 'solely in the light of illustrations of national manners' (Vol. 3.4, viii). This statement is in itself significant, not least because, ironically, Frances Trollope's controversial *Domestic Manners of the Americans* had appeared at the very moment when Austin was publishing her translation of the Prince's view of English domestic manners. A review of Trollope's scathing attack on American republicanism by Basil Hall appeared in the Tory *Quarterly* in March 1832 just weeks after the first volumes of Austin's translation had been reviewed in the same *Quarterly* in January 1832. In a letter to Pückler of May 1832 Austin mentions Trollope's book as having been 'hailed with enthusiasm by the same people who detest yours ... it is by a woman and full of the vilest mis-representations'. In a later letter she tells him '*Our* book ... has made unspeakable *furore* in America; I hear there have been eight editions! There's news for you! Of course the Yankees are enchanted at your picture of the English'.[28] Austin is probably correct in assuming the American press would be delighted to see English domestic manners examined in such

26   Venuti, *Scandals of Translation*, 5.

27   'Briefe eines Verstorbenen', *Athenaeum* (18 February 1832), 105; 105–107. See also (25 February 1832), 122–3 and (3 March 1832), 141–2.

28   Quoted in Hamburger, *Contemplating Adultery*, 239 and 108. Austin's emphases. A search of the National Union Catalog reveals only two editions by Philadelphia publishers in the years 1833 and 1835.

similar negative detail. Certainly the author of 'Prince Pückler Muscau and Mrs. Trollope' comments in the *North American Review* that 'His book, without having the least reference to America, is the best possible answer to Mrs. Trollope'.[29]

For Austin, a self-declared radical and certainly a Whig, the politics of the issue of national identity in the great reform year of 1832 would have been a topic hotly debated in the circles in which she moved and one in which she would have participated with relish. Her interest in politics is very clear from her letters. While in residence in Germany in 1828 she complained of being kept in 'ignorance of all that can grieve Whig or Liberal hearts ... In God's name, therefore, write, my dear Mrs. Grote!' And in 1830 she writes of her evening visitors, like the Member of Parliament who 'is a violent Liberal, and ... likes ... to sit and talk politics for ever and ever'. She adds, 'John Mill is ever my dearest child and friend'.[30] With this intense interest in mind, it is noticeable the degree to which negative comments about the English aristocracy, or anecdotes which show the aristocracy in a bad light, occur in Pückler's travels.

Conservative reviewers attribute the Prince's negative comments to 'wounded pride and bitterness of spirit', terms used by the *Fraser's* reviewer, because the Prince felt he was not given the kind of reception he might have expected by the English upper classes.[31] But reading various passages in his work suggests rather that what he is expressing is a genuine interest in English politics. He remarks, for instance, 'I think I see many indications that England is advancing towards a reform; and indeed, that it is, from various causes, quite inevitable' (297–8). He also reveals complex awareness of the undercurrent of ferment in the country:

> England is now – viewed, certainly, with relation to a totally different universal
> spirit of the age – in a similar state to that of France thirty years before the
> revolution. And it will fall out with her as with her great rival, if she does not
> avert the storm by radical but continuous reform. Nearly-allied fundamental
> evils are present here, as there. On the one side, the undue preponderance,
> misused power, inflexible stony arrogance, and heartless frivolity of the great;
> on the other, selfishness and rapacity are grown into the national character of the
> mass of the people. (331)

Pückler elaborates on this by considering the absence of republicanism in English politics:

> In the relations and tone of society ... not a trace of any element of republicanism
> is to be found ... The English aristocracy has indeed the most solid advantages
> over those of all other countries – from its real wealth, and yet more from the

---

[29] 'Prince Pückler Muscau and Mrs. Trollope', *North American Review* 36(1833): 1; 1–48.

[30] Quoted in Ross, 72 and 81.

[31] 'Tour of a German Prince', *Fraser's Magazine* 5(1832): 537; 533–44.

share in the legislative power allotted to it by the Constitution: *but as it is not upon these grounds that it chooses to assert or to justify its supremacy, but precisely upon its assumed noble blood and higher extraction*, the pretension must, unquestionably, appear to the rest of the world doubly ludicrous. (332–3; translator's emphasis)

Such statements, so much in accord with radical thinking, must have struck a chord with Austin. The Whigs and the radicals, vociferous supporters of reform, would have been in this period exceedingly frustrated with the actions of the British House of Lords and their continual rejection of the Reform Bill. Their frustration is voiced by Austin in a letter to Pückler of May 1832 when she describes a meeting of three London parishes and compares this British reform agitation with the July 1830 revolution in Paris:

it was a grand sight, – for hours one unceasing tide of men, cheerful, quiet and resolute. Your friend the Queen has played a disastrous game. She can never recover it. I pity her for I have no doubt her English advisers are the causes of it. Lord Munster and his sister Lady Sophia Sidney are also done for. What idiots, not to see that [reform was] their only means of gratifying their rapacity and ambition … It was their interest to be ultra reformers instead of affecting the claims of high birth.[32]

Austin's recognition of political impact in offering the Prince's opinions of English life is confirmed in the 'Preface' to Vol. 1.2, for instance, where she remarks in response to criticism of his errors of fact that it is difficult for a traveller to obtain 'accurate and impartial information … in a country so divided by party and sectarian hostilities and prejudices as England' (v). This is reinforced by Henry Southern's review of her translation in the radical *Westminster Review*. For instance, he praises Pückler's negative opinions on England's treatment of Ireland, reminding his readers that 'Ireland is in fact a bye-word (sic) of reproach against this country all over Europe'.[33]

The Prince's book had one other serious drawback, its chronology. The first two volumes to appear are the later stages of the Prince's travels, and when Austin began the translation Pückler's volumes on his time in London at the start of his tour, material which she thought would be the most 'taking' in England, had not yet appeared. In the end the translation was published in the same way, with the first two volumes dealing with the later stages of his travels. According to the *Athenaeum* reviewer of *Briefe eines Verstorbenen*, it was suggested in this original German publication that the first two volumes were withheld because they 'contained remarks on persons and things, which might be unpleasing to parties still living'.

---

[32]   Quoted in Hamburger, *Contemplating Adultery*, 239–40.

[33]   Henry Southern, 'Tour of a German Prince', *Westminster Review* 16(1832): 235; 225–43.

The reviewer then cynically remarks that once the published material proved popular, then such niceties vanished, offered up 'at the shrine of prurient curiosity, and … individual profit'.[34] This highly publicized background must have made the proposition of translating the work a very attractive marketing opportunity.

Austin is not named as translator on the title page of the early editions as she so very clearly is on her other published translations, offering evidence of some circumspection on her part about being too openly associated with the work. The identity of the translator was clearly an open secret, however, because the *Athenaeum* reviewer assures the readers that his or her translation of various passages will not 'interfere with the labours of the accomplished lady, to whom the public are indebted for the two volumes already before them'.[35] The reviewer for *Fraser's* was far less circumspect, baldly announcing 'The translation is the work of Mrs. Austin'.[36] But it should be noted that the original in the German and the translation do not carry Prince Pückler-Muskau's name either, although his authorship was also very quickly just as open a secret. Austin's supposed anonymity nevertheless enables her to give voice to a certain high-handed tone of defiance with regard to the criticisms levelled against the original German publication in her 'Translator's Preface' to the first two published volumes, combined as Volume 1.2, in which she refers to herself in the third person as 'he', and remarks that the fact that the Prince's opinions 'are not those of the mass of Englishmen, will, it is presumed, astonish no reflecting man' (Vol. 1.2, vi). And she adds an even more determined defiance in the preface to Volume 3.4 in which she responds to the various adverse comments regarding her translation. Her response is telling. She declares that anything she terms 'objectionably personal' she has tried to obscure, stating that 'any such material change I should have made myself, in some sort, responsible for its contents: which, as a mere translator, I can in no way be held to be' (Vol. 3.4, viii).

Austin's construction of herself as a 'mere translator' is equivocal. To begin with no translator can achieve that degree of objectivity and in her private correspondence with Pückler it is clear Austin never contemplated such objectivity for a moment. At one point he even warns her not to add anything to the text because, although it might be better than the original, it will be clear to readers that it is not genuine.[37] This kind of complicity between author and translator is interesting because it is probably far more common than most readers suppose. Certainly Austin was always careful, where she could, to contact the authors of the various works she translated and to consult with them. Venuti has even suggested that translators are complicit in the exploitation of translated material and we can safely assume that in her rewriting of Pückler's book Austin certainly domesticated the text and adapted it to accommodate the dominant values and ideologies of the

34   'Briefe eines Verstorbenen', 105.
35   'Briefe eines Verstorbenen', 105.
36   'Tour of a German Prince', 544.
37   Hamburger, *Contemplating Adultery*, 106–107.

target readership.[38] Her prefaces nevertheless suggest that she is very aware of the ways in which this material might be exploited politically, and so it is possible for Pückler's casual remarks and anecdotes on the English upper classes to be read as discourses to arouse public awareness of the political and social inadequacies both of that class and the class system. Even when the text arouses outrage, the very reaction fuels a political position. Henry Southern, in his favourable review of Austin's translation remarks, 'It is the nature of men to habituate themselves even to enormities: custom blinds: the traveller lends us a renewed vision'.[39] Southern's remarks reveal the extent to which, for the reader, this translated book is a form of journey. He also reveals his awareness that Pückler's views offer a politicized domain open to readjustment.

In her 'Translator's Preface' Austin also attacks English intellectual complacency and ignorance. She states, with a certain contempt, that once the English public are likely to accept the kind of German literature 'it would be my greatest pride and pleasure to render into my native tongue', she would also be willing to 'share with the illustrious and humanizing poets and philosophers of Germany any censure' (Vol. 3.4, viii–ix). This indicates her unwillingness to share condemnation with the Prince for his various excesses and lapses in good taste, disclaiming his book indeed as 'this slight but clever work' (Vol. 3.4, ix). But her statement also indicates that she believes the English to be too insular, in particular because, as Christoph E. Schweitzer has argued, she felt that translation as an art was not held in very high regard in England, an issue I address early in Chapter 3.[40]

This is not, however, the only factor. In being too insular, Austin is suggesting that the English are not interested in other literatures and philosophies, and are not prepared to learn from or profit by the observations of outsiders. Indeed, Austin remarks in the 'Translator's Preface', with some bitterness of tone, that up until now 'I have found no encouragement to hope that any such work as I should care to identify myself with, would find readers' (Vol. 3.4, ix). Austin later remarks to Pückler, in a letter dated May 1832, that she is about to embark on some translations of Goethe and Schiller and adds that the '[fool] public won't understand one word in ten of Göthe and Schiller when I have done it ... sordid, manufacturing creatures. *Mes hommages* to M. Schefer. Tell him our souls are in cotton and steam'.[41] Nevertheless, she embarked, as I have shown, on a series of translations from the German over the ensuing decade, which in part placed before the English reading public a variety of German prose writings and scholarship. Incidentally, Thomas Carlyle complains in a letter to John Stuart Mill dated 16 October 1832 in similar vein that his publisher 'informs me ... that the general or

[38]   Venuti, *Scandals of Translation*, 4.
[39]   Southern, 225–6.
[40]   Schweitzer, 150.
[41]   Quoted in Hamburger, *Contemplating Adultery*, 243–4. Leopold Schefer (1784–1862) was manager of the Pückler-Muskau estates. See http://en.wikipedia.org/wiki/Leopold_Schefer, accessed 27 April 2011.

rather universal opinion about the *Goethe* production was – *unfavourable!*' adding that to '*elucidate* that subject to English readers, at this point of time, lying beyond me, nothing remained but to coruscate round it with what fireworks one had'.[42]

Not surprisingly, however, the Prince was unhappy with Austin's transformation of his text into something more bland than the original, designed to accommodate a culture which he himself describes as 'religious and decorous England' (84). She had turned what he termed a 'consommé' into 'breadsauce'.[43] His metaphor likening his work to a thin dish to be consumed indicates the degree to which both the impoverished Prince and his translator sought optimum commercial success for the work. Finally he suggests that he may have to seek for a more faithful translator. Sarah Austin's response to Prince Pückler-Muskau's threat to replace her because of what he describes as her prudishness and cowardice, demonstrates the extent to which her rewriting was designed to produce a marketable commodity, aimed not at the 'Victorian drawing room' as the Hamburgers' would put it,[44] but at an interested and informed readership capable of appreciating the 'renewed vision' which Henry Southern praised, of their country's domestic politics. For the marketing to succeed, the book had to be cleaned of its sexual excesses and discursive crudities. Austin, in her high-handed and inimitable way, made this plain to the Prince:

> I have been a guardian angel to your book, and you abuse me. You seem unconscious of having offended people here, and you have not the least conception of the thing[s] they accuse you of ... it was in the most anxious and tender regard for *you* ... that I wished to take out all that might be thought disloyal or disgusting ... I shall be *trop charmée* to be rid of you and to see you delivered over, with the aid of your *faithful translator*, to all the rage, scorn and vituperation of the whole press of England ... to hear myself congratulated by all decent people for having washed my hands of you.[45]

Austin's riposte amply reveals her confidence that her translating practice, in accommodating the text to this particular target audience, with a sly focus on politics rather than sex, is perfectly legitimate. Venuti, in exploring Milan Kundera's critiquing of translations of his own work, points out that authors must 'recognize the linguistic and cultural differences that a translation must negotiate' and that Kundera's belief in the possibility of 'faithful renderings' fails to recognize that

---

[42]   Thomas Carlyle and Jane Welsh, *The Collected Letters of Thomas and Jane Welsh Carlyle*, 7 vols ed. Charles Richard Sanders (Durham, NC, 1977), 6: 240–41. The reference is to Carlyle's essay 'Goethe's Works', *Foreign Quarterly Review* 10(1832): 1–44.

[43]   Quoted in Hamburger, *Contemplating Adultery*, 104. Bread sauce is 'made of milk infused with onion, bay leaf and pepper, and strained over breadcrumbs', *Macquarie Dictionary*.

[44]   Hamburger, *Contemplating Adultery*, 103.

[45]   Quoted in Hamburger, *Contemplating Adultery*, 104–105. Austin's emphases.

a foreign author's intention cannot 'travel unadulterated across a linguistic and cultural divide'.[46] This is precisely what Austin is telling the prince.

The Hamburgers argue that Austin's blue-pencilling of the text was 'out of fear that it might offend propriety and cast a shadow on her reputation',[47] and to a certain extent that assessment is a fair one. But the idea of a Sarah Austin who is timid and squeamish is difficult to accommodate to the strong voice of the Translator in the prefaces. Certainly she is reluctant to brave public opinion but she is clear in her own mind about the role of the translator because she explains to Pückler that as a translator 'I should appear to stand quite neutral and indifferent'.[48] Unquestionably, however, politically she is neither neutral nor indifferent. Austin was targeting a politically aware audience with a strong and lively sense, not only of the rising status of the English nation, but of the way in which the reform debates would renew and invigorate an ever more powerful middle class. Austin's blue pencil removed the erotic and the sexual as mere detritus, as mere encumbrance, to those far more important passages which accorded with her own political position.

By way of contrast, Austin's political engagement in her next translation of a German traveller's account of England, Frederick Von Raumer's *England in 1835: being a Series of Letters Written to Friends in Germany, during a Residence in London and Excursions into the Provinces* (1836), is far more obvious and open. She played hostess to Von Raumer during his London stay, which Anna Jameson records in a letter to Ottilie von Goethe dated 7 May 1836:

> Every one is talking of von Raumer's book about England, and it is generally approved of. He is himself a great Lion in all societies and much caressed. Mrs. Austin's preface to her translation of his book is quite admirable … Raumer called this morning and offered us seats in the Duchess of Kent's box at Drury Lane for the 11 – this was arranged by Mrs. Austin … After the play we joined a party at Mrs. Austin's, where we met von Raumer; Millman, the poet and author of *Fazio*. (Needler, 38–9)

As will be addressed more fully in the next chapter, Sarah Austin also apparently inculcated the visitor with the Whig political position. In the opening letters of *England in 1835*, von Raumer refers to 'Mrs. A – ' who took him to parties in the evening, or invited him to breakfasts. At one such meeting 'We fell upon Irish affairs. A gentleman said that the rule of Prussia over her Catholic subjects was tranquil and undisturbed, only because she was a military despotism'. Such meetings lead von Raumer to conclude, in his discussion of the two dominant parliamentary parties: 'Had the Tories always done the right thing at the right time, the Whigs would never have come into power. But they carelessly let the

---

46   Venuti, *Scandals of Translation*, 6 and 5.

47   Hamburger, *Contemplating Adultery*, 100.

48   Quoted in Hamburger, *Contemplating Adultery*, 101.

clock run down, and then the Whigs stepped in and wound it up'.[49] It is this kind of commentary which so aroused the ire of Tory journals and critics.

Unlike most women translators in this period Austin produced lengthy explanatory prefaces to her translations as my earlier discussion of the Pückler-Muskau translation shows. Unlike the Prince, Von Raumer, it seems, offered her carte blanche: 'he gave me full powers to omit, abridge, and alter', although she then goes on to outline the extent to which she uses this power in the work. I employ the term 'power' deliberately because Austin herself labels it 'my discretionary power' and in one notable instance used it to the full. She writes:

> The name of Mr. Bentham occurs not unfrequently in the work as the supposed representative of the opinions of an existing party, and always accompanied with expressions of disapprobation or of contempt. I have constantly omitted it, when used in this manner, and have only inserted it in one place, where some remarks on Mr. Bentham's opinions occur. Allusions and insinuations, founded on what I believe to be an entire misapprehension of the character and sentiments of Mr. Bentham, were, as I thought, neither instructive nor convincing; and to me, who had much cause to know the warmth, singleness and kindness of heart of the venerable man of whom Herr v. Raumer has conceived such erroneous impressions, would have been, I confess, most painful to write. I am anxious, however, that this unfairness, if such it be, should be understood to be the effect of grateful and affectionate regard for the memory of a revered friend, and to have no relation to speculative systems of politics and ethics, which it is quite beyond my objects and my province to affect to judge.[50]

Once again I would argue that Austin, despite her claim to the contrary, was as much motivated by political as by personal considerations in undertaking such excisions. That she and Von Raumer were politically in accord, however, seems very clear, despite Austin's disclaimers. At one point she writes:

> I must protest against being made a party to the opinions of any author whatever. It is the peculiar and invaluable privilege of a translator, as such, to have no opinions; and this is precisely what renders the somewhat toilsome business of translating attractive to one who has a profound sense of the difficulty of forming mature and coherent opinions, and of the presumption of putting forth crude and incongruous ones; not to mention the more individual feeling of the unsuitableness of any prominent and independent station in the field of moral and political discussion, to a person naturally withdrawn from it.[51]

---

[49] Raumer, I: 14 and I: 17–18.

[50] Sarah Austin, 'Translator's Preface', *England in 1835: Being a Series of Letters written to Friends in Germany, During a Residence in London and Excursions into the Provinces* by Frederick Von Raumer (London, 1836), I: xi–xiii.

[51] Austin, 'Translator's Preface', *England in 1835*, I: xiv.

She then goes on to remark, almost casually, that his political opinions 'appear to be such as a loyal subject of Prussia, where reform has so long been the exclusive business of the government, would naturally fall into', and she concludes by stating that while she is not sanctioning his opinions, she is nevertheless 'helping to give utterance to the sentiments of an honest, courageous, faithful and enlightened friend to the highest interests of humanity'.[52] Under any terms, this is an extraordinary statement revealing the degree to which Sarah Austin was a partisan and bold political advocate. The discussion in Chapter 3 will explore in greater detail this particular translation.

Sarah Austin's translations of two very different German travellers, from two very different strands of German society, take her English readers on journeys into their own country and enable them to consider their own various institutions as seen through the eyes of strangers. Most of the reviewers do celebrate the opportunity to consider their own nation against a European backdrop. As Christian Isobel Johnstone remarks of Von Raumer, '[W]herever he gives the result of his observations upon our manners and social usages, and contrasts them with those of the continental nations, the work rises in interest'.[53] In the following chapter I address the writings of Mary Margaret Busk, who, unlike Sarah Austin, wished to persuade her readers that despite the interest aroused by such travellers' accounts, nevertheless England remains the superior nation.

52   Austin, 'Translator's Preface', *England in 1835*, I: xv and xvii.
53   Christian Isobel Johnstone, 'Raumer's England in 1835', *Tait's Edinburgh Magazine* 3(1836): 315; 315–25.

Chapter 3
Mary Margaret Busk
and the Business of Culture

Mary Margaret Busk, writer, traveller and translator, is known today, if at all, only through her journalism. As a professional journalist whose output was based almost entirely on translation from a range of European languages, German, French, Italian, and Spanish, Busk seemed worth investigating, given that she appears to have also travelled extensively. While there is little extant evidence for such travels, her occasional remarks in her correspondence with the Blackwoods alone indicates journeys and long stays in Holland, Paris and Germany, and in 1823 she had visited Waterloo. Her translations were also accompanied with commentary and it is this style of review which dominates her contributions to *Blackwood's Edinburgh Magazine* from 1825 to 1827. I first discovered Mary Margaret Busk in an article by Eileen Curran in *Victorian Periodicals Review* (1998) and wish to acknowledge here my indebtedness to her meticulous scholarship and the piquant writing that so captured my interest and led me not only to the Blackwood files in Scotland's National Library, but more importantly, to Busk's periodical publications themselves.

D.E. Latané Jr. for the *Oxford Dictionary of National Biography* describes Busk as a 'writer and translator' and notes that she and her husband travelled frequently on the continent. She was proficient in a range of European languages, as noted, via her education and her travels, and, writes Latané, 'served as an intermediary between intellectuals on the continent and in Britain, through both review essays and translations, and helped broaden the cultural climate after the end of the Napoleonic wars'.[1] There is a deceptive simplicity about this retrospective account, because Mary Busk's professional journey was not performed with the ease, nor with the success, this neat summary might imply, even though she was indeed one of very few women contributors to periodicals of the 1830s, and a prolific contributor at that. Her translations were not simply the shifting of a text from one language into another, rather her correspondence with Blackwoods seems to indicate that translations were made via personal choice and interest, that is, where she was herself intellectually engaged. See for instance her letter of 28 February 1825:

> The flattering approbation you have bestowed upon the Article already inserted, induces me to ask whether you would like a Spanish play treated in the same

---

[1] D.E. Latané Jr., 'Mary Margaret Busk', *ODNB* 9: 102.

manner? I have by me a translation of a Comedy of Calderón, the most celebrated
Spanish Dramatist, and although I cannot ascribe to it equal intrinsic merit with
Wilhelm Tell, it would I think afford an interesting Article, inasmuch as the
Spanish Theatre is very little known in this country, and possesses many peculiar
and curious characteristics.[2]

Busk gave the readers of various periodicals, particularly in the 1830s, the
opportunity to experience the foreign, even if that experience was nevertheless
predicated upon her very strong sense of a superior Englishness, emphasised for
the Tory reader, but later modified in her two articles for the more radical readership
of the *London and Westminster Review* then under the unnamed editorship of
John Stuart Mill.[3]

Between February 1833 and December 1834 she published approximately
20 items for the *Athenaeum*; between 1825 and 1838 over 30 for *Blackwood's
Edinburgh Magazine* (referred to as *Maga*); and between 1828 and 1839 over
60 items for the *Foreign Quarterly Review*. Her contributions included straight
translations (particularly prior to 1832), full-length review articles, or slighter
column pieces consisting of blocks of translation linked by plot synopses and
some brief commentary. John Wilson, writing for the Tory journal *Blackwood's* in
1832, in *Noctes Ambrosianae*, using the conceit of a dinner conversation between
a cast named as North, Tickler and Young Gentleman, includes Mary Busk in a
list of translators of 'genius and erudition, who in general improved upon their
originals, often changing geese into swans, and barn-door fowls into birds of
Paradise' (693).[4] Wilson's comparisons indicate ambivalence, even distrust,
of translation as a useful intellectual tool and signal what the correspondence
between Busk and *Blackwood's* reveals, and which Curran explores, a fraught,
even painful relationship between contributor and publisher. In the commissioned
history of their magazine, *Annals of a Publishing House*, written by their long-
time, prolific contributor Margaret Oliphant, names like those of Busk are
nowhere to be found. As David Finkelstein has shown, 'financial details and
mundane tasks that characterize much of daily editorial and literary duties ... are
inevitably subsumed into narratives emphasizing personalities and connections
to perceived literary and cultural touchstones'.[5] A quick check of the index to
Annals of a Publishing House confirms this assessment. Busk was too early in
her career, chosen from necessity, and doubtless she was too demanding: in the

[2]   National Library of Scotland, Blackwood Papers, MS4014, ff. 103–104.

[3]   Walter E. Houghton, et al. (eds), 'The Westminster Review, 1824–1900', *Wellesley
Index to Victorian Periodicals 1824–1900* (5 vols, Toronto and London, 1979), III: 537.

[4]   John Wilson (Christopher North), 'Noctes Ambrosianae No. LXI', *Blackwood's
Edinburgh Magazine* 31(1832): 693; 693–720.

[5]   David Finkelstein, '"Long and Intimate Connections": Constructing a Scottish
Identity for *Blackwood's Magazine*', in *Nineteenth-Century Media and the Construction
of Identities*, ed. Laurel Brake, Bill Bell and David Finkelstein (Basingstoke, 2000), 333.

late nineteenth century she would have already disappeared from view and would never have ranked as a 'literary and cultural touchstone'. In vivid contrast, Joanne Shattock points out that *Blackwood's* gave Margaret Oliphant 'a central platform from which to speak throughout her career', a career begun nearly two decades after that of Busk had ended.[6]

Wilson's *Noctes* number is in fact about patriotism and nationalism, beginning with reference to Thomas Carlyle's championing of Goethe. The Young Gentleman asks how Goethe could possibly compete with Shakespeare and North complains that Carlyle 'cannot conceal his pity, perhaps his contempt, for all whose vision is confined within the limits of the horizon of England's poetry'. The love of country is the theme, and with the exclamation 'Woe to the Citizen of the World!', the journey ends where it began, in the Blue Parlour.[7] Notably, Busk's straight translations for *Blackwood's*, such as extracts from Schiller's *Wilhelm Tell* which appeared in 1825 or Grillparzer's *Sappho* in 1826, among others,[8] virtually ceased after the publication of Wilson's piece and her subsequent contributions to *Maga* are mostly review articles which nevertheless call on her combined skills as a translator and her experiences as a traveller. She did attempt to interest *Blackwood's* in some political satire, verses she describes as 'stanzas against Ministers, entitled either Whig Constancy, or a Whig's Resolve', but there appears to have been no response. The verses do indicate, however, a possible personal adherence to the Tory cause.[9]

As has been previously discussed, this book argues that travel and translation are interconnected terms and therefore form a kind of by-product within the travel book industry. The two terms come together almost naturally when considering the business of culture and the journalism of Mary Margaret Busk. Anna Jameson, standing before the cataracts of Niagara in January 1837 and experiencing a common traveller's reaction, disappointment, wrote 'I am metamorphosed – I am translated'. She captures, I think, far more than merely a simple negative tourist moment. Rather, it is surprise at discovering a self who is journeying with preconceptions, a self who has been, until this moment, foreign and unknown. And in contradistinction, the practice of translation itself, produces, to quote Jameson again, 'A world ever at hand'.[10] For her, this suggests a journey of the

---

6   Joanne Shattock, 'Work for Women: Margaret Oliphant's Journalism' in *Nineteenth-Century Media and the Construction of Identities*, ed. Laurel Brake, Bill Bell and David Finkelstein (Basingstoke, 2000), 171.

7   John Wilson, 694 and 715.

8   Mary Margaret Busk, 'Horae Germanicae (No. XX): Schiller's *Wilhelm Tell* (Part 1)', *Blackwood's Edinburgh Magazine* 17(1825): 299–318 and (Part 2), 417–36; 'Horae Germanicae (No. XXI): *Sappho* by Franz Grillparzer', *Blackwood's Edinburgh Magazine* 19(1826): 404–15.

9   National Library of Scotland, Blackwood Papers, MS4032, f. 73 dated 4 October 1832.

10   Jameson, *Winter Studies and Summer Rambles in Canada*, 57 and 103.

mind crossing national borders with ease and enabling like journeys for those readers for whom translations are prepared. But some minds are more open than others, more prepared to traverse or even transgress national boundaries, and as John Stuart Mill warns, it can happen that historians and travellers 'see only what they already had in their own minds'.[11] Mill, many years before, in an essay on the *Edinburgh Review*, accused that journal of pandering to national prejudices, remarking:

> English and excellent it employs as synonymous terms; that a foreigner admires England, is a sure passport to its praise; that he does not, is of itself sufficient to draw down upon him its censure. The habits and institutions of other nations are praised exactly in proportion as they approach to the English standard; blamed in proportion as they depart from it.[12]

These distinctions, and in particular Mill's comments, should be kept in mind when considering Mary Busk's contributions to the burgeoning Victorian periodical press and the impact of travel and translation on the dissemination of culture.

As mentioned briefly in the 'Introduction', one of the most prolific industries in the Victorian age was publishing, evidenced clearly by a continuing upward trend in book production from the 1830s on as Simon Eliot's exhaustive investigation of available publishing statistics shows.[13] In the same period, the periodical press was having an increasing and significant impact. Through the pages of the press in all its various forms journeys of cultural significance took place, including the dissemination of European culture into English homes. Books on travel, and this includes translated travels, proved a major category in the publishing industry, and the major subject of reviews in the press. What I want to argue in this chapter, however, is that in terms of import and export, Mary Margaret Busk, writer and journalist, qualified the ideas from the Continent that her work imported into England, more for the purpose of affirming England's superior standing in the world, and explaining European literatures against their English counterparts, rather than seeking to appropriate an unqualified European culture for English consumption, which seems unquestionably to have been Sarah Austin's position in producing translations from the German in particular. As Austin notes in her 'Translator's Preface' to Raumer's *England in 1835*, she has prefixed a biographical memoir of Von Raumer to the work 'because the lives and writings of the eminent men of Germany are not in general familiar to English readers'.[14]

Statistically, interchanges between England and the Continent were profound. For instance, Walter E. Houghton suggests that up to 1835, just two book-sellers

[11]   John Stuart Mill, *The Subjection of Women* (1869; New York, 1986), 28 [see Chapter One, Part 19].

[12]   Mill, 'Periodical Literature', 521.

[13]   Simon Eliot, 28.

[14]   Sarah Austin, 'Translator's Preface', *England in 1835*, I: xv.

alone imported into England an average of 400,000 French books annually.[15] Given the date, and the relatively small proportion of the population able to read at this time, this seems to me an extraordinary figure. By 1884 Florence Fenwick Miller could celebrate the printing-press and modern technology generally as enabling intellectual progress: 'Mind will be more and more valued and cultivated, and will grow more and more influential; and the condition and status of women must alter accordingly'. Barbara Onslow tellingly remarks that this is 'almost a Whig view of progress and enlightenment'.[16]

This chapter then explores the early journey of this particular woman, Mary Margaret Busk, and the way in which she shaped her periodical contributions discursively to the business of cultural exchange in the first decade of Victoria's reign. Busk also shaped her politics according to that of the journal to which she was contributing. When dealing with the Blackwoods she offers a steadfast Tory view of the world, either to accord with the well-known Blackwood conservatism as a means of assured *entrée* into the magazine, or as an expression of her own orthodox politics. This steadfastness may well have been a discursive ploy, given her struggle to hold her own both intellectually and financially in a field dominated by men. An extract from just one of her many letters to the Blackwoods demonstrates this possibility:

> As I unfortunately cannot afford to devote my time to literary pursuits without remuneration, you must pardon my again soliciting the return of the papers which appear to have forfeited the approbation they once obtained, and for some of which at least I have customers.

> I do not exactly know how our account stands, but as I conceive the last 10£. I received from you in September 1829 covers the Duke of Rovigo, Autobiography and Mad. de Genlis, I should imagine that some trifle must remain due to me.[17]

Busk produced a number of full-length review articles for both *Blackwood's* and the *Foreign Quarterly* (although not necessarily of the lengthy, substantial kind which appeared in the major review quarterlies) and it is on these that I will focus, concentrating both on the 1832–1838 period, and on her discussions of continental literatures that interconnect France or Germany, with England. These analyses will allow investigation of the complex and occasionally dynamic processes that occur when travel and translation intersect with the business of cross-cultural exchange. When I use the word *exchange*, however, it must not be assumed that this is either

---

[15]   Walter E. Houghton, et al. (eds), 'Foreign Quarterly Review, 1827–1846', *Wellesley Index to Victorian Periodicals 1824–1900* (5 vols, Toronto and London, 1979), II: 130.

[16]   Quoted in Barbara Onslow, *Women of the Press in Nineteenth-Century Britain* (Basingstoke, 2000), 12.

[17]   National Library of Scotland, Blackwood Papers, MS4029, ff. 99–100, dated 31 March 1831.

even-handed or balanced. While for both journals Busk's style is for the most part robust, forthright and lively, it is nevertheless at times heavily biased both in terms of national identity and politically. I should note too that the *Foreign Quarterly*'s putative editor, John George Cochrane, stated at the journal's outset in 1827 that he wanted the journal to make 'the nations of Europe better acquainted with each other' and encouraged contributors from both sides of politics. This policy positions that journal quite differently to *Blackwood's*.[18] The *Foreign Quarterly*'s interest in building and reinforcing an intellectual relationship, a form of journey, between Britain and the Continent, takes on significant force in this pre-Reform period. The necessity for impartiality in constructing a useful rapport between nations must surely have formed a crucial part of John Stuart Mill's later thinking on liberty, in particular the contribution such rapport could make to individuality and to alter what Mill termed 'collective mediocrity', striking a blow against the 'despotism of custom', which, so Mill argues, hinders human advancement and national development.[19] Mill praised Cochrane as an 'impartial arbiter' and claimed that the *Foreign Quarterly* represented 'more correctly the attitude which English minds of all parties and sorts have taken up towards foreign nations'.[20] Possibly Cochrane achieved such balance in accepting articles from contributors as diametrically opposed politically, for instance, as Sarah Austin and Mary Busk, both of whom could bring to their work extensive knowledge of European languages and writings, of which more anon. Unlike the long-running and conservative *Blackwood's*, the *Foreign Quarterly* ran for only 20 years.[21]

In March 1835, writing for *Blackwood's*, Busk offered their readership an essay titled 'French and German Belles Lettres' supposedly based on reviews of two novels, *Le Magnetiseur* [*The Mesmerist*] by Frédéric Soulié and *Die Feindliche Brüder* [*The Hostile Brothers*] by Ernest Raupach, both published in 1834. The essay insists that a cross-cultural journey has taken place and that the work of these two authors offers evidence of a 'marvellous interchange of national character', or what she terms a 'mutation'.[22] It seems that the Germans, or our 'Teutonic cousins', have abandoned a mysticism disregarding morality for 'metaphysical development and graphic representation of the character of an individual, of a nation, or of an age' (513). This is subsequently claimed to signal progress for Germany in cultivation, civilization and refinement (513). The French, our 'Gallic neighbours', have on the other hand now embraced incomprehensible dogma,

---

[18]   Houghton, 'Foreign Quarterly', II: 131.

[19]   John Stuart Mill, 'On Liberty', *On Liberty, Representative Government, The Subjection of Women. Three Essays by John Stuart Mill*, introduced by Millicent Garrett Fawcett (1859; London, c. 1912), 81 and 87.

[20]   Houghton, 'Foreign Quarterly', II: 131.

[21]   Houghton, 'Foreign Quarterly', II: 131. Houghton describes Busk as a 'literary hack' (131).

[22]   Mary Margaret Busk, 'French and German Belles Lettres', *Blackwood's Edinburgh Magazine* 37(1835): 513; 513–22. All subsequent references are to this article.

and abandoned reason and morality, claimed by Busk as the 'demoralizing effect of violent political excitement' (513). For Busk, revolution lowers 'the tone of national feeling' (513) and has had a consequent negative impact on French *belles lettres*. This will prove a very different position to that located in her subsequent journalism discussed later in this chapter. She claims that on the French stage 'adultery and murder are frigid, are absolutely *perruque* – the fashionable word for old-fashioned and stupid – if not enlivened by a due admixture of incest and parricide' (515) but does admit that novels are tamer, 'the murder of a beloved bride upon the wedding-night by the adoring bridegroom, and a few tiny peccadilloes of the like nature, answer their purpose' (515). This British anxiety about morality in literature was ongoing and critics could be excessive in their language. John Steinmetz, writing for the *Dublin Review* in 1840, opens by stating he cannot conceal his disgust and proceeds, in a long paragraph to list 'depravity', 'horrors', 'diabolical invention', 'highly seasoned immoralities', 'fiendish traffic' and 'moral gangrene', forewarning 'the public against the moral cholera, which our Gallic neighbours are spreading far and wide, aided, as they are, by the mercantile avidity of the Belgian booksellers'. He was reviewing the work of Sand, Hugo, Balzac, Soulié and de Kock.[23] Busk manages to avoid this hysterical note, and when resorting to stereotypes, at least resorts to less obvious ones, expressing her own disapprobation in far more mild, even wryly humorous terms, commenting for instance that Soulié's novel 'is by no means deficient in the ordinary allowance of adultery, incest, etc. etc. etc.' (516). It is a tone very similar to that of Thackeray whose 1842 review 'The German in England' for the *Foreign Quarterly* addresses the French/English divide a number of times. The German author is described as 'a very strong Anglomaniac' to which Thackeray adds, 'We give this passage up to the French, as a proof of the blind and unjust admiration which the German Naturforscher exhibits for our country'.[24]

But to return to Busk's 'French and German Belles Lettres'. With regard to German literature in this same article Busk directs those of her readers who are 'German scholars' to particular German authors, but 'mere English readers to the accounts of the productions of these and other admired German novelists, in the periodical expressly devoted to foreign literature, namely, the *Foreign Quarterly Review*' (513), a form of self-advertising, perhaps, given that she had been contributing to the 'Critical Sketches' review column of the *Foreign Quarterly Review* for some years.[25] Moreover, she digresses into a discussion of French novelist George Sand, pointing out that an earlier article in *Blackwood's*

---

23   Steinmetz, 'Modern French Romance', 353–4.

24   William Makepeace Thackeray, 'The German in England', *Foreign Quarterly Review* 29(1842): 377; 370–83. The work under review is *Mittheilungen aus dem Reisetagebuche eines Deutschen Naturforschers. England* [Extracts from the Travelling-Journal of a German Naturalist. England]. No author is indicated.

25   Busk also refers her readers to a *Foreign Quarterly* article in the essay 'Philosophy of Fiction'. See the *Westminster Review* 7(1838), 87.

needs correction, adding, one should have imagined embarrassingly, both for *Blackwood's* and the reviewer, but employing the universal 'we' and assuming the authoritative editorial voice of *Blackwood's*:

> here we must pause to correct, or, in parliamentary phraseology, to explain, what Maga said, in the month of January last, touching that highly gifted, but singularly unwomanly, at least unhonest-womanly authoress, Madame Dudevant, *alias* George Sand ... We have, we blush to say, shown ourselves precipitate, and, what we are not often, credulous. We spoke of this lady and her novels upon report, upon the strength of French praise, without having seen either; and having now made ourselves better acquainted with the subject, we here solemnly revoke our hearsay verdict, and correct our erroneous statements. (515)

Busk had herself reviewed six Sand novels for the *Foreign Quarterly Review* in 1834 (in which she also notes general 'want of delicacy and of moral sense' in French literature),[26] and felt free to make her statements with all the confidence of a full knowledge of her subject and with an apparently intensely political and national bias. As she had pointed out to the Blackwoods in her letter of 22 January 1835, there is:

> a slight mistake in your last Number touching Mad. Dudevant, which, had you read her novels you would surely not have suffered to pass. She does not call herself Mad. Sand, but plain George Sand, writing in the character of a man, and that probably because her novels are so indelicate and immoral that no woman of character could acknowledge them. Should you wish to know more of them, I would refer you to my critique of them in the last number of the *Foreign Quarterly*.

> I wish not to suffer this erroneous praise [of Sand] to pass, and thought the occasion favourable for offering a few remarks upon the noxious influence of revolutionary excitement upon National literature, and though the two odd little works that I have taken as illustration are not very important, their queerness makes them answer my purpose.[27]

The article to which Busk refers is 'Prince Talleyrand', by Arnout O'Donnell in which he alludes to Sand's 'pleasing and successful romances'.[28] Busk's letter can I think be construed as Busk's actual opinion and while she later praises Sand's

---

[26]   Mary Margaret Busk, 'Madame Dudevant's Novels – *Indiana – Valentine, etc.*', *Foreign Quarterly Review* 14(1834): 272; 271–97.

[27]   National Library of Scotland, Blackwood Papers, MS4040, ff. 126–7.

[28]   Arnout O'Donnell, 'Prince Talleyrand', *Blackwood's Edinburgh Magazine* 37(1835): 76; 76–81.

style in 'Philosophy of Fiction' for the *Westminster*, to be addressed at the end of this chapter, she nevertheless in that same review addresses what she terms 'the social condition of woman' as a question exercising 'the French mind', and asks 'Is it the *honnête homme* [honest man] of the novels whom a wife is to make happy? It is against this notion of the moralists that Sand has protested, and by it offended all our prejudices'. The novels under review are *Lea Cornelia* [Anne Marie Texier, Countess d'Hautefeuille]; *Les Romans et le Mariage*; and *Histoire de la Grandeur et de la Décadence de César Biroteau, Parfumeur* [Balzac].[29]

Busk's review essay 'English Literature' for the *Foreign Quarterly* in July 1835 also addresses French and German authors in relation to reception in England. The article is not of itself a balanced critique, even though the essay opens with a very clear statement from Busk capturing the business associated with the travelling of culture to a nicety, and in particular placing England, naturally enough, as the pivot in any cross-cultural exchange:

> There are few kinds of works more entertaining and informing, alike to the philosophic inquirer, to the man of letters, and to the general reader, than sketches or critical histories of the literature of foreign nations, which, in truth, afford means and opportunity for that enlargement of mind and views, by extension and variety of knowledge, which constitutes the real advantage derived from foreign travel ... the literature of the world is brought home to the reading public, at least of England, France and Germany.[30]

The broad positive embrace of these opening remarks is initially continued in Busk's appraisal of her authors. M. Mézières, author of *Histoire Critique de la Littérature Anglaise* [*A Critical History of English Literature*] (1834), is criticised for the narrow range of literature he explores. However the layout of the work is praised as pedagogically sound for his French readership. For instance he translates complete essays from the *Spectator* and the *Rambler* and includes English critical opinion on the various titles, and thus 'makes his French readers acquainted with English taste and criticism, as well as with English literature of one or two kinds' (350). Busk clearly has no problem with the quality of said translations, although she regrets that he did not include 'a ratiocinative French *critique*' which would have 'given it value in this country' (350). The process Busk describes here is a complex one of cross-channel interaction, and she is acutely aware of what would sell, be of 'value' in Britain and of opportunities lost. Unfortunately, and this seems often to be the case in this period, both author and critic (Busk) are locked into historic nationalistic rivalries that impact with some complexity on the business of cross-cultural exchange. The apparent openness of Busk's initial comments at

---

29   Mary Margaret Busk, 'Philosophy of Fiction: Balzac, Dumas, Soulie, Etc.', *London and Westminster Review* 29(1838): 85; 73–98. All subsequent references are to this article.

30   Mary Margaret Busk, 'English Literature', *Foreign Quarterly Review* 15(1835): 347–8; 347–60. All subsequent references are to this article.

the start of her review is undercut by her subsequent comment, of M. Mézières's book, that 'it is always amusing, and often instructive, to learn the opinions of intelligent foreigners upon the productions of our national genius' (350). The word 'amusing' subtly denigrates and reduces her 'intelligent foreigners' as opposed to 'our national genius' (350).

Mézières's German counterpart, Dr. Wolff, has, however, sinned egregiously by criticizing spoken English, causing Busk to anticipate how startled the English readership will be 'that a German, whose national guttural enunciation they have probably been accustomed to regard as the *ne plus ultra* of cacophony, reprobates our speech as singularly and pre-eminently inharmonious' (353). This form of attack is unusual in the period given the degree to which German literature was being enthusiastically praised and circulated at this time. Wolff's work, says Busk, will, however, offer English readers 'some idea of the nature of German *aesthetic* criticism' (353), and she examples Wolff's critique of Byron. By italicizing the word *aesthetic* throughout, as well as adopting a rather dry tone, she quickly signals that such criticism is to be treated as suspect because the criticism is based on aesthetics alone with no regard for morality. Her use of the word 'aesthetic', as a form of blunt instrument, signals an inherent amorality in the critical stance taken. As an instance, Dr. Wolff, it seems, finds Byron's *Don Juan* innocuous:

> an Englishman must needs be somewhat astounded by the ease with which Dr. Wolff, addressing a mixed audience, composed of both sexes, either mentions or omits to mention, the immorality or the indecency, even when tolerably gross, of the writers of whom he may have to speak. (356)

The review concludes with Busk addressing both authors' very favourable critiques of Sir Walter Scott. Wolff's is, she declares, a mixture of 'much subtle acumen and sound judgment ... blended with much unintelligible aesthetic Germanism' (359). She concludes: 'We ... will frankly confess that the school of fiction founded by Sir Walter Scott overspreads the continent, and that there, likewise, ay, even in Germany, the disciples are immeasurably inferior to their mighty master' (359). The cultural exchange, as this review demonstrates, is not even-handed, but rather an opportunity to assert English superiority: linguistic, literary, and moral. Busk's English readers learn only that continental critics are capable of appreciating English literature even if the forms their critiques take are of dubious value to the serious English scholar. Incidentally, Scott's impact on the Continent is often remarked in English critical writing from this period. The anonymous author of 'French Criticism of English Writers' claims that the 'kind, warm, noble, gentlemanly vein of feeling, that runs in the most trivial dialogues of Scott, ... is completely lost on the French. It is only the dramatic part of the fiction which strikes them', nevertheless, as I noted in Chapter 1, this same critic claims that Scott, along with Byron, won French admiration through translation, despite critics initially withstanding 'the invasion'.[31]

As Eileen Curran confirms, 1835 marks the beginning of the end for Busk with *Blackwood's*. They published only four more of her articles, one in 1836, two in 1837 and the last in 1838. She had been, Curran claims, supplanted by much younger contributors, and all of them men.[32] Her replacements too, may have been less inclined to offer such stern correctives as that regarding George Sand. *Blackwood's* may, of course, have simply wearied of her importunities, but in saying that I would have to add that women in this period were so placed as to be forced to be importunate if they were even to begin to achieve both their financial and their intellectual goals.

Busk's January 1837 review 'Lucien Bonaparte and Friedrich Von Raumer', again for *Blackwood's*, offers a further example of the way in which the modes of travel and translation coalesce because of the intellectual journey offered to the English reader. In reviewing for *Blackwood's* her Whig rival Sarah Austin's translation of Raumer's *England in 1835*, alongside Raumer's German original, Busk complains shrewdly that Raumer has 'queerly metamorphosed into an English Radical' and that he is 'an observer of England through the spectacles or the eyes of Mrs. Austin and the Whig Ministry'.[33] As discussed in Chapter 4, Austin's 1832 translation of Baron Pückler-Muskau's *Tour in England, Ireland and France, in the years 1828 and 1829* had received a mixed reception, depending on the politics of the reviewing journal in question but nevertheless demonstrates with marked clarity Austin's own political position. Furthermore, as also previously noted, Austin's political position is even more specific in the Raumer translation, despite her disclaimers to the contrary. Busk's review for *Blackwood's* is the third of three significant reviews of Friedrich Von Raumer's *England in 1835*, the first appearing in the *Foreign Quarterly* in April 1836 and possibly by Busk herself, which reviews Raumer's German edition only, published in Berlin in 1835; and the second in the *Quarterly*, in July 1836, by John Wilson Croker which addresses Raumer's German edition published in Leipsig in 1836 and Austin's English translation published by John Murray, also in 1836.

Like Austin herself, Busk's writing is generally coloured by the politics of the journal for which she writes to produce a version of culture that is personally skewed. However, while she goes on to accuse Austin in the *Blackwood's* review of unduly influencing Raumer during his visit to England and of having perverted his politics, she nevertheless acknowledges him as a 'diligent, lucid, and judicious historian' (22) only to express her disappointment that his letters concerning 'living England' (26) do not match this esteemed historian's earlier

---

[31]　'French Criticism of English Writers', 8 and 3.

[32]　Eileen Curran, 'Holding on by a Pen: the Story of a Lady Reviewer Mary Margaret Busk (1779–1863)', *Victorian Periodicals Review* 31/1(1998): 22; 9–30.

[33]　Mary Margaret Busk, 'Lucien Bonaparte and Friedrich Von Raumer', *Blackwood's Edinburgh Magazine* 41(1837): 22; 21–31. All subsequent references are to this article.

work. She writes that she had anticipated Raumer would regret the changes 'which had tended to assimilate this country to theorizing, centralizing France', instead she asks 'why should we trouble ourselves to take at second-hand, in German or English, translated back from German into the original language ... what we can so easily get, spick and span new, from the Whig statesmen and orators, ladies and gentlemen, from whom Professor Von Raumer received his observations, views, and opinions?' (27) The trafficking in ideas expressed in this sentence, the dynamic journeying back and forth between the two languages, combined with the discourse of consumerism inherent in the statement, is quite extraordinary and indicative of what is most powerful and insightful in Busk's work.

The outrage voiced in Busk's *Blackwood's* review, that Raumer should endorse the business of 'exploring, understanding, and appreciating England and the English' (27) from a Whig perspective only, possibly takes its tone from that second review essay by Croker noted above, which appeared in the *Quarterly* in July 1836. The mandarin *Quarterly*, as Barbara Onslow succinctly puts it, 'dominated public discussion of cultural and social issues' in the early decades of the nineteenth century.[34] In deliberately purple prose Croker rails that Mrs. Austin:

> communicated to [Raumer] her own Whig opinions – this clique of people are naturally propagandists; but what we do complain of is, that Raumer retails the *ex parte* statements ... – the cavils of this coterie, the prejudices of his *prompter*, as if they were the *natural and spontaneous results of his own impartial inquiry and observation*. If he had told us honestly and truly that he knew nothing of what he was writing about ... the public in Germany and here would have known what to trust to, and would have listened, with a due appreciation of its value, to the prating of the parrot.[35]

Austin's translation of *England in 1835* was also noticed, anonymously, in the *Dublin Review* and in *Tait's Edinburgh Magazine*, unaccompanied by the German original. Michael Quin, writing for the *Dublin Review*, uses the opportunity, again politically, to rail against English 'bigotry, suspicion, treachery, cupidity, unrelenting tyranny, and remorseless crime' with regard to Catholic Ireland. Quin was a co-proprietor of the *Dublin Review* and a supporter of Catholic emancipation.[36] By way of contrast, Christian Isobel Johnstone, the chief reviewer for *Tait's Edinburgh Magazine*, takes that journal's more liberal line in a long and thoughtful appraisal noting that there 'is nothing inveterate or bigoted' in Raumer's 'enlightened and impartial' analyses, and expresses the hope 'that not a few of our Tory legislators may find leisure to benefit by the perusal of this

---

[34]   Onslow, 62.

[35]   John Wilson Croker, 'Raumer's *England in 1835*', *Quarterly Review* 56(1836): 534; 530–83 [Croker's emphases].

[36]   M.J. Quin, 'Raumer's *England in 1835*', *Dublin Review* 1(1836): 133; 131–51. See G. Martin Murphy, 'Michael Joseph Quin (1796–1843)', *ODNB* 45: 696–7.

Conservative foreigner's reasoning, before the Irish Church Bill shall come to be again discussed'.[37] Austin's translation was also noticed by the *Athenaeum* and later, in their column 'Our Weekly Gossip on Literature and Art', this weekly took the *Quarterly* to task, complaining both that the Raumer review is 'laborious trifling' and 'the attack on Mrs. Austin, with its inroads on private life, coarse and ungentlemanly; and not even justified as criticism, for the writer, in more than one instance, blunders in his German, and accuses her of mis-translation – finds out omissions, which she has acknowledged in her Preface, and accuses her of suppressing passages'.[38] Perhaps, more surprisingly, the work was briefly noticed in the *Magazine of Domestic Economy*, which celebrates in no uncertain terms Raumer's intelligent interest in 'our manners [and] our national character'.[39] This broad interest in the book signals a significant development in cross-cultural exchange, and can also be attributed to the steadily growing interest in German philosophical and intellectual developments, but at the same time reveals the extent to which the reception of translation by the target readership was deeply politicised in the period. Each review, nevertheless, takes the reader on a particular journey in the company of those deemed 'intelligent foreigners' as Busk had put it.

However, as noted earlier, Busk may well have previously reviewed Raumer's German original, *England im Jahre 1835* published in Berlin in 1835, in the *Foreign Quarterly Review* for 1836, well before the *Quarterly* attack. The attribution to Busk is by the *Wellesley Index* editors. There is some minor evidence for this attribution but if it is by her, certainly the general tone of this earlier review is far more moderate than her piece for *Blackwood's*. Croker's vituperative review perhaps gave her the imprimatur to produce that more strongly-worded assessment for *Blackwood's*, or as I suspect is more likely the case, she merely cut her cloth to suit the editorial style of the various periodicals to which she contributed. This first review by Busk for the *Foreign Quarterly* acknowledges that Raumer's 'official recommendations naturally brought him chiefly into contact with the Whig party ... We cannot, therefore, be much surprised, if he has adopted, in general, their opinions on many subjects'. Moreover his comparison of school education in England and Prussia, and his assertion that education is the responsibility of every government, is documented by Busk who adds: 'How far this could or should be done in England is a different question, which is well worth the sincere consideration of every real friend to the happiness and prosperity of his country'. Despite her strong engagement with the politics of the piece, Busk (if it is indeed by her) also admits that the English can feel gratitude to Raumer for the 'highly favourable view of their country, their character, and manners' and that his is the 'voice of a friend'. The defects of his work can be ascribed to

---

[37]   Johnstone, 'Raumer's England in 1835', 316.

[38]   'Our Weekly Gossip on Literature and Art', *Athenaeum* (23 July 1836): 523. The earlier review noted is *Athenaeum* (26 March 1836): 218–21.

[39]   'Reviews', *Magazine of Domestic Economy* 1(1836): 305.

his 'continental education'.[40] The three major reviews nevertheless demonstrate that the value of cultural exchange in this case is once again heavily weighted against the Europeans and is valuable only for the light that it shines on the British themselves. Busk's journey with Raumer has been a two-fold one, she obviously translated for herself passages from his work in that initial review of his German edition, but then took another excursion with Austin's translation. Culturally, according to Susan Bassnett, the 'map-maker, the translator and the travel writer are not innocent producers of text. The works they create are part of a process of manipulation that shapes and conditions our attitudes to other cultures while purporting to be something else'.[41] Bassnett's insight usefully describes Busk's process and works even when Busk merely reviews a straight-forward travel text by an English lady traveller.

If Europeans travelled to England in this politically-charged period of the 1830s and wrote about their experiences (Baron Pückler-Muskau, Friedrich Von Raumer, Flora Tristan to name just a few), the English also travelled abroad, English women in particular, and kept their observations and encounters in an array of personal letters, journals and diaries, just as Busk herself doubtless did. Busk wrote to the Blackwoods on 17 November 1837 that she had 'just returned from a continental excursion', adding 'I ... venture to send a few sonnets, written in the scene that most impressed me during my journey ... I think to offer you something more, in prose, of what I saw ... Perhaps, Fragments, or Scraps of a Travelling Tutor's Diary, might not be a bad form, as admitting reflection, burlesque, history, and whatever else occurs'. Needless to say, this offer was not taken up.[42] In 1838, in her final published article for *Blackwood's*, Busk reviewed the politically controversial writer Frances Trollope's latest travel book, *Vienna and the Austrians* (1838), which had been published by Richard Bentley that same year. Presented as a series of letters, addressing an anonymous, even amorphous 'you', and asserting truthfulness, Trollope writes:

> For some time to come my letters are likely to be a sort of Morning Post for Vienna, containing a full, true, and particular account of all sorts of fêtes and festivals. So if it should happen that diamonds and pearls, beautiful ladies and magnificent gentlemen, come and go in my letters with something like puppet-show rapidity, you must not wonder at it.[43]

Busk's review juxtaposes Trollope's book with another by Wenzel Blumenbach, *Austria and the Austrians*, an anonymously translated work published by Colburn in 1837. Busk clearly believes the author to be 'liberal', that is, politically opposed

---

[40]   Mary Margaret Busk [?], 'Raumer's *England in 1835*', *Foreign Quarterly Review* 17(1836): 211, 215 and 216; 209–16.

[41]   Susan Bassnett, *Comparative Literature. A Critical Introduction* (Oxford, 1993), 99.

[42]   National Library of Scotland, Blackwood Papers, MS4714, ff. 146–7.

[43]   Frances Trollope, *Vienna and the Austrians*, 2 vols (London, 1838), II: 133.

to Trollope's Toryism. Curran argues of these two books that Busk found 'beneath their differences they shared a view of contemporary Austria that contradicted English preconceptions' and notes that the origins of such preconceptions are also briefly considered.[44] Busk, however, begins by considering Trollope's prodigious output of novels and travel books, *Vienna and the Austrians* being Trollope's ninth book since 1832:

> Her literary activity astounds us, she really so overwhelms the reading public
> with travels and with novels, with pictures, some professedly matter of fact,
> others satirically idealized, of manners foreign and domestic, European and
> Transatlantic, that we ask ourselves ... where she was present corporeally, where
> only in imagination, which is truth, which fiction?[45]

It's a clever critical positioning, apparently impartially objective, and the decision to compare Trollope's work to 'her brother and sister writing-travellers' (494), described by Busk as an 'experiment', is suggestive of a careful, scientifically controlled, survey. Busk's aim in solving the questions posed, is to enable the reader to accept Trollope's 'vivid and graphic descriptions of foreign lands, manners, and customs' as a true record of a journey which actually took place. In other words, Busk is testing and validating the imported cultural product by which the English reader will learn more about Austria.

Busk initially returns to Trollope's earliest work, *Domestic Manners of the Americans* (1832) and compares that with Harriet Martineau's recently published *Society in America* (1837), Martineau being constructed as one of a number of writers who are Trollope's political polar opposites and with whom Trollope 'has to do battle for her views and statements' (495). Busk clearly saw this comparison as central to her essay's argument, writing to the Blackwoods on 11 March 1838 that she is 'writing an article, Trollope versus Martineau & Co'.[46] Busk attacks Martineau to defend Trollope, referring to the former pejoratively as 'the new champion of women' and as Mary Wollstonecraft's successor, an alignment, given Godwin's notorious *Memoir* of Wollstonecraft (1798), specifically designed to denigrate Martineau and her radical politics (496).

Busk makes it clear that the argument of the review is a defence of Trollope regarding the 'censures so virulently lavished upon her by some of our critical fraternity' (494). These censures Busk reduces to 'superficiality' and 'Toryism', the latter a word Busk asserts is interpreted 'by the critics to whom we allude to include or imply bigotry, obstinate ignorance, want of philosophy, and all the other intellectual crimes of omission or commission laid to the charge of our author' (494). Busk does, however, attack the word 'superficial' as one used commonly

---

[44]   Curran, 17.

[45]   Mary Margaret Busk, 'Mrs. Trollope's Vienna and the Austrians', *Blackwood's Edinburgh Magazine* 43(1838): 494; 494–508. All subsequent references are to this article.

[46]   National Library of Scotland, Blackwood Papers, MS4046, ff. 90–91.

of women writers but then claims, while assuming an apparently masculine voice, that men writers too are superficial because it is an 'age of superficial writers in general' (494) and that women are disadvantaged because not classically educated (494). She then proceeds to extract from Blumenbach's study *Austria and the Austrians*, to show that his work, like Trollope's 'appears to be rather a pleasant sketch of the surface of things, than the fruit of a politico-philosopher's deep researches into the arcana of Austrian policy' (498).

Busk concludes from her reading of both Trollope and Blumenbach that Austria is making advances politically and may well eventually enjoy a constitution 'more analogous to the English than the continental model' (500). She advocates gradual reform as opposed to what she terms 'theoretic', an epithet Busk commonly uses with regard to France and revolutionary politics. In summing up she claims her English readership will be amazed that the descriptions of Austria by both authors, despite their opposing politics, reveal a very different version 'from all the notions we had for years been imbibing of a people sunk in and stupified by sensual and vicious indulgences – of a blindly bigoted Government sedulously promoting ... ignorance'. And proceeds to account for this by blaming the French as 'inimical to Austria' and thereby inducing 'the rest of Europe, England included' to accept 'their opinions, true or false, with an undoubting confidence' (507). Surprisingly, however, the final paragraphs engage with Austria's occupation of the Lombardo-Venetian empire. Assuming again the editorial *Blackwood's* voice, she confesses 'We ourselves, Conservative as we are ... must confess that the same revolutionary movement which, in Austria, would shock us ... we should, in Italy, feel to be a gallant though injudicious struggle for national independence' (507–8). This sentiment is, however, quickly countered at the last, dismissed as 'philanthropic', by a warning that such an 'abstract love of liberty' if acted on could only prove premature, unsuccessful and unjustifiable (508). Just five years later Nicholas Wiseman reviewing Dickens's *American Notes for General Circulation* with Frances Trollope's *A Visit to Italy* remarks of the latter 'while she is a thorough enemy to revolutionary and *sans culotte* movements and parties in England, she worships them in Italy'.[47]

This, Busk's final review for *Blackwood's*, is, intriguingly, a defence of women writers (Martineau excepted of course) even as Busk implies a male persona by claiming to be 'chivalrously taking up the gauntlet' (494) on their behalf. The review's over-arching argument attempts to adjust the critical balance in favour of Frances Trollope regarding those earlier critical censures and is a masterly display (no pun intended) of a subtle evocation of the craft in the way she informs, directs and even at times enlightens her readership about continental politics across a broad spectrum.

Late in her career Busk published twice with the *London and Westminster Review*. In a surprising turnabout, given the dominant conservative tone of her earlier work, the article 'Philosophy of Fiction' (1838), noted previously, on

---

[47]   Wiseman, 265.

modern French fiction, so roundly condemned in Busk's *Blackwood's* article 'French and German Belles Lettres' (1835), is explained, and even condoned, as an inevitable outcome of the French Revolution, an event Busk describes as a 'terrible explosion of the forgotten part of her citizens – barbarians desiring to enter the pale of her civilization' (77). France is described as young again, all the old landmarks, Busk explains, have been 'washed away and old conventionalities broken' (82) and she argues that because of this, French fiction writers have no old models or ideals to call upon, rather, everything must be re-created and made new, a circumstance which allows the French writer to take the kinds of liberties a British writer would not. It's an astonishing, even dynamic, description of modernity we are offered here. The article is notably erudite and balanced. Busk observes with keen insight: 'If the moral edifice be unfinished, and consecration not yet poured over the fane, it is because what is great, and worthy, and original, must begin with unshapely parts, like scattered giant's limbs' (90). She declares that the English 'misjudge' French fiction in part because French authors as 'children of new France' must prove to be without prejudice (91). Again, in this review, she argues that the writing style of George Sand is 'so clear, pure, keen, we seem to breathe some mountain air' (92) and Balzac is praised for his descriptions of bourgeois life, an acknowledgement of other people's lives which causes Busk to reflect 'we feel that the streets and shops of our great city are filled with human beings, not merely with people of whom one buys' (93), almost as if this recognition of other human existences is indeed a revelation to her.

In all of these details the Tory author, if not obliterated (the word 'barbarians' can cause unease) is at least modified, and at some points substantially obscured. The process of writing for the radical *Westminster*, of adapting her statements to their agenda, comparatively late in her career, leaves the reader uncertain as to what Mary Margaret Busk's political position might actually have been. She appears to have embarked on a personal political journey in this regard, and to have understood that journey in terms of translation. Towards the end of 'Philosophy of Fiction' for the *Westminster* she writes about this journey as undertaken by herself in company with the reader:

> There is a great vitality in this literature; though unfinished, immature, it will and must one day strongly affect ours. We English do not yet give much welcome to its lighter portion. We are too near, and not near enough. A language of which every one acquires a smattering, does not possess sufficient dignity to invite attention from the learned, except for the important matter it conveys. We even translate from it carelessly, adopting every word we cannot easily render, and thus entering little into the new beauty and riches which it has been acquiring … It is not till *after* the grand epoch of a literature, that it finds its way into the hearts of other lands. … we are only now going *back* to the loftiest productions of Goethe and Schiller. (97–8)

As professional translators, women like Mary Busk and Jane Sinnett, took considerable interest in their practice. Busk's remarks above regarding careless translation practice might be compared with those of Jane Sinnett in a review for the *Westminster*, of Edouard Servan de Sugny's *La Muse Ottomane*. Sinnett complains that the 'Ottoman muse here makes her appearance in a very Parisian looking costume', not surprising, she intimates, given de Sugny's theory of translation, a theory it appears developed very much in economic terms given how pronounced the metaphorical language of barter and merchandising is:

> Whoever undertakes to translate contracts a debt. In order to discharge it he must pay, not in the same coin, but in the same sum. When he cannot render an image, let him supply it by a thought – if he should be less energetic let him be more harmonious – if he should be less precise let him be more rich.

Sinnett's response accords quite precisely with Busk's anxiety about careless translation while she cleverly maintains the merchandising metaphor:

> This is like the plan of an eloquent shopkeeper we have somewhere heard of, who, when a customer came in for a pair of pistols, persuaded him to accept in lieu thereof a fiddle.[48]

Moreover, while Sinnett would probably not deny the debt owed by the translator to the targeted reader, nor the business of cultural exchange generally, her dry comment denies emphatically that the contracted goods can be of just any shape or kind as long as the size and weight are the same.

For Mary Margaret Busk, the business of culture, of travel and translation, was the business of financial survival. Curran suggests that she could be politically disloyal and the two disparate reviews of *England in 1835* demonstrate this. She could also be ambivalent about issues such as slavery.[49] But such careful tightrope walking is the lot of most women writers in the 1830s and in subsequent decades. Busk's oeuvre is predicated upon travel and translation, but the journey always leads her readers back to England where the 'literature of the world is brought home'[50] to be considered and critiqued, but predominantly only understood and appreciated in terms of 'English institutions, English liberty, and the English character'.[51]

---

[48]   Jane Sinnett, '"Belles Lettres", Review of Edouard Servan de Sugny's *La Muse Ottomane'*, *Westminster Review* 61(1854): 312–13; 301–15.

[49]   Curran, 27.

[50]   Busk, 'English Literature', 348.

[51]   Mary Margaret Busk, 'Russell de Albuquerque', *Foreign Quarterly Review* 12(1833): 244; 241–5.

Chapter 4
Anna Jameson's
Sentimental Journey Elsewhere

Altogether elsewhere, vast
Herds of reindeer move across
Miles and miles of golden moss,
Silently and very fast.

(W.H. Auden, 'The Fall of Rome')

W.H. Auden's poem 'The Fall of Rome' in its entirety captures synchronic moments in time across politics, history and untamed geographical spaces. Jameson, too, demonstrates a similar synchronous impulse but hers is a politics of sensibility, women's history and domestic geography.[1]

Section I

In the Winter of 1836–7 the successful writer and critic, Anna Jameson, found herself snowed in at Toronto, Canada where she had travelled to reunite with her uncongenial husband, a reunion based on the practical needs of both: his to demonstrate, for the purposes of promotion, a functional marriage; hers to obtain a formal separation and some financial maintenance. Rather surprisingly, she openly expresses her feelings of desolation and loneliness in her published travels, *Winter Studies and Summer Rambles in Canada* (1838) abandoning the generally bold, brisk tone of the British lady traveller in the first part of the narrative at least. Her discontent emerges through various modes, the quotation of relevant poetry and prose, landscape description summed up as 'sublime desolation', and simple forthright complaint.[2] A January sleigh trip to Niagara provokes this landscape in which the words 'waste', 'melancholy' and 'drearily' are more a reflection of mood than an accurate account of the terrain over which she travels:

---

[1]   W.H. Auden, *W.H. Auden. Collected Poems*, ed. Edward Mendelson (London, 1976), 257–8. Thanks to Gail Jones for drawing my attention to the poem and to the anonymous preliminary reader for this elegant exposition of its significance to Jameson's Canadian journey.

[2]   Jameson, *Winter Studies and Summer Rambles in Canada*, 49.

> The whole earth was a white waste: the road, on which the sleigh-track was only just perceptible, ran for miles in a straight line; on each side rose the dark, melancholy pine-forest, slumbering drearily in the hazy air. (49)

She does not record seeing herds of reindeer, but does note the 'only living thing I saw in a space of about twenty miles, was a magnificent bald-headed eagle' (49). She also produced several sketches of this particular winter excursion.[3] Anna Jameson did not wish to be in Canada, complaining: 'I lose all heart to write home, or to register a reflection or a feeling – thought stagnates in my head as the ink in my pen – ... I *must* rouse myself to occupation; and if I cannot find it without, I must find it from within' (29).

I wish to argue in this chapter that while the reference to home here is to Jameson's dependent parents and sisters back in England, it is not to this 'home' that Jameson journeys in her mind during the long, bitter winter months in Canada, of which the first third of *Winter Studies and Summer Rambles in Canada* is comprised. Rather, 'home' has become somewhere altogether elsewhere and unexpected, not Canada, not England, but Germany. John Leonard writes of 'the exasperations and romance of Elsewhere' and captures Jameson's situation with these precise terms.[4] Elsewhere, which is Germany, is not unproblematic for Jameson but nevertheless is the site of a deeply-seated romance with that country on a number of grounds. First, her feelings for Ottilie von Goethe, daughter-in-law of Germany's supreme man of letters, as expressed in a letter dated 30 November 1833: 'Leaving Germany was leaving *you*, you, round whom some of the deepest feelings of which my nature is capable, had imperceptibly twined themselves' (Needler, 17. Emphasis Jameson's). Second is her cordial reception and ready *entrée* into the highest literary circles. As she tells her parents in a letter from Bonn, dated 30 July 1833: 'it is gratifying to find that I am no stranger in this foreign country – that my name and the opinions and sentiments I advocate are well known ... every where I find friends and people anxious to talk to me'. In this same letter Jameson notes that the 'celebrated Schlegel', as she puts it, was introduced to her but had avoided meeting Frances Trollope, remarking that 'the Germans generally seem quite afraid of her – as of a woman who is come, as they express it *to make a book*' (emphasis in original).[5] Third, is her sense of independence, in part generated by the ease with which travelling in Germany could be accomplished where the regulations 'are so precise, so admirable, and so strictly enforced, that no where could an unprotected female journey with

---

[3]   See 'Starting out by sleigh for Niagara from Toronto in January, 1837' and 'The Forest Road to Niagara, 1837' in *Early Canadian Sketches by Mrs. Jameson* Intro. G.H. Needler (Toronto, n.d.), n.p. See reproductions of these drawings in Wendy Roy, *Maps of Difference. Canada, Women, and Travel* (Montreal and Kingston, 2005), 66–7.

[4]   Leonard, xv.

[5]   Beinecke Rare Book and Manuscript Library, Yale University, Speck Collection, MS J23b M833 7:30, Anna Jameson to Johanna and Denis Murphy, 30 July 1833.

more complete comfort and security. This I have proved by experience'.[6] The problems consist in her struggles to learn the language, and to make herself *au fait* with the writings of the most noted of the German literary intelligentsia, and the demands and recriminations generated by Ottilie von Goethe who, as Needler perhaps unkindly puts it, inflicted 'the recurrent whims of her naïvely emotional temperament' on the long-suffering Jameson (Needler, vii). In this regard, however, I have always felt in my extensive reading of the extant correspondence that Jameson was, for the most part, enjoying herself.

Jameson's Canadian travel book is shaped as a letter-journal, in common with many women's travel publications from this period. It is addressed directly, I would suggest, to a primary reader, Ottilie von Goethe. In the 'Preface' to *Winter Studies and Summer Rambles*, the book is described circumspectly as 'these "fragments" of a journal addressed to a friend' (9). Jameson nevertheless remains conscious of secondary readers and throws herself 'upon "the merciful construction of good women," wishing it to be understood that this little book, such as it is, is more particularly addressed to my own sex' (10). The first section, titled 'Winter Studies', records Jameson's intellectual excursions into a German literary landscape, interleaved with actual excursions confronting the Canadian environment, so that as she translates her travels in the New World into a new, subjective reality, this parallels what is a very similar journey into another unknown territory, the literature of the Old World, translations that produce commentaries on her feelings and emotions and on the socio-cultural situations she confronts. In the 'Preface' there is no attempt to explain the presence of these 'Winter Studies' except for noting an 'impertinent leaven of egotism' a clear reference to her expression of personal feelings (10). I want to extend my argument regarding Jameson's journey to Elsewhere to suggest that all the material in her book about Canada is very much a part of the travel writing genre as described by Rita Monticelli: 'a genre constructed through a process of translations and intertextual movements … a process that is directed towards women's education and emancipation in an international, trans-European dimension'.[7] This description can be applied to both the Canadian travels as a whole, and to the 'Winter Studies' as another kind of travel writing. Right at the start of the narrative Jameson declares that wherever the mind is, that mind can be 'its own world, its own country, its own home' (17) and this statement is upheld by her intellectual excursions into the other world of Elsewhere, a form of travel writing which, despite appearances to the contrary, still conforms to Monticelli's depiction of the travel writing genre as a process.

Jameson's travel narratives address an unspecified 'you', a reader with whom she appears to be on easy, familiar, conversational terms, and comparison of some sections of the published narrative with Jameson's letters to Ottilie von Goethe help to confirm that von Goethe is indeed the reader to whom these pages are

---

[6]   Jameson. *Visits and Sketches*, II: 137.

[7]   Monticelli, 300.

addressed. For instance, Jameson's letter of 12 February 1837 to von Goethe describes the return journey from Niagara:

> One thing I cannot forget. We crossed the upper lake upon the ice, the distance of 7 miles and it was a dark gloomy night. There was danger of losing the track and in that case destruction, as the lake is not *equally* frozen over. As we glided along the smooth surface, the darkness, the solitude, the recollection of the abyss of waters beneath, the cracking and hissing of the ice, the sense of danger gave me a feeling of more sublime excitement than even the falls of Niagara. (Needler, 79)

In *Winter Studies and Summer Rambles in Canada*, this episode is similarly described, and there are many other instances of this kind where the private letters and the published text correspond:

> it was found expedient to cross Burlington Bay on the ice, about seven miles over, the lake beneath being twenty, and five-and-twenty fathoms in depth. It was ten o'clock at night, and the only light was that reflected from the snow. The beaten track, from which it is not safe to deviate, was very narrow, ... All this, with the novelty of the situation, the tremendous cracking of the ice at every instant, gave me a sense of apprehension just sufficient to be exciting, rather than very unpleasant ... (63)[8]

Jameson had met Ottilie von Goethe in Weimar in 1833 and initially von Goethe's attraction for Jameson rested in her impeccable literary connections, expressed in Jameson's travel book on Germany, *Visits and Sketches at Home and Abroad* (1834), which contains a long description of Ottilie von Goethe without actually naming her. The published description offers a detailed and fulsome assessment of her new friend, written up chiefly in terms of the ways in which she was the ideal companion for her famous father-in-law: 'Quick in perception, yet femininely confiding, uniting a sort of restless vivacity with an indolent gracefulness, she appeared to me by far the most poetical and genuine being of my own sex I ever knew in highly-cultivated life'.[9] Part of Jameson's thesis for *Visits and Sketches* was the idea of trans-national understanding, morally, politically and socially, which she argues can best be achieved through the relationships of women exploring each other's cultures and addressing the differing gender ideologies which impact on each other's lives: 'For my own part I slipped so quietly and naturally into all their social and domestic habits, and cared so little about the differences and distinctions, which some of the English thought it fine to be always remarking and lamenting, that my German friends used to express their surprise'.[10] Notably the position of women is a recurring theme in *Winter*

---

8   See also Roy, 19.
9   Jameson, *Visits and Sketches*, I: 165.
10   Jameson, *Visits and Sketches*, I: 203.

Studies and Summer Rambles in Canada as well. One contemporary reviewer, Margaret Mylne, astutely notes that both parts of Jameson's Canadian book, both 'her winter studies and summer rambles', have 'the same object – the nature and situation of women', adding 'her thoughts … are acute and profound, displaying an intimate acquaintance with life (ladies' life especially)'.[11]

Jameson's private appreciation of Ottilie von Goethe was as fulsome as her public published version. She was soon addressing letters to her expressing eternal love and affection. From Dresden in 1833 for instance she writes: 'do not doubt, that I am really happier with you than elsewhere, and when I return to you it will be as to my heart's sister, and my *home*'.[12] In 1835 Jameson became embroiled in a sexual scandal which threatened to destroy von Goethe's reputation. Even Sarah Austin, exiled in Boulogne, had heard rumours, asking Jameson what her German correspondent could have meant by the words 'Poor Mme. de Goethe who would have thought it?'[13] Von Goethe had had an affair with a young English clergyman and gave birth to a baby girl, and Jameson, with old friend Robert Noel, spent many weeks attempting to place this child with foster parents and came close to compromising her own good name. The child subsequently died, possibly from neglect. Nevertheless this involvement generated a close relationship and Jameson's letters reveal sufficient detail to gain a sense of von Goethe's own, more ambivalent, commitment to the friendship.

It is during Jameson's stay in Germany in 1835 that the need to travel to Canada was first mooted only to become gradually more imperative with the passage of time. In the August Jameson informs von Goethe that her husband has asked her to state when she will be travelling to Canada to join him (Needler, 26–7). In the same letter Jameson declares her own plans are unchanged and she will spend the coming winter with von Goethe.[14] By November, 1835, however, writing from Dresden, there is a more dramatic announcement. There is much that is not being said here, in particular about the 'suffering' and the 'struggle' which suggests a possible love affair, but with whom is never clear:

> my fluctuating resolutions are fixed immutably. I go to Canada. I see it must be so. I cannot brave the alternative. If, when we meet, you ask any questions about myself, I will answer them honestly. I have suffered much, but I have no reason to blush before any human being … I have had a hard struggle of about 18 months duration, but it is past; and having made my choice, shall I weakly sit down and wring my hands over the inevitable, the irremediable? (Needler, 31)

---

[11] Margaret Mylne, 'Woman, and her Social Position', *Westminster Review* 35(1841): 31; 24–52.

[12] Goethe und Schiller Archiv, Weimar, Germany. MS GSA 40/VIII, 9, 1. This portion of the letter, numbered 12 in Needler's edition, was not included in his published version.

[13] Beinecke Rare Book and Manuscript Library, Yale University, Osborn Files, Sarah Austin to Anna Jameson, 26–28 September 1835. No accession number.

[14] Goethe und Schiller Archiv MS GSA 40/VIII, 4.

In May 1836 Jameson is still planning to spend two to three months in Germany to 'assiduously study your language', adding that her 'departure for Canada is now absolutely final – I MUST GO – but not till next year. The interval I shall spend chiefly in Germany' (Needler, 41). The desire to put off the inevitable seems poignantly clear in that wishful 'not till next year'. By July Robert Jameson's demand that she make the necessary preparations for the voyage has become, to use her word, 'peremptory' and she declares 'I hate the idea of Canada and all that belongs to it at this moment' (Needler, 47). In late August 1836 she writes 'I shall in all probability sail for Canada the 20th of September. If I cannot go at that time it will be too late to go this year ... I feel that I belong to you and that we must spend our existence together. This is my hope, my wish, my thought, my dream' (Needler, 52). In the event, after strenuous urging indirectly from her husband in the interval (she claims in June 1836 not to have heard from him personally for 13 months – he appears to have used others as proxies in the negotiations) she sailed on the 'Ontario' in October 1836 without, after all, returning to Germany (Needler, 46, 50 and 57).

Mixed in with her lamentations about having to make this journey to Canada are very specific plans for furthering her German studies. Back in July 1835 she had confessed that her 'greatest anxiety is to improve myself in German, it has become a source of extreme vexation to me. I suffer at every moment ... I am studying very hard' (Needler, 24) and in October that same year confesses 'my ignorance of German is a daily and hourly torment to me' (Needler, 29). Sarah Austin, in exile in France herself because of the failing mental health of her husband which prevents his working and earning an income, begins her letter to Jameson of September 1835 by expressing sympathy regarding the projected travel to Canada, and countering her initial advice, 'Don't go', with the contrary view, that for women performing their duty within certain bounds is essential despite 'the prospect of passing a winter a hundred miles from any creature with whom I can exchange a thought or a feeling'. Jameson must surely have felt that the exigencies of Boulogne would probably prove nothing in comparison with Toronto, both in terms of climate and distance. Austin does, however, note 'I am to be ready to translate M. Raumer's letters on England in November and he wants these *out* in February so I will have no time for *ennui*' and this casual remark may well have helped to spur on Jameson's own translation ambitions.[15]

On the eve of embarkation Jameson claims (perhaps not quite truthfully) that for the first time she will consider earning money from her publishing to achieve independence (one assumes from her husband) so that she can go where she chooses. She has learned that she is popular in New York and her publishers, Saunders and Otley, propose that a new edition of her *Characteristics of Women* (1832) be produced *in situ*. She prepared new plates for this edition and it was published in New York in 1837, possibly as early as February. Needler also offers

---

[15]   Beinecke, Osborn Files, Sarah Austin to Anna Jameson, 26–28 September 1835. Contractions and punctuation have been normalized.

a detailed account of this New York edition described on its title page as 'The Author's Edition, illustrated by a series of her own vignette etchings, with a new preface, original notes and other important additions'.[16] This embarkation letter also includes a description of the articles taken on board: 'in my cabin I take the *Rahel* you marked for me, and all the M.S.S. notes which you made for me, I intend to read these during the voyage. Most of my German books go in the ship with me' (Needler, 57).

On arrival in New York in early November 1836 Jameson is feted in similar fashion to other British and European authors, writing: 'before I had time to deliver my letters of introduction, my door was crowded with visitors, my table covered with cards. The people in short are beyond measure enthusiastic and kind, engagements were pressed upon me' (Needler, 66). Jameson notes that New York women dress in the latest Paris fashions and that 'it has been in the fashion to study German' (Needler, 66). Jameson does not leave for Toronto until early December travelling at the very worst time of the year. Toronto will not prove nearly as welcoming or as enjoyable as New York but to what extent the presence of her husband affects her first impressions it is difficult to say. She tells von Goethe:

> when I begin to write to you (and I have two or three times taken the pen to do so
> since I came to this far *far* off place) the idea of the distance which separates us,
> the seas, the lands that come between us, the long time which must elapse before
> these words reach your eye, so overwhelms me that I throw down the pen and
> throw myself down on the sopha (sic) in a despair. (Needler, 67–8)

Writing in German Jameson adds that she is unhappy, that she prays and works, reads German every day and will, in her next letter, say what she has been studying, which clearly includes Goethe's most noted dramatic works.[17] These details from Jameson's private letters show the degree to which Canada as the one travel destination and Germany as the other are so intertwined that it would be almost impossible to unravel them and in part explains the presence of Germany as a prospective Elsewhere in a book about Canada.

Stranded in Canada, the idea of Ottilie von Goethe as tutor and mentor to her German studies, as well as her ultimate destination, becomes ironically (given that she would rather be with von Goethe than elsewhere as she states in her letter from Dresden noted earlier) the very Elsewhere to which Jameson can return and where she can indeed be happier, the discovery of which she celebrates ecstatically: 'A word, a name, has sent me from Toronto to Vienna; what a flight! what a contrast! – it makes even Fancy herself breathless!' (*Winter Studies*, 39). Jameson captures here the idea of travelling in the mind: an excursion in which memory and desire

---

[16]   For further details see Clara Thomas, *Love and Work Enough. The Life of Anna Jameson* (London, 1967), 115 and Needler, 55–6.

[17]   Translated by G.H. Needler. See 71. Needler later notes 'In the text I have left Mrs. Jameson's imperfect German as she wrote it' (84).

are both important components which enable the journey to Elsewhere, a place that is always specifically 'not here'. H.F. Chorley, reviewing *Winter Studies and Summer Rambles in Canada* for the *British and Foreign Review* naturally, given the declared political interests of that particular periodical in fostering 'more intimate acquaintance with the Continent',[18] was far readier than other reviewers to accept Jameson's winter studies as a legitimate expression of what he terms her 'real position' (snow-bound in Toronto) with her 'ideal journeys to those cities of art and pleasure, Vienna and Munich', and remarks that 'Not the least engaging of Mrs. Jameson's "Winter Studies" are the personal and biographical sketches' – that is, her notes and commentaries on various German writers.[19] In Chorley's terms, then, Elsewhere also becomes an ideal destination. Ali Behdad has commented on the difficulty of 'finding an elsewhere, of finding alternative horizons to explore'.[20] This is not Jameson's problem. Her problem is to regain her desired Elsewhere.

Jameson combined her imaginative capacities and desires with a more pragmatic approach when it came to her journey Elsewhere. To function professionally in her preferred Elsewhere, Jameson needs to develop her language skills and her knowledge of German literature. Her Elsewhere not only has a deep personal attraction, therefore, but a professional one as well. Christopher Bird, writing the prospectus and introduction to the new journal, the *British and Foreign Review*, at the start of its publication run in 1835, was very clear on the importance of German scholarship to those undertaking classical and historical studies and claims a 'peculiar advantage to be derived to this country, by a concentration within it of European knowledge'.[21] Jameson would instantly have recognized the latent opportunities such attitudes would foster, endorsing both her earlier travels to Germany in the first place, and why the Canadian winter is spent exploring possibilities for book and essay publication based on German literature and culture.

The very new and lively interest in German scholarship in this period, although not yet widespread or popular, also offers a professional, as well as a personal, explanation as to why these studies remain in a book ostensibly about Canada, a fact which produced considerable complaint from the various reviewers, Chorley excepted. Christian Isobel Johnstone in *Tait's Edinburgh Magazine* straightforwardly accuses Jameson of book-making, noting 'A great part of this work is filled with reminiscences of Germany, criticism, and speculation on German dramas, and other matters quite foreign to Canada, though perhaps bearing closely on the means of filling three volumes'.[22] The reviewer for the *Monthly Review* more

[18]   Christopher Bird, 'Introduction', 6.

[19]   H.F. Chorley, 'Mrs. Jameson's Winter Studies and Summer Rambles', *British and Foreign Review* 8(1839): 137; 134–53.

[20]   Ali Behdad, *Belated Travelers. Orientalism in the Age of Colonial Dissolution* (Durham and London, 1994), 92.

[21]   Christopher Bird, 7 and 5.

[22]   Christian Isobel Johnstone, 'Mrs. Jameson's Winter Studies and Summer Rambles in Canada', *Tait's Edinburgh Magazine* 6(1839): 70; 69–81.

querulously states that the reader would be right to complain about 'reminiscences and criticisms which have no more right to intermeddle with Canadian sketches and affairs than with Constantinople … We allude to the dissertations about Germany, and what is purely German'.[23] The *Spectator* sees 'no necessity … for reminiscences of German actresses, and criticisms on German authors, in a book on the Canadas'.[24]

When travelling in Italy, Mary Shelley had noted that 'I read a great deal to beguile the time, chiefly in Italian; for it is pleasant to imbue one's mind with the language and literature of the country in which one is living'.[25] The newly arrived Jameson has not yet discovered the language and literature of Canada (although eventually she will learn much about the First Nations people and will come to embrace that knowledge with an openness that is endearing) and so between occasional excursions and visits in and around Toronto, with the snow deep on the ground and the temperature below freezing point, she journeys to her German Elsewhere where she struggles with German language studies and valiantly tries to engage with German literature and culture. As a successful and ambitious writer Jameson was, naturally enough, very aware of the intensified interest in German writings generally so apparent from the early 1830s, an industry in which her friend Sarah Austin was playing such a key role, and was keen to be a part of that inner circle of English literati espousing all things German and to contribute her part to the 'circulation of knowledge' as Rita Monticelli so astutely puts it.[26] The sheer number of articles about German language, literature and culture in the mainstream British periodicals such as the *Quarterly*, the *Edinburgh Review*, as well as more obvious journals like the *Foreign Quarterly Review* in the mid-1830s substantiates my reading of this activity as a form of industry. Jameson also doubtless saw this wave of interest as a definite publishing opportunity and would later capitalize on it to produce a translation of the plays of the Princess Amelia titled *Social Life in Germany* (1840). G.H. Needler says of her translation of the plays that the 'cordial reception [Jameson's] translation met with marks them, with Mrs. Jameson's enlightening commentary, as a not insignificant contribution to the understanding of German literature and thought at that time' (Needler, 75).[27] At the same time in her work she never loses an opportunity to proselytize regarding the Woman Question.

I want now to turn to *Winter Studies and Summer Rambles in Canada* to map Jameson's Elsewhere journey. And I want to begin with the epigraphs that work as signposts pointing the way. The entire book has two epigraphs, one from the

23 'Mrs. Jameson in Canada', *Monthly Review* 148(1839): 67; 65–79.

24 'Mrs. Jameson's Winter Studies and Summer Rambles in Canada', *Spectator* 11(1838): 1166; 1166–8.

25 Shelley, *Rambles in Germany and Italy*, 124.

26 Monticelli, 301.

27 See Johnston, *Anna Jameson*, Chapter Five, for a full discussion of this translating and publishing venture.

writings of Rahel Von Ense which appears under the title on the title-page, and reads 'Leid, und Kunst, und Scherz' [Sorrow, and Art, and Joy], a quotation from Rahel Varnhagen Von Ense whose writings were published by her husband, after her death in 1833, under the title *Rahel. Ein buch des Andenkens für ihre Freunde* [*Rahel. A Memorial Book for her Friends*] (1834), the same book obviously which Jameson had taken with her on board ship.[28] After the 'Preface' and before the 'Contents' in the original 1838 edition, there is a second epigraph, this time a quotation from Spenser's *The Faerie Queen*, book iii, an exhortation to '*Be bold*' with the proviso, '*Be not too bold*', which I have always read as a necessary quality to be embraced by any lady traveller in the early Victorian period (emphasis Jameson's). There is, however, a third epigraph, which prefaces the first section of her Canadian travels titled 'Winter Studies', a quotation from Bettine von Arnim: 'Sind denn die Bäume auch so trostlos, so verzweiflungs voll in ihrem Winter, wie des Herz in seiner Verlassenheit?' (15). [Are the trees then as desolate, as full of desperation in their winter, as the heart is in its loneliness?]. Von Arnim had published only one work prior to 1838, *Goethes Briefwechsel mit einem Kinde* [*Goethe's Correspondence with a Child*] (1835) presumably the source of this quotation. The two women to whom the German epigraphs are attributed moved in the same literary circle in Berlin. Rahel's *salon* was 'the most notable social focus of Berlin literary life', and Bettine Von Arnim, from 1831 on, addressed social questions which had at their core the role and emancipation of women, a politics which accorded with Jameson's own and which emerges in all of her writings.[29] Both epigraphs, as quotations from published writings by women, not only give expression to the emotional turmoil aroused by the need to travel away from Germany, which is evidenced in Jameson's personal correspondence quoted previously, but also authorize, even legitimate, that emotion, even as the epigraphs are disrupted by that clarion call to boldness and courage. Moreover, by these judicious quotations, Jameson writes herself into a circle of German women (I am including von Goethe), all of whom have literary and artistic connections, a writing-in which perhaps eases the pain of displacement and exile. However, as previously noted, she also appeals to women readers beyond the work's first and most intimate putative reader, Ottilie Von Goethe, readers who are both English and German, as *Winter Studies and Summer Rambles in Canada* was translated and published in Braunschwieg (near Hanover) by F. Biewig in 1839.

The 'Preface' to *Winter Studies and Summer Rambles in Canada* is typical of Jameson's careful discursive management not just in terms of gender but also in her consciousness of the expectations accompanying professional authorship.

---

[28] The words can be found in a letter from Rahel to Regina Frohberg dated 13 December 1807 reprinted in *Märkischer Dichtergaren*, ed. Günter de Bruyn and Gerhard Wolf (Berlin, 1983), 62. My thanks to Prof. Jacqueline Van Gent for this and the following translation.

[29] Henry and Mary Garland (eds), *Oxford Companion to German Literature* (Oxford, 1997), 860 and 37.

The usual disclaimers are there in the modifiers she uses to describe her work, 'fragments', 'little', 'crude' (9), while simultaneously she reveals herself as a professional in discussing preparation of the text for the press; in designating her readership; and in assurances that the work conforms to the travel genre, as it was then understood, in embracing 'reality' and 'essential truth', while at the same time is sufficiently personal to retain its 'original character', 'grace of ease' and 'pictorial animation' (10), qualities which reviewers over and over again seek in critiquing the many travel books published by women in this timeframe. In the 'Preface' Jameson does not mention her literary and translation studies, or Germany, which figure so prominently in the first part of her book. The real excitement and interest of her Summer Rambles had, in effect, overshadowed that initial despair she had experienced in confronting and undertaking the Canadian journey. Her Elsewhere as a destination has, at the end of her Canadian sojourn, faded from sight.

The account of both journeys begins in Toronto on 20th December. Jameson spares her readers the inevitable rigours of the sea voyage, rather she thinks seriously and profoundly about her role as a traveller, emphasizing the need for observation and for 'recording faithfully the impressions made by objects and characters on my own mind – or, rather, the impress they *receive* from my own mind – ... to be corrected, or at least modified, by observation and comparison' (16). Such a credo suggests a traveller who is translating what she sees and what is more, unconsciously invoking the then accepted idea of translating practice as faithful and true to the original and applying it to the process of travel writing. The word 'truth', for instance, is repeated four times in this one paragraph. Jameson follows this writing, this translation practice, in both the journeys she undertakes, the journey to Elsewhere and the travels within Canada itself.

Section II

Books, dreams, are each a world; and books we know,
Are a substantial world.[30]

Jameson misquoted Wordsworth for her own purposes. His lines read 'Dreams, books, are each a world; and books, we know,/ Are a substantial world, both pure and good'. Inverting 'books' and 'dreams' may have been a deliberate choice on Jameson's part to place the emphasis on 'books'. The lines inspire her as the remedy to manage 'the strait in which I am placed' because books are a 'world ever at hand' (103). On 21 January 1837 Jameson began her German studies in earnest. She chooses first to work on the Danish writer Adam Oehlenschläger's tragedy *Correggio* (1808) which he had originally written in German, and Adolf Müllner's

---

30   William Wordsworth, 'I am not One who much or oft delight', *William Wordsworth*, ed. Stephen Gill (Oxford, 1984), ll.33–4, 269.

Die Schuld [*Guilt, a Tragedy in Four Acts*], published in 1816, performances of which enjoyed widespread success in Germany.[31] The frequent choice of plays to work on suggests that she may have found translating dialogue, or forms of dialogue, easier than more complex, philosophical works. She flirts with the idea of translating *Correggio* for performance on the English stage, asking her reader 'would it be possible, think you, that the tragedy of "Correggio" could be exhibited in England with anything like the success it met with in Germany?' although subsequently doubting it will find a sympathetic audience (34–5). Jameson is acute, though, in locating the play's originality as a tragedy that is not about ambition and kingly pride, but rather 'high art – its power as developed within the individual soul – its influence on the mind of others' (35). The comment indicates her interest in and knowledge of art, Italian art in particular. Moreover, throughout her career Jameson was interested in the theatre, participating in the preparations for the acting debut of Fanny Kemble and dedicating *Characteristics of Women* (1832) to her, based as that work is, on Shakespeare's heroines.

In *Winter Studies*, the investigation of these two lesser dramatists proves to be a dead end. Jameson's next excursion Elsewhere in *Winter Studies* is dated 24 February [1837]. As she puts it, 'I took refuge in another and a higher world, and bring you my ideas thereupon' (76). That higher world is, perhaps inevitably, four works by Goethe, *Iphigenia in Tauris* (1787), *Tasso Torquato* (1789), *Egmont* (1787) and *Clavigo* (1774). Of the four, it is *Iphigenia* and the eponymous heroine's internal monologues which can be best understood as giving Jameson a high, classical form of expression to her personal feelings and to her feminist politics. Such lines as the following (which I take from David Luke's translation) must surely have struck Jameson with their pertinence to her own condition, both personally and ideologically:

How lamentable is the lot of women!
A man rules in his home, and rules in war,
And in a foreign land he finds recourse;
Possessions gladden him, victory crowns him,
He lives assured of honourable death.
But strict and narrow is a woman's fortune. (Act I: 24–32)[32]

The question 'Can a strange land become our native soil' (Act I: 76) must also have exercised Jameson's mind, in particular in those encounters she later has with unhappy women immigrants to Canada. Unlike such women, Jameson always retains the freedom of the traveller in that she never has any intention of remaining in Canada. No matter how long and wearisome the winter seems,

[31]   Garland, *Oxford Companion*, 636 and 603.
[32]   Johann Wolfgang von Goethe. *Iphigenia in Tauris. A Play in Five Acts*, trans. David Luke, *Goethe's Collected Works. Volume 8. Verse Plays and Epic*, ed. Cyrus Hamlin and Frank Ryder (Princeton, NJ, 1987), 2.

no matter how intense at the start her emotional engagement with feelings of exile and estrangement, Canada will not be her permanent home. Eventually, like Iphigenia, she will be free to go.

Jameson's actual analyses do not directly articulate such thoughts but her letter to Ottilie von Goethe of 26 May 1837 confirms that her studies have prevented 'the mind from wasting itself away and being weakened and disordered with the struggle ... solitary in the midst of strangers, in a cold strange country' (Needler, 88). She offers basic truisms regarding the plays: 'Iphigenia is all repose; Tasso all emotion; Egmont all action and passion. Iphigenia rests upon the grace and grandeur of form – it is *statuesque* throughout. Tasso is the strife between the poetic and prosaic nature. Egmont is the working of the real' (*Winter Studies*, 76). However, the focus of Jameson's critiques of the various plays is always the women characters, thus Leonora d'Este in *Tasso* Jameson reads as 'true to itself, as a character – true to all we know of her history' (76) and asks of *Egmont*, 'what can be finer than the two female portraits ...?' (76). In discussing Goethe's attitude to women as 'like that entertained by Lord Byron, rather oriental and *sultanish*' (78), she adds of Iphigenia that this character is Goethe's 'only heroic and ideal creation ... she is as perfect and as pure as a piece of Greek sculpture', a characterization which reveals that 'if he did not understand or like the active heroism of Amazonian ladies, he had a very sublime idea of the passive heroism of female nature' (79). David Pugh remarks of Iphigenia that 'older scholarship ... glorified her as a statuesque ideal', pointing out that in fact the character 'undergoes violent changes during the course of the five acts',[33] the kinds of change Jameson sought in women's lives.

Nevertheless, Jameson has clearly tapped into the commonly-held critical view. For instance, Sarah Austin in her *Characteristics of Goethe* (1833) mentions the 'severe, chaste, antique beauty of his *Iphigenie*', and in doing so reveals how long-held that older scholarly critical positioning was.[34] Austin praises William Taylor's translation of *Iphigenie* which may be the version published in Taylor's *Historic Survey of German Poetry*, famously reviewed by Thomas Carlyle, who notes an 'entire *Iphigenia*' among 'dense masses of Translation, sometimes good, but seldom of the characteristic pieces' and damns with faint praise Taylor's publication with the comment 'there is, if no map of intellectual Germany, some first attempt at such'.[35]

Notably, Jameson is not attempting to read in the original German those works of Goethe which attracted the bulk of English critical commentary in the first three decades of the nineteenth century, his *Wilhelm Meisters Lehrjahre* [*Wilhelm*

---

[33] David V. Pugh, 'Goethe the Dramatist', *Cambridge Companion to Goethe*, ed. Leslie Sharpe (Cambridge, 2002), 76.

[34] Sarah Austin, trans. *Characteristics of Goethe. From the German of Falk, von Müller, etc. with Notes, Original and Translated, illustrative of German Literature* (1833; Philadelphia, 1841), 188. I use Austin's German spelling of Iphigenie where appropriate.

[35] Carlyle, 'Historic Survey of German Poetry', II: 171 and 164.

Meister's Apprenticeship] and the two key dramatic works, *Götz von Berlichingen mit der eisernen Hand* [*Götz of Berlichingen with the Iron Hand*] and *Faust*. In part this may well be because these three key publications had already been translated into English. *Wilhelm Meister's Apprenticeship* was translated by Thomas Carlyle and published in 1824. Walter Scott had published his translation of *Götz* in 1799, and Rose Lawrence published her translation the same year. Lord Francis Gower translated and published *Faust* in 1823. The 1830s saw considerable discussion of Goethe's literary output in the periodical press, in particular articles by Thomas Carlyle, J.S. Blackie and Sarah Austin. Critics and translators of Goethe had also included Coleridge, De Quincey and Shelley to name just a few. Indeed, a critic for the *Dublin University Magazine*, John Anster, remarks with a singular lack of prescience: 'Shelley is more likely to be remembered by his noble translations from Goethe, than by his original writings'.[36] Just five years on Jane Sinnett remarks that translations 'of *Faust* for instance – have been "as plenty as blackberries" – the regular *pièces de résistance* for every tyro to try his "'prentice hand" upon'.[37] For Jameson's "'prentice hand', however, these major works by Goethe may also have proved more challenging to read for a woman whose struggles to learn German I have already noted. As late as 1 April 1837 she tells von Goethe 'I read German every day, and I think I make progress – but I am dissatisfied with myself' (Needler, 85). Sarah Austin had noted in *Characteristics of Goethe* that Sir Walter Scott's translation of *Götz* 'is little read; nor indeed is it deserving of more notice than it has received' and remarks that it is 'much to be regretted that Goethe's best tragedies are not attempted again'.[38] A remark such as this, in a book which Jameson must surely have read, given her interest in the topic and her friendship with Austin, may have proved a spur to Jameson's translating ambitions which also are the remedy she needs to keep boredom and despair at bay.

On 10 March [1837] she announces 'I shall take to translating' (*Winter Studies*, 103) and the work she decides on is Johann Peter Eckermann's *Gespräche mit Goethe in den letzten Jahren seines Lebens* [*Conversations with Goethe in the final years of his Life*] first published in the German in 1836. Needler notes that von Goethe gave Jameson a copy on her departure from Weimar (87). She may also have read J.S. Blackie's 30-page review 'Eckermann's *Conversations with Göthe*' published in the *Foreign Quarterly Review* in October 1836, the same month in which she set sail for Canada. What follows are Jameson's thoughts and reflections as she journeys slowly through Eckermann's *Conversations*. As with travel narratives, there is an expectation on the part of the reader in the Victorian age that truth will inform biographical accounts. Ottilie von Goethe, thinly disguised in *Winter Studies* as someone 'intimate with the domestic life of Goethe' (103–104) is several times quoted in asserting the truth of Eckermann's *Conversations*.

36   John Anster, 'Goethe', *Dublin University Magazine* 8(1836): 350; 350–66.
37   Sinnett, 'Schiller', 478.
38   Austin, *Characteristics of Goethe*, 192.

One conversation between Goethe and Eckermann which Jameson notes particularly regards 'German poetesses'. It is recorded that the only successful women writers 'were almost universally women who had been disappointed in their best affections' (118). Marriage and children is the activity that is deemed 'best' for women. This discussion triggers a comprehensive outburst from Jameson. In a footnote she writes that such an attitude 'applies more to Germany than with us' (118) but nevertheless, in confronting what she dismisses as 'the old saw' (120), her words appear to include English society as well. Jameson is notably aware of the difference between ideology and reality. Women, she states, are placed in a false position by a society 'becoming every day more artificial and complex' (118), by men who merely 'pretend to admire' domestic devotion and submissiveness but nevertheless create these as the 'staple of the womanly character' which Jameson condemns as promising 'sunshine and roses' but producing instead a life in 'the arctic zone' (118). She writes of the 'cruel prejudices' once practised against women and calls for 'no more caricatures of methodistical, card-playing, and acrimonious old maids' (119). She reminds her readers of Coleridge's statement that men would like an Ophelia or a Desdemona for wives and drily comments: 'No doubt; the sentiment is truly a masculine one: and what was *their* fate? What would now be the fate of such unresisting and confiding angels? ... No, no; women need in these times *character* beyond everything else; the qualities which will enable them to endure and to resist evil' (119). Jameson is always polemical when it comes to the condition of women. Bringing up women to be 'happy wives and mothers' is, she says dangerous and wicked, because 'we know that hundreds, that thousands of women are not happy wives and mothers – are never either wives or mothers at all' (120). Rather what is needed is the cultivation of 'moral strength and the active energies of a woman's mind, together with the intellectual faculties and tastes' (120). In all her journeys Jameson never shifts from this demand for women that even when denied 'love and happiness' women should still be enabled 'to find content and independence' (120). This outburst is dictated by her own personal circumstances of course but it has also shifted her a long way from Eckermann's conversations with Goethe, and even further from Goethe's own position with regard to women. Ideally, the journey back to Elsewhere must enable the expression of the need for a radical shift in the gender ideology of the day. I suspect that for this reason the *Conversations* disappoints her because the book cannot be used or manipulated to this end.

Jameson's English model for a literary biography is, inevitably, Boswell's intimate account of Samuel Johnson, which she argues is a flawed model: 'we should be careful not to trust entirely to any one portrait, even though from the life, and of undoubted truth' (105). For Jameson, Boswell intrudes himself too often, 'the man's personal character is always in the way' (131), while Eckermann has an 'unsullied' mind, unable to 'perceive or speak other than the truth' (104). Yet when Jameson decides not to translate Eckermann's *Conversations* because it would not suit an English readership, it is on the grounds that it fails to deal in 'facts' and lacks 'anecdotes and personalities' (132), the very features which make Boswell's *Life of Johnson* so lively. She decides that the *Conversations* would be of as little interest to the English reader as Coleridge's *Table Talk* would be to the German reader. This consideration causes Jameson to address the issue of national character. She claims that the English have political liberty but not 'the social liberty of the Germans' (134) and comments on Goethe's belief that Germans achieve individual freedom as opposed to the English and the French who conform to each other. Jameson writes:

> This appears to me very true, and must, I think, strike every one who has been in Germany, and felt the interest which this kind of individuality imparts to society; though certainly I have met with travellers who were not a little put out by it … The women appear affected, and the men quizzical, precisely because the former are natural and the latter original, and all very unlike the ladies and gentlemen they have left behind, whose minds, like their bodies, are dressed in the same fashion. (135)

Her Elsewhere is thus a territory which needs to be negotiated through knowledge and understanding. Jameson attempts this by citing Sir James Mackintosh who, she says, described German literature and criticism 'as a sort of *terra incognita*' (136).[39] Mackintosh had reviewed Madame de Staël's *De l'Allemagne* [Germany] for the *Edinburgh Review* in 1813 and interestingly Jameson brings the two names together as explicators of German national character.[40] Jameson is on firmer ground here in considering Elsewhere as a *terra incognita* which she can, like Madame de Stäel, like the navigators of the fifteenth century seeking the western continent invoked by Mackintosh, open up the German national character and culture to the English gaze as if she might produce a Murray's handbook that navigates the tourist through the uncharted wilderness that is German literature and culture and national identity, and which constitutes her own territory Elsewhere. Her premise is that the 'Germans understand us better than we understand them' and claims that the language 'lends itself with wondrous richness and flexibility to translation from every tongue' (136) even as she struggles to acquire it. Her research into Eckermann's *Conversations* ends here. In concluding her Goethe studies she pays lip service to him as one who promotes 'the progress of the whole human race' (145) but Jameson herself travels down another road.

The last literary by-way Jameson takes is prompted by a notice titled 'Sternberg's *Tales and Novels*' in the February number of the *Foreign Quarterly*

---

[39]   Jameson mentions reading *Memoirs of the Life of the Right Honourable Sir James Mackintosh* (London, 1835) to von Goethe in a letter dated 17 May 1836 (Needler, 43–4).

[40]   See James Simpson, 'The Authority of Culture: Some Reflections on the Reception of a Classic' in *Goethe and the English-Speaking World. Essays from the Cambridge Symposium for his 250th Anniversary*, ed. Nicholas Boyle and John Guthrie (New York, 2002), 188 and n. 8, 196.

Review lent to her by a Mr. Hepburne.[41] The review was, in fact, written by Mary Margaret Busk and reveals, as her critiques consistently do, her strong predilection regarding English supremacy. In taking up English 'works of imagination', writes Busk, the reader can be assured of 'truth and vividness' in the portrayal of 'natural feelings, strong passions, individual character, and the manners of times past or present' but this is no longer the case with regard to 'novels, romances, and tales poured in upon us from the continent, more especially from Germany'.[42] For Busk the problem is the style of these novels which she labels 'dissertating' and asks 'what do we find?' The answer is:

> Dialogues upon religion, politics, ethics, metaphysics, aesthetics, or any other topic of discussion under the sun, loosely tacked together by the walks, visits, and amours, sometimes by the loves, of an artist Otho, or a Count Hermann, or any other human being, high born or low born.

Jameson appears at first to dismiss Busk's review of Sternberg's novels as 'not very well done' although this is promptly qualified by her concession that it 'is true, as far as it goes; but it gives no sufficient idea of the general character of his works, some of which display the wildest and most playful fancy, and others again, pictures, not very attractive ones, of every day social life' (181). Oddly, however, this precisely echoes what Busk is saying in the review. Jameson's opening defensiveness is accountable probably because this is German popular literature which she is considering making better known to an English readership via translation, and moreover, Sternberg is personally known to her, although again she qualifies her appraisal of the man who is young, handsome, and elegant, but cold and cynical.

In Busk's thumbnail sketch of the plot and characters of Sternberg's *Die Zerrissenen*, a title which she mockingly declares she is unable to satisfactorily translate, suggesting as possibilities 'the lacerated', 'the dilaniated', or 'the torn to pieces', we have a coterie of men who are profligate and licentious, anti-religious and amoral. The following nicely captures the general tone in Busk's plot précis:

> Another worthy, an old Englishman ... appears to have been a member, but he forthwith shoots himself, for no assignable reason but a taste for suicide, and impatience to be buried in the air, by being hung, after death, upon a gallows – a testamentary disposition duly executed by his friends.[43]

---

[41]   Alexander Ungern-Sternberg or Alexander von Sternberg (1806–68) attracts only a very minor biographical entry in Garland, 853.

[42]   Mary Margaret Busk, 'Sternberg's *Tales and Novels*', *Foreign Quarterly Review* 18(1837): 433–4; 433–54.

[43]   Busk, 'Sternberg's *Tales and Novels*', 435.

In her critique as part of her *Winter Studies*, Jameson oddly applies Busk's description of the men in the novel to the personal lives of a broadly-labelled group, the 'accomplished and popular authors of the day' (181) as she puts it, claiming:

> They are a set of men who have drunk deep, even to license, of the follies, the pleasures, and the indulgences of society, even while they struggled (some of them at least) with its most bitter, most vulgar cares ... A power is gone from them which nothing can restore – the healthy, the clear visions, with which a fresh, pure mind looks round upon the social and the natural world ... They wish us to believe, that in order to produce anything true and great in art, it is necessary to have known and gone through all this, to have been dragged through this sink of dissipation, or this fiery furnace of suffering and passion. ... Goethe, at least, did not think so ... I hope it is not so. I hope that a knowledge of our human and immortal nature ... does not depend on this sort of limited, unhealthy, artificial experience. (182)

Like Busk, who remarks 'that all Baron Sternberg's heroes are weak, whilst all his heroines are strong-minded',[44] Jameson admires his women for their 'individual character' (186) but complains that 'his men are almost without exception vile, or insipid, or eccentric – and his heroes (where could he find them?) are absolutely *characterless* – as weak as they are detestable' (186–7). Both women condemn Sternberg's latest novel *Galathee, ein Roman* (1836), Jameson calling it a 'painful book', remarking of the heroine's death of a broken heart: '"The more fool she!" I thought, as I closed the book "to die for the sake of a man who was not worth living for!"' (186). Busk writes with similar but even blunter asperity: 'We feel that she never could have been happy with him, and is better dead'.[45]

Jameson's determination once again that a translation, this time of Sternberg's *Die Gebrüder Breughel* [*The Two Breughels*] would not 'please generally in England' because it is 'too discursive and argumentative' (Busk uses the term 'dissertating') and would require 'a familiar knowledge of art and artists' (189) is deeply influenced, I believe, by Busk's article, both with regard to Sternberg's general style and on the grounds that the works are morally 'repugnant' to use Busk's term.[46] Despite a few admirable women characters it is clear that for Jameson's purposes this author too will not answer.

The German work Jameson finally translates is the plays of a woman dramatist, the Princess Amelia of Saxony as she is designated on the title page. The translation is cleverly framed as an investigation of German domestic life, and the plays collected under the title *Social Life in Germany, illustrated in the Acted Dramas of Her Royal Highness the Princess Amelia of Saxony*. Just as Jameson had used Shakespeare's heroines to write a treatise on the position of women in England in

---

44 Busk, 'Sternberg's *Tales and Novels*', 452.
45 Busk, 'Sternberg's *Tales and Novels*', 452.
46 Busk, 'Sternberg's *Tales and Novels*', 453.

1832 with an intelligent and lengthy introductory dialogue expressing the work's polemic, a device used again in *Visits and Sketches at Home and Abroad* (1834), so this dialogue strategy is re-introduced in *Social Life in Germany*, allowing Jameson at the outset to disclaim modestly her ability to translate in the very first line, but more importantly to explain:

> the particular purpose I had in view. English readers, English travellers, even English critics, had been, in some degree, interested by the very slight and imperfect sketches of German life and literature scattered through my little books. Now it happened that, when these comedies came under my notice, I was just looking round for some vehicle through which I might hope to convey a more detailed and finished picture of the actual state of society in a country which I have learned to love as my own.[47]

This introductory essay runs to just over 70 pages and, as with her earlier books, contains strong feminist statements regarding the condition of women and the existing gender ideology which so disadvantaged women in the period. In all her travels, whether to France, to Italy, to Canada or Elsewhere, it is this issue which occupies Jameson's mind, and is often expressed the most forcefully of all her observations as a traveller.

But it is now June, and the long winter is over. The journey to Elsewhere, achieved through that process of translation and intertextual movement described by Monticelli, comes haltingly to an end with a random selection of what Jameson herself dismisses in the page header as 'Detached Thoughts'. Detachment is significant. Imperceptibly as the weather has thawed so she has formed friendships, or as she puts it 'lived in friendly communion with so many excellent people' (193). All her thoughts are now focused on her Canadian tour and the epigraph from Sir Henry Taylor's verse drama *Philip van Artevelde* (1834) signals her change of heart and a newly revived emphasis on the independent woman traveller:

> It was to feel her fancy free,
> Free in a world without an end:
> With ears to hear, and eyes to see,
> And heart to apprehend. (193)

As Wendy Roy has shown, Jameson used her ears and her eyes to remarkable effect in producing what Roy terms an 'ethnographic project' in which, unusually for the time, contact with the First Nations people proves a two-way encounter demonstrated by Jameson's 'interest in the good opinion of her First Nations friends'.[48] Against all expectation Canada will prove both an intensely satisfying

---

[47] Anna Jameson, *Social Life in Germany, illustrated in the Acted Dramas of Her Royal Highness the Princess Amelia of Saxony* (London, 1840), I: viii–ix.

[48] Roy, 46 and 39.

intellectual encounter and a profitable publishing venture. Although she visits Germany again in later years, Jameson will spend much more time in France and Italy. The friendship with Ottilie von Goethe lessened in intensity with the passage of time but the exchange of correspondence continued until Jameson's death in 1860. Jameson's ethnography might, in some ways, be compared to the practices of my next translator, Lady Charlotte Guest, except that the differences in personal situation and social position produce a completely different story.

Chapter 5

Charlotte Guest,
Wales, and Cultural Appropriation

Through the translating practice of Charlotte Guest, and viewing her journey to Wales as a form of emigration, I want to consider the issue of cultural appropriation and the role of gender in such appropriation. I read Guest's work as part of an imperialist enterprise because translation gives access not only to prevailing ideas and philosophies, but also to myths, tales, legends and songs; a journey that takes the form of cultural colonization. Stephen Copley and Peter Garside in their work on the politics of the picturesque have commented on the way in which 'the discourse of the Picturesque intersects with and is shaped by the discourses of colonialism at various points', using the sentimentalisation of the Scottish landscape as an example.[1] Just as they have read the picturesque as helping to shape colonial discourse, so I wish now to consider translation as an enterprise also helping to shape colonial discourse. It seems to me that it is not the act of translation per se that is appropriative, rather, it is that translation, in time, forwards the colonial project.

The colonial project is forwarded in part because translation assists appropriation and can also risk the downgrading of colonized language and culture, in particular in cases where myths and legends are turned into stories for children. Language, as Lefevere has shown, is not the main problem in translation, the problem lies in ideology, poetics and 'cultural elements that are not immediately clear, or seen as completely "misplaced" in what would be the target culture version of the text to be translated'.[2] The target language, shifted out of its culturally significant context, reappears in another form: in the case of tales and legends, for instance, that form is most often locked into a particular mode: quaint, noble savage, child-like. I am using the term 'appropriation' here as defined by David Spurr in *The Rhetoric of Empire*. Spurr describes appropriation as a two-fold process in which the colonizer, as if by natural inheritance, takes over a territory and its products/ productions, and at the same time disguises this act of appropriation by pretending to be acting 'on the part of the colonized land and people'.[3]

---

[1] Stephen Copley and Peter Garside (eds), 'Introduction', *The Politics of the Picturesque. Literature, Landscape and Aesthetics since 1770* (Cambridge, 1994), 6–7.

[2] André Lefevere, 'Translation: its Genealogy in the West', *Translation, History and Culture*, ed. Susan Bassnett and André Lefevere (London, 1990), 26.

[3] David Spurr, *The Rhetoric of Empire. Colonial Discourse in Journalism, Travel Writing, and Imperial Administration* (London, 1993), 28.

I wondered to what extent this particular scenario might be applied to other translations, particularly by women, which had taken place across the nineteenth century, and decided to begin with the translation, by Lady Charlotte Guest, of the Welsh *Mabinogion*, and other tales, from *The Red Book of Hergest*. The tales are traditional mythic accounts of bygone Welsh pre-history, with heroes, otherworld adventures, magic encounters, prophecies and maidens. They are an important part of the Welsh literary tradition. Charlotte Guest's translation is therefore invasive, because it can be read very much as part of the rise of English nationalism and the celebration of Englishness. Thus the key questions I confronted at the outset of this chapter were, why Lady Charlotte Guest took this project on, and what prompted her to learn Welsh in the first place and to become involved in Welsh culture. Rhys Phillips, posing this identical question in 1921, attributes her incentive merely to a life-long habit of self-education and study, noting from her son's publication of her Journals that 'with the aid of her brother's tutor, she studied Greek, Latin, Hebrew, and Persian, for all things oriental appealed strongly to her'.[4] Of course this may have been *part* of the reason, but in considering my own answers to these questions, my response is indebted in particular to Janet Wolff's book *Resident Alien*. In its opening chapter Wolff offers an examination of the condition of dislocation through the writing of twentieth-century women, insights which are also applicable to nineteenth-century women as Wolff herself shows.[5]

Lady Charlotte Guest was indeed a stranger in town, a young 21-year-old escaping from an unhappy home-life through marriage, in July 1833, to a man of 48, a dissenter, a man in 'trade', but also, redeemingly, extremely wealthy and a Member of Parliament. After the honeymoon the pair set off to visit their Welsh home at Dowlais, an unexpected neighbourhood one would imagine, and an event she dramatizes in her diary suggesting the extent to which a sense of displacement preoccupies her mind:

> The country *did* smile as we started on our route and I could not have entered my new abode under more favourable circumstances ... By the time we reached the house it was quite dark and the prevailing gloom gave full effect to the light of the blazing furnaces, which was quite unlike all I had ever before seen or even imagined ... My first impulse was to establish myself in the library, by far the pleasantest room in the house. From the very moment I entered it I felt quite settled and at home.[6]

---

[4]   Rhys D. Phillips, *Lady Charlotte Guest and the Mabinogion* (Carmarthen, 1921), 13. All subsequent references are to this edition and will use the abbreviation 'Phillips' throughout.

[5]   Janet Wolff, *Resident Alien. Feminist Cultural Criticism* (Cambridge, 1995), 4.

[6]   Lady Charlotte Guest, *Lady Charlotte Guest. Extracts from her Journal 1833–1852*, ed. Earl of Bessborough (London, 1950), 16. All subsequent references are to this edition and will use the abbreviation 'Journal' throughout.

What strikes me about the language Charlotte Guest uses, the way the furnaces dominate the landscape, is its similarity to the travel-writing of women in Canada or Australia in the 1830s and 1840s, that mixture of seeking 'home' and at the same time the celebration of difference, the exotic, for instance, native figures lit by firelight are a common motif in travel writing from this period. Charlotte Guest was not alone in this. See for instance Moira Dearnley, addressing the novels of Anne Beale, in which she writes of the 'new world' in which Beale found herself on taking a position as governess at Llwynhelig. In her first prose work of 1844 set in Wales, she comments on the 'language of its primitive inhabitants'. Similarly, in Elizabeth Gaskell's short story, 'The Well of Pen-Morfa' (1850), Gaskell writes 'I could tell you of a great deal which is peculiar and wild in these true Welsh people'.[7] Victorian author and traveller George Borrow records of Merthyr 'only a vision of a fiery inferno occupied by "throngs of savage-looking people"'.[8] Linda Colley also makes a strong case for the distinctness of Wales at this time, quoting an English writer on tourism in 1831: 'If nothing can please him but what is *foreign* ... he will find the language, manners, and dress of the inhabitants [of Wales] ... as completely foreign as those of France or Switzerland'.[9]

The ultimate confirmation that Charlotte Guest's Welsh sojourn is intrinsically linked to travel and then tourism comes in 1860 when John Murray published *A Handbook for Travellers in South Wales and its Borders, including the River Wye*, adding to their already extensive travel guide list of continental destinations, a far more localised selection of guides for the British Isles, responding, in part perhaps, to increasing interest in the nation state. Moreover, the 'Introduction' to the 1877 edition was considerably expanded with 'Part X. Additional Information about Dowlais', offering the area as a particular tourist destination and the Guest connection there a tourist attraction. The tourist is given very precise locations for the four iron works and is told that the town of Merthyr owes its existence and survival to their presence. The *Handbook* then proceeds to eulogize the ironmaster Sir John Guest as doing 'more than any single man to leave it a populous town, larger than, and as opulent as, many cities'. The *Handbook* provides the tourist with various routes to choose. Route 9 includes the ironworks which are described again in terms which can only be thought of as a further panegyric. The *Handbook* also uncannily reflects Charlotte Guest's own reaction to the way the furnaces light the night sky as well as offering a typical traveller's reaction to local people in the comments about the previous state of the indigenous population as neglected and degraded. The tourist is told that there are 17 furnaces in all:

---

7   Moira Dearnley, '"I Came Hither, a Stranger": A View of Wales in the Novels of Anne Beale (1815–1900)', *New Welsh Review* 1(1989): 27; 27–32 and Elizabeth Gaskell, 'The Well of Pen-Morfa', repr. in *The Moorland Cottage and Other Stories*, ed. Suzanne Lewis (Oxford, 1995), 124.

8   Quoted in Basini, 35.

9   Quoted in Linda Colley, *Britons. Forging the Nation 1707–1837* (New Haven, 1992), 373.

The aspect of the works at night is a sight not to be forgotten, and the beacons are lighted up with their glow for miles round. They were brought to their present perfection by the energy and perseverance of the late Sir John Guest, who ranked as one of the foremost iron-masters in the country. A story is told, that Lady Charlotte Guest (now Lady Charlotte Schreiber) received the balance sheet of the works during a large entertainment that was being given at her mansion in London, and that the greatest sensation was created by a noble lady looking over her shoulder and observing that the profits of the year were represented by five figures. Under Sir John's care the sanitary and social condition of the people, who number at this work about 20,000, was considerably raised, after having been for many years in a state of neglect and degradation horrible to contemplate.[10]

The political bias of this statement should be balanced against the anger felt and expressed by Taliesin Williams in 1835 regarding the threat posed by the 'powerful foreign ruling caste' to his language and culture. The one exception Williams made in his protest against English 'incomers' was Lady Charlotte Guest.[11]

Oddly enough, in 1839 the reviewer in the *Spectator*, discussing Part II of Charlotte Guest's translation, the tale of Peredur, calls on analogies associated with exotic travel to explicate the translated tale itself. The reviewer is exercised about the 'impossibilities' of the tale, citing giants and dragons, the sudden acquisition of skills, and in particular the class issues: sudden intimacy between people, perfect strangers recounting family troubles and concerns, easy access to princes, and the familiar treatment of princes. The reviewer discovers a parallel however:

> in the narratives of American and African travellers, or even amongst the petty potentates of the East. The still more strange facility, shocking to our sense of moral feeling, with which a substitute is found for the dearest ties, also obtains amongst nations in an early stage of society, where necessity and hourly hazard prevent the growth of refined sentiment. When the Red Indians have slaughtered part of a family, they think they make full reparation, should mercy touch them, by finding the survivors with husbands or wives; and stranger still, this sort of recompense seems admitted.[12]

Lady Charlotte was a displaced woman both in regard to locality and to class, and it is significant that she almost immediately set about learning the local language. Within two months she was taking lessons in modern Welsh from the rector, Evan Jenkins, and in November 1833 writes in her diary: 'Welsh my study, and Ariosto and

---

[10]   'Introduction', *A Handbook for Travellers in South Wales and its borders, including the River Wye* (1860; London, 1877), xl and 97.

[11]   Basini, 34–5.

[12]   'National Literature – The Mabinogion: Legends of the Rhine', *Spectator* 12(1839), 761; 760–61.

Chaucer once again my relaxation' (*Journal*, 20). A year later, September 3, 1834 she records 'Baby leaves but little time for anything, and that time must be spent on Welsh' (*Journal*, 35). As Wolff remarks, in discussing contemporary accounts by women who have found themselves outsiders, some women 'have stressed the crucial importance of … foreign language as a catalyst in change, in development, and often, in literary and other forms of creativity'.[13] Guest's relationship with the working people through language is marked once again as typically colonial in its limitations as can be located in this brief vignette from her diary dated 17 July 1837 when she went to hear her husband speak at a political meeting:

> Far from the incivility they talked of at Dowlais the crowd was quite obliging to me; when first I came up there was a buzz of one asking another to make room for me, and when I put my finger to my lips and said "goshey goshey", they smiled at my Welsh and were as quiet as possible. (*Journal*, 51)

Janet Wolff's reading of Caren Kaplan's article on deterritorialization highlights the way in which 'the position of outsider enables a special vision', relating both to the idea of home, and to the idea of exile.[14] Although marginalized socially in Wales by her upper-class rank, and by her husband's powerful position as the Iron Master, a reversal of the usual process, Guest's mobility of class and geography gave her both intellectual and critical advantage. But throughout the published sections of her journal that I have been able to examine, the reader gains an overwhelming sense that Charlotte Guest's was indeed both an imperialist and a feminist project, although never expressed in either of those terms. As a feminist project she sought for both identity and position, 'in opposition', as Wolff puts it in another context, 'to linear narratives of the self and essentialist conceptions of gender and place'.[15]

I have put together the following extract from Charlotte Guest's journal, dated 27 April 1839, from two separate sources. It gives, I think, a sense of Guest fulfilling exactly this style of feminist project. It is important to note her use of the possessive: 'my house', 'my works', 'my blood', 'my book'. The extract is written in triumph at being 'complimented' (her term) with her own room at the new offices of her husband's firm in London, a room of one's own having, as we know, particular feminist significance:

> I think it is a retreat that I shall often be tempted to resort to from the gaieties and interruptions of Grosvenor Square. I have so schooled myself into habits of business that it is now more congenial to me to calculate the advantage of half per cent commission on a cargo of iron than to go to the finest Ball in the world. But whatever I undertake I must reach an eminence in. I cannot endure

---

13   Wolff, Resident Alien, 2–3.
14   Wolff, Resident Alien, 9.
15   Wolff, Resident Alien, 9.

anything in a second grade. I am happy to see we are at the head of the iron trade. Otherwise I could not take pride in my house in the City, and my works at Dowlais, and glory (playfully) in being (in some sort) a tradeswoman. Then again, my blood is of the noblest and most princely in the Kingdom, and if I go into Society, it must be the very best and first. I can brook no other. If I occupy myself in writing, my book must be splendidly got up and must be, as far at least as decoration and typography are concerned, at the head of literature, and I delight in the contrast of the musty antiquarian researches and the brilliant fetes and plodding counting house, from all of which I seem to derive almost equal amusement. And then I can sit and laugh at the gravest of them all as vanities, and moralise upon the thought of how soon the most important of them will cease to be of any avail or interest to me. Yet while they last and while there is youth and health to enjoy them, surely it cannot be wrong to take pleasure in the various blessings of this life. (*Journal*, 89 and, for the two additional sentences at the end, Phillips, 15)

The note of triumph is at first undisguised but as the entry proceeds so Guest attempts to restore her sense of what is appropriate both to gender and to class by using parenthesis. If she glories in being a 'tradeswoman', it is only 'playfully' and she is only 'in some sort' a tradeswoman as she remembers what is due to her rank. Lady Charlotte Guest's ambition for her book is clearly defined by herself in the foregoing extract more in terms of book-making, of appearance, than in terms of literary quality, which might seem to narrow the intellectual significance of the enterprise considerably, except that she put extraordinary work into both the translation and the notes as almost every modern reviewer comments.

Charlotte Guest's translation of these Welsh tales is a tale in itself of cultural appropriation that still remains a considerable success story. She would never have understood her process in that way however and in 1837, attending a Cymreigyddion Meeting, she laments that it seemed:

there was not the same display of genuine and native enthusiasm among the lower order of Welsh Literati themselves, which had been so animating and gratifying in 1835. I am afraid the Society is beginning to be tamed down to the conventional rules of English taste. (*Journal*, 61)

It is clear that Wales, and its language, dress and customs, represents for her an exotic location.

Perhaps not surprisingly then, Charlotte Guest's actual moment of decision to translate the *Mabinogion* is not included in the edited version of her Journal produced by her grandson, the Earl of Bessborough in 1950, from which many entries are omitted. Moreover, a subsequent family biographer, Revel Guest, with Angela John, has commented on the numerous errors of transcription in this publication, particularly of Welsh words.[16] They also pinpoint more accurately the project's timeline. On 17 October 1837 Charlotte Guest records in her journal that there will be an attempt to obtain Owen Pughe's manuscripts and notes but this is never mentioned again and appears to have been unsuccessful (Guest and John, 101). Guest and John name the particular scholars linked with Lady Guest's translation as Tegid (Rev. John Jones) and Carnhuanawc (Rev. Thomas Price) and in fact declare that these two men were 'crucial to the success' of the project (Guest and John, 106). Charlotte Guest's Journal entry for 30 November 1837 records that:

> Mr. Justice Bosanquet, has, through Tegid, kindly lent me his copy of the Llyfr Goch y Hugest, the Mabinogion, which I hope to publish with an English Translation, notes, pictorial illustrations. Price of Crickhowel and Tegid have promised their assistance, and by God's blessing I hope I may accomplish the undertaking. (*Journal*, 63–4)[17]

It is easy to misread the extracts from the Journal which come hard upon this one. She writes on 4 December 1837 of reading 'part of the Tale of Kilhwch and Olwen translated by Justice Bosanquet from the Mabinogion. It pleases me much. There is a great field for annotation' (*Journal*, 64). I believe this translation is from medieval Welsh into modern Welsh because on 8 December she writes of needing 'some plan for translating Justice Bosanquet's Copy, as I do not feel inclined to give up my scheme of publishing it myself'. She then writes that Mr. Jones (Tegid) 'has taken Justice Bosanquet's M.S. and is to copy from it one story at a time in a fit manner to go to the Press, viz: in Modern Orthography which would be more generally useful, and send them to me to translate' (*Journal*, 64).

The subsequent published translation (including both Modern Welsh and English) originally appeared in seven parts between 1838 and 1845. In 1849 it was published as a three-volume edition. In 1877 Quarich published a one-volume reprint which omits the Modern Welsh text. Charlotte Guest's English translation was published by Dent (Everyman) in 1902, by Fisher Unwin in 1902, and by David Nutt in 1902, the publisher in the 1890s of a range of 'folk lore' translations from various colonial sites including Australia, New Zealand and New Guinea; and by the Folio Society in 1980. Everyman reprinted their edition consistently until 1937. At first praised in contemporary reviews of her day for giving access to an 'old Welsh national literature', it is clear from reading the various reviews which appeared between 1838 and 1844, that this celebration of nationalism shifts from a focus on Wales to Britain.[18] A review of 'Kilhwch and Olwen' in the

---

[16]   Revel Guest and Angela V. John, *Lady Charlotte. A Biography of the Nineteenth Century* (London, 1989), 115. All subsequent references are to this edition.

[17]   Guest and John note that Lady Guest actually wrote 'Llyfr Coch o Hergest'. The misspelling is a typographical error (Guest and John, 115).

[18]   'The Mabinogion, Part II', *Monthly Review* 150(1839), 132.

Monthly Review in 1842 declares the tale to be 'strictly and purely British',[19] and from then on a case is consistently made that Welsh literature 'was not confined to the mountains of Wales'.[20]

This indeed is Lady Guest's own position, writing in the 'Introduction' to the 1849 three-volume edition:

> The Mabinogion however, though thus early recorded in the Welsh tongue, are in their existing form by no means wholly Welsh. They are of two tolerably distinct classes. Of these, the older contains few allusions to Norman customs, manners, arts, arms, and luxuries. The other, and less ancient, are full of such allusions, and of ecclesiastical terms. Both classes, no doubt, are equally of Welsh root, but the former are not more overlaid or corrupted, than might have been expected, from the communication that so early took place between the Normans and the Welsh ...[21]

By 1840, when Part 3, 'Gereint the Son of Erbin' was issued, the shifting of cultural significance had already begun. The *Monthly Review* in its 'Notices' announces the publication, and quotes from a speech by Dr. Thirlwell, Bishop of St. David's at the Abergavenny Cymreigyddion meeting, 8 October 1840: 'I am inclined to believe, that there must be some particular charm in that literature, which has found grace in ladies' eyes'.[22] In an age when the current ideology maintained a rigid separation of male and female spheres of activity, literature for ladies carries very particular implications: less challenging, less erudite, simple, charming and other such epithets. Earlier, however, the same London journal, the *Monthly Review*, in noticing 'Part 2, Peredur the Son of Evrawc', had celebrated Lady Guest's considerable achievement in quite different terms that suggest some measure of colonial supremacy over 'the principality' as Wales is termed:

> The tale, according to the agreeably quaint translation, is even more interesting than its predecessor. Lady Charlotte Guest is doing more to popularize and make the English reader acquainted with the old Welsh National literature than all the other living antiquaries in the principality, boastful as some of them are of its treasures.[23]

---

[19]   'The Mabinogion, Part IV', *Monthly Review* 158(1842), 284; 284–7.

[20]   'The Red Book of Hergest', *Saint Pauls* 3(1868), 310; 308–20.

[21]   Lady Charlotte Guest, 'Introduction', *The Mabinogion from the Llyfr Coch o Hergest and other Ancient Welsh Manuscripts, with an English Translation and Notes* (3 vols; London, 1849), xvii–xviii. All subsequent references are to this edition and will use the abbreviation Mabinogion.

[22]   'The Mabinogion, Part III', *Monthly Review* 153(1840), 610.

[23]   'The Mabinogion, Part II', 132.

The issue of local nationalism as a failed enterprise in Wales itself, as hinted at here, is interesting. Linda Colley remarks that English nationalists 'were much less repelled by their union with Wales, partly because this connexion was so much older, but primarily because the Welsh seemed so much less threatening'.[24] Colley goes on to note particularly that what distinguished the Welsh from the Scottish was the retention of their language which three out of four still spoke by choice as late as the 1880s and which has had, of course, an unprecedented revival in the late twentieth, early twenty-first centuries. Guest's project was undertaken just as the concept of a united kingdom, and thus a nation state, was becoming more fully developed. Despite David Powell's claim that Wales, in comparison to other states in the kingdom, was more fully assimilated into the British State, I would want to argue that Wales was nevertheless perceived as having a 'semi-colonial status' to use Powell's words regarding Ireland.[25] The review of Part III, from 1840, already quoted, praises in particular Lady Guest's 'liberality and patriotism in this grand undertaking'.[26] It seems clear to me that the 'patriotism' being celebrated here is not a Welsh one, but rather, her work as contributing to English Nationalism, or in other words, to the project of uniting the kingdom as a necessary corollary to the Empire as a whole. If this is so, then reception of the translation is confirmed as appropriation as the following comments from the earliest reviews (1838–9) reveal.

The *Spectator*, for instance, notes that for the last 12 years, the special Society for the Publication of Ancient Welsh Manuscripts had failed to achieve anything towards their aims, having 'neither money nor Welsh' and the *Athenaeum* remarks that when:

> the Cymreigyddion, from the difficulties in the way, (a whole nation find difficulties in translating and publishing what might easily be compressed into a couple of octavos!) and from past disappointments, were about to abandon the enterprise, Lady Charlotte Guest at once declared that she would both translate the book and publish it at her own expense.[27]

The *Monthly Review*, noticing 'Part 1, The Lady of the Fountain', also remarks on the Society's failure 'owing either to a want of knowledge of the Welsh language, the want of money, or the want of manuscripts' and continues:

> At length to rescue the province from the disgrace which apathy or deficiency of one sort or another entailed, and also to circulate the "Llyfr Coch o Hergest",

---

24   Colley, 13.

25   Powell, 6.

26   'The Mabinogion, Part III', 610.

27   'The Mabinogion – Early Welsh legends', *Spectator* 2(1838), 1067; 1067–8 and 'The Mabinogion', *Athenaeum* (24 November 1838), 833; 833–5,

or "Red Book of Hergest", which contains a collection of Welsh legendary tales, Lady Charlotte Guest of Dowlais volunteered her talent and her purse.[28]

It should be clear from these examples that the London-based periodical press celebrated the translation of the Welsh legends in terms both nationalistic and acquisitive, fulfilling Spurr's definition of appropriation to a nicety. While at times the reviews blur national boundaries, nevertheless a very particular prejudice develops, notably when the scorn of the *Athenaeum* is so palpable, emphasized both by parentheses and exclamation: '(a whole nation find difficulties in translating and publishing)', clearly the Welsh nation is intended here, while the *Monthly Review* believes the 'province' is rescued from 'disgrace'.

While each tale in Lady Guest's *Mabinogion* is presented in modern Welsh orthography up front, followed by the English translation and then the copious notes, also in English, the presence of the Welsh is not specifically commented upon in the English press until 1843. The *Monthly Review* notes only that the work is 'curiously illustrated with fac-similes', or as the *Spectator* puts it:

> The getting-up of the work is magnificent; and in its typography, its vellum-like paper, and the different fac-similes of manuscripts, as well as the wood-cut vignettes, reflects the highest credit upon its provincial publisher.[29]

In 1843, however, the *Monthly Review* produced a long article titled 'Welsh Fiction' which considers the first four parts, 1838–1842, of Lady Guest's translation and draws attention to the fact that to:

> the Welsh text has been added a literal English translation, some few explanatory notes, and fac-similes of the oldest manuscripts in this and other countries, of the romances corresponding to each Mabinogi.[30]

It should be noted that the Welsh text is missing from later editions such as that of 1902, edited by Owen Edwards and published by Fisher Unwin. Ironically, 'Welsh Fiction' addresses a further act of acquisition, Villemarqué's Paris edition of the *Mabinogion*. This was claimed to be a direct translation from the Welsh into French but Lady Guest, and the *Monthly Review*, insisted it was in fact a rendering of her English translation into French – but that is another story.

While it can be argued that Charlotte Guest made these medieval manuscripts available to the Welsh, it is difficult to estimate how many people in 1838 could read and write Welsh, or for that matter how many people could actually read and write at all. The London-based Welsh school teacher William Owen Pughe had produced the two-volume *Dictionary of the Welsh Language* (1832) and

---

28   'Mythology and Legends', *Monthly Review* 148(1839), 24; 20–29.

29   'Mabinogion, Part II', 132 and 'The Mabinogion – Early Welsh Legends', 1068.

30   'Welsh Fiction', *Monthly Review* 160(1843): 453; 431–68.

his translation of 'Pwyll', along with the text, was serialised in the first Welsh periodical, the *Cambrian Register*, from 1796. Lady Charlotte used both his *Dictionary* and his *Cambrian Biography* (nd) for her 'Notes' accompanying the translations (Guest and John, 96). Guest and John in their 1989 biography also provide, as Appendix 4B, a list of the books in Lady Guest's possession in 1852 relevant to the Mabinogion. The list includes another *English and Welsh Dictionary 1798–1805* by Richards. The knowledge of Middle Welsh in the period is less easily determined but appears not to have been widespread if we go by Charlotte Guest's own evidence. It seems the scholar Elijah Waring 'provided the initial impulse for her particular project' (Guest and John, 99), and when he visited Dowlais in October 1835 Lady Guest noted 'he is somewhat acquainted with ancient literature ... He is the only person I have found so in this country except George Clark' (Guest and John, 100).

Subsequent editors of the English versions of these tales insist that through lack of knowledge or poor instruction, sadly, Lady Guest incorrectly titled the tales as *The Mabinogion*. Most subsequent editions or new translations, while doggedly pointing out her error of transmission, nevertheless appear under the very sobriquet she provided. All those editors and translators who are Lady Guest's successors, well into the twentieth century, explain with care and precision her 'error', and invariably attribute it to misunderstanding of the Welsh term, offering very rational explanations as to how the mistake might have occurred. For instance, Jeffrey Gantz, translator of the 1970s Penguin edition writes:

> Each of the Four Branches ends with some form of the phrase, "So ends this Branch of the Mabinogi". Inasmuch as the Welsh word *mab* means "boy", Lady Charlotte concluded that *mabinogi* was a noun meaning "a story for children" and that *mabinogion* was the plural of the word. In fact, the word *mabinogion* does not exist in Welsh, though it appears once by mistake in "Pwyll". *Mabinogi* is a genuine Welsh word, but in these texts it applies only to the Four Branches in which it appears. Strictly speaking, this collection ought to be called "The Mabinogi and Other Early Welsh Tales", but that is cumbersome, while "The Mabinogion" is established and convenient.[31]

Jones and Jones believe the word is better interpreted as 'a tale *of* youth' (a meaning gradually reduced to simply 'a tale'), rather than *for* children, and Rachel Bromwich has suggested 'a tale of descendants'.[32]

I should make it clear at this point that I have no quarrel with subsequent translators, nor with their translations. I know no Welsh myself, ancient or modern. My interest is solely in translation as an imperialist project, as a means of cultural colonisation and in the part women played in that project. Guest's real

---

[31] Jeffrey Gantz, *The Mabinogion* (Harmondsworth, 1976), 31.

[32] Gwyn Jones and Thomas Jones, *The Mabinogion* (1948; London, 1974), xii and Bromwich, quoted in Gantz, 32. Emphases mine.

part in creating the title is in fact very minor. It is apparent from her journal that the name 'Mabinogion' for some particular Welsh tales was in common parlance well before her first translated tale appeared in print. As Jones and Jones point out, her understanding that 'mabinogion' was the plural of 'mabinogi', was an error in common with most Welsh scholars of her time.[33] Few subsequent editors have been able to resist the title's usefulness as a neat package label, a cultural commodity or 'brand' conspicuously marketable. As Jeffrey Gantz so rightly sums up, it is 'established and convenient'.

Thus by accident, Lady Guest's mistake places her imprimatur both on the received English title of these early Welsh tales and therefore on the translation of them as a whole. Because of the title, every subsequent edition pays some form of acknowledgment to Charlotte Guest with a consistency that seems to me to be remarkable, if based solely on that error in the title. It is even more remarkable because of the difficulty in determining to what extent she fully translated from medieval Welsh, the translated tales which appear under her name. Guest and John note that the early twentieth-century Welsh scholar W.J. Gruffydd believed 'the main credit should go to the two scholars who "devilled" for her, Tegid and Price' (Guest and John, 113). The Preface written for the first part in 1838, and republished for the 1849 edition, acknowledges the copy Tegid produced of Justice Bosanquet's manuscript but the expressed indebtedness is to the Justice for its use, rather than to Tegid for the work. She does however express her obligation to Tegid 'for the trouble he has taken to forward my wishes with respect to publishing the MS. as correctly as possible' (*Mabinogion*, vi). There is no acknowledgement in the 1849 edition of the work of Thomas Price with whom Lady Guest worked so closely throughout the production of the Tales from 1838 to 1845. Meic Stephens believes the:

> extent of Charlotte Guest's labours as a translator is an open question: she was certainly acquainted with Welsh and her children were taught the language, but it seems likely that her part in the venture was the rendering into graceful English of her collaborators' literal translation rather than any close involvement in the basic task of translating the original texts.[34]

Modern translators of the tales vary in the extent to which they address the question of Guest's translating ability. In 1977 Patrick Ford acknowledges Guest's translation as important because it is the earliest into English, noting tactfully that hers 'is a graceful and romantic rendition, which was well suited to the tastes of her mid-nineteenth century audiences'.[35] Jones and Jones in 1948 give a full translation history, carefully pointing out the names of Guest's Welsh collaborators

---

[33]   Jones and Jones, ix.

[34]   Meic Stephens (ed.), *The Oxford Companion to the Literature of Wales* (Oxford, 1986), 233.

[35]   Patrick K. Ford, *The Mabinogi and other Medieval Welsh Tales* (London, 1977), ix.

and deciding that hers is 'a charming and felicitous piece of English prose, and has been justly esteemed by every succeeding generation of readers as a classic in its own right'.[36]

Although in 1929 Ellis and Lloyd praise her translation's 'charm and literary qualities', they are far more severe regarding the translation project itself:

> Only one attempt has been made hitherto to render into English the whole of these romances, namely, that by Lady Charlotte Guest, with the assistance of Tegid, in 1838–49. The intention of Lady Charlotte Guest appears to have been to produce a version which could be used for the instruction and amusement of her own children, with the result that parts of her translation are either inaccurate or bowdlerized.[37]

The accusation that the work is 'inaccurate or bowdlerized' appears to be unsubstantiated. It seems to me that subsequent editors, Jones and Jones for instance, would have commented on extensive inaccuracies and alterations had they existed and none of the subsequent translators do take issue with the translation itself. A random check of the Jones and Jones translation of various tales against those of Charlotte Guest reveals few variations. In 'Pwyll Prince of Dyfed' for instance at the start:

> *Guest*: Once upon a time, Pwyll was at Narberth his chief palace.

> *Jones and Jones*: And once upon a time he was at Arberth, a chief court of his.

The ending is rendered by both as follows:

> *Guest*: And Pryderi ruled the seven Cantrevs of Dyved prosperously, and he was beloved by his people, and by all around him.

> *Jones and Jones*: And Pryderi ruled the seven cantrefs of Dyfed prosperously, beloved by his people and by all around him.

'Branwen the Daughter of Llyr' similarly reveals few variations, as did other tales I checked. The concluding lines of 'Branwen' for instance:

> *Guest*: In Ireland none were left alive, except five pregnant women in a cave in the Irish wilderness;

---

[36] Jones and Jones, xxxi.

[37] T.P. Ellis and John Lloyd, *The Mabinogion. A New Translation* (Oxford, 1929), viii and vii.

Jones and Jones: In Ireland no person was left alive save five pregnant women in a cave in the Irish wilderness.

The comment by Ellis and Lloyd that the work may have been produced merely to instruct and amuse her children is also unfounded. Lady Guest certainly dedicated the 1849 publication to her two eldest sons, but had no children when the project began. The dedication, 'To Ivor and Merthyr', however, reinforces the notion that Wales was, for Charlotte Guest, a site of positive, rather than negative, displacement, which she invests with romantic and sentimental associations. She tells her sons, in the dedication, to cultivate the literature of the country 'in whose beautiful language you are being initiated, and amongst whose free mountains you were born', adding in even more intensely romantic style:

> May you become early imbued with the chivalric and exalted sense of honour, and the fervent patriotism for which its sons have ever been celebrated.

> May you learn to emulate the noble qualities of Ivor Hael, and the first attachment to your Native Country, which distinguished that Ivor Bach, after whom the elder of you was named. (*Mabinogion*, n.p.)

In 1921 Rhys Phillips's publication *Lady Charlotte Guest and the Mabinogion* begins with a section titled 'The English Version of the Mabinogion' in which he defends Lady Charlotte from 'unlettered gossips and certain village writers' who had 'found it difficult to believe that an English lady could effectually surmount the difficulty of rendering into English a series of texts written in early Medieval Welsh' (Phillips, 9). This discussion carefully sets out Guest's due acknowledgment of any existing translations and her revising of same into modern English prose, and cites her journals as evidence of her participation in translation where none, or only partial ones, existed. The argument is, unfortunately, predominantly and least effectively developed, from a class position. The denigration implicit in 'unlettered gossips' at the beginning culminates in a citation from Burke's *Peerage* of Lady Guest's pedigree at the conclusion.

The 1989 biography authored by Guest and John produces more positive evidence of Lady Guest's exact role in the translation. Her Deed Box, held in the National Library of Wales, was explored and they found that the Welsh text is 'presumably in Tegid's handwriting'. They conclude that Lady Guest translated into English from the copy in modern Welsh supplied by Tegid and that then Price 'worked with her on this, improving it', a version thence turned into 'the graceful and elegant English which was her hallmark'. Admitting that Price's role is never acknowledged in the 'Preface' of the 1849 edition, they suggest this might be explained by his death before its publication (Guest and John, 115). However, the Preface is actually to the first tale of 1838 as I have shown and Price's name appears nowhere in it. It is very clear that Lady Guest never properly acknowledged the extensive work of her two Welsh collaborators. However, Guest and John note that Rachel Bromwich has done some comparative work based on segments of translation of 'Pwyll' and 'Math' and found that the Guest translation 'clearly owes nothing to the earlier versions and is in several instances more accurate than Owen Pughe's' (quoted in Guest and John, 101), despite the fact that it was probably 'more of a collaborative effort than she fully acknowledged' (Guest and John, 116).

Rhys Phillips makes much of the evidence of Lady Guest's own journals regarding the issue of the extent to which she actually translated the medieval Welsh into English and the extent to which she used modern Welsh transcriptions provided for her. I wondered if Guest was using the word 'translate' loosely for 'transcribe' but that appears not to be the case, as in this very precise statement from 6 January 1838, that she finds translation 'rather difficult for me, being so little conversant with the Welsh, and the *Mabinogion* being in such a cramped and ancient style' (Phillips, 19), which might suggest medieval Welsh but could also simply mean that rendered into Modern Welsh the ancient style made translating more difficult. On the 22 January 1838 five days after the birth of her fourth child, she had been given permission 'to set to work with my dictionaries on a fresh sheet of the Mabinogion, which I finished' (*Journal*, 65) which suggests translating from modern Welsh to English. However, by July she is pleased to discover she can understand *old* Welsh words (my emphasis) without a dictionary. In March 1839 she records that the *Dream of Ronabwy* 'is very tiresome and difficult Welsh, and I did not get on much with it' (Phillips, 23). Of *Peredur* she boasts 'I have transcribed it, translated it, written the notes, provided the decorations, and brought it almost out of the printer's hands' (Phillips, 25). This last quotation does seem to suggest that the word 'transcription' denotes rendering medieval Welsh into modern. The advantage she did possess was the money and the social position to command considerable assistance. For instance, someone she names Nethercliff is recorded by Lady Guest as having 'made me a facsimile of Sir John Bosanquet's MS. of *Peredur*';[38] she notes that researches 'are being made for me at the British Museum'; she comments that it 'would be a great advantage if [Tegid] would correct the press of *Peredur*'; and Colonel Vaughan lent her MS fragments of *Gereint* and Lord Mostyn promised to lend his copies of the *Mabinogion* (Phillips, 24, 25, and 26).

Guest's introductory essay to the 1849 three-volume edition, however, deals not with translation at all, but with the question of antiquity and origins, of comparative philology, with in fact the wealth of information she had gathered along the way, writing:

> it is one thing to collect facts, and quite another to classify and draw from them their legitimate conclusions; and though I am loth that what has been collected with some pains, should be entirely thrown away, it is unwillingly, and with

---

[38] The facsimiles of medieval manuscript material in the 1849 three-volume edition of her work are signed 'J. Netherclift, lithog'.

> diffidence, that I trespass beyond the acknowledged province of the translator.
> (*Mabinogion*, xii)

It is clear, despite this disclaimer, that this is the area of the work in which she took the most interest and felt herself to be on very sure ground making comfortable comparisons with other romance texts in the, by now, very familiar style of other nationalizing scholars like Joseph Ritson and Walter Scott.

Philological investigation was only just developing as a popular field of intellectual activity at the time, linked to attempts to establish a common source of all languages, a study in part produced by colonial encounters. Guest determines that the Mabinogion, although 'early recorded in the Welsh tongue' is 'by no means wholly Welsh' (*Mabinogion*, xvii) but nevertheless although 'mixed up, indeed, with various reflex additions from beyond the border, ... still containing ample internal evidence of a Welsh original' (*Mabinogion*, xxii). In more recent times Ceri Davies confirms that the 'so-called *Mabinogion* ... (The Four Branches of the Mabinogi) are tales which belong entirely to the Celtic world, largely unaffected by the legacy of classical writing'.[39] Rachel Bromwich has shown that *Culhwch ac Olwen*, for instance, shows evidence of 'having been shaped by an author familiar with Christian customs and practices'.[40] One would imagine that this would also apply to the four Mabinogi tales as well.

Guest and John suggest that the four branches of the Mabinogion, 'Pwyll', 'Branwen', 'Manawyddan' and 'Math' may have existed in manuscript form since about 1200 'but they were most probably relayed orally over several generations before ever assuming written form' (Guest and John, 97). When removed from an oral culture, a written translation's production and reception, as much as the work of the translator, effects a form of appropriation such that the culture subjected to the imperialism of another is brought to a standstill, locked, in this case, by the printed English into a time-frame and a category from which it is difficult to escape. In the case of Lady Guest's translations from written medieval sources, publication into English naturally does not have this effect, the written tales are already locked into their medieval time-frame. However, the categorization of the work is a different matter. To begin with, as I have already mentioned, the translation was critiqued as woman's work. The *Spectator* writes of the 'fair translator', and the *Athenaeum* believes the 'translation is a good one – clear, simple – preserving much of the quaintness so apparent in the original', while the *Monthly Review* also remarks the 'agreeably quaint translation' and elsewhere calls it a 'translation quaint and happy'. A later *Spectator* review believes the tales will have considerable attraction 'not only for the most childish vulgar, but for persons

---

[39]   Ceri Davies, *Welsh Literature and the Classical Tradition* (Cardiff, 1995), 39.

[40]   Rachel Bromwich and D. Simon Evans, *Culhwch and Olwen. An Edition and Study of the Oldest Arthurian Tale* (Cardiff, 1992), lxxviii.

perfectly competent to detect their critical faults'.[41] All of these remarks might be considered qualified to some degree, and reductive, playing into the prevailing idea that women's publishing of this kind might be considered mere popularizing and educative, designed for under-educated, female and/or child readers.

Nevertheless, women had a particular part to play in cultural colonization via translation: the female translator is like the female colonist, not only does she participate in the enterprise, she contributes to its effectiveness, even if she sees herself as at one with her new land. The *Monthly Review* remarks in 1843 that 'Lady C. Guest could not have bestowed a more acceptable gift upon her adopted countrymen than the collection of the Mabinogion'.[42] It is thus clear that the English periodical press saw her relationship with Wales in that light. Rita Kranidis has commented on emigrant women's roles in imperialism that: 'emigrant women are neither colonizer nor colonized, yet they may be said to be both. Insofar as they manifest the nation's perpetually expanding cultural borders, they are national subjects who are simultaneously not integral, legitimated parts of the empire',[43] and Frederic Will raises questions in *Literature Inside Out* (1966) 'about naming and meaning and indirectly suggests that translation can be viewed as a form of naming, fiction-making, and knowing'.[44] Translation thus expands cultural borders, and might be likened to colonial botanizing, an activity undertaken more by women than men. Once you name, and transcribe, you acquire.

But there is another facet to the process. It is a woman's sense of exile, or displacement. Edward Said defines exile as a 'discontinuous state of being' but he elaborates this by suggesting that the exile creates 'a new world to rule'.[45] Charlotte Guest's class and wealth permitted her an opportunity to dominate ('unfair domination' is Said's term in *Culture and Imperialism*) and her elaborate production of a translated *Mabinogion* represents her own attempt to locate a place for herself that was different from her husband's world yet well within the acceptable parameters of the ideology of the day: the woman's sphere. If John Guest, the iron master, dominated industrial production in Wales in the 1830s, his wife discovered a role for herself in dominating cultural production, a domination the reviews of her day, to which I have already referred, make very clear.[46]

Other spheres existed of course, apart from the ideologically gendered ones I have just described. Edward Said writes of an 'isolated cultural sphere' and a 'debased political sphere', pointing out that these are not separate at all, but

---

[41]   'Mabinogion – Early Welsh Legends', 1067; 'Mabinogion', 835; 'Mabinogion, Part II', 132; 'Mythology and Legends', 29; and 'National Literature', 761.

[42]   'Welsh Fiction', 453.

[43]   Rita Kranidis, 'Introduction: New Subjects, Familiar Grounds', *Imperial Objects. Essays on Victorian Women's Emigration and the Unauthorized Imperial Experience*, ed. Rita Kranidis (New York, 1998), 14.

[44]   Quoted in Gentzler, 29.

[45]   Edward Said, 'Reflections on Exile', *Granta* 13(1984): 163 and 167; 159–72.

[46]   Edward Said, *Culture and Imperialism* (1993; London, 1994), xxiii.

rather that 'the two are not only connected but ultimately the same'. He goes on to show that culture is mistakenly regarded as separate from power, adding that 'representations are considered only as apolitical images to be parsed and construed as so many grammars of exchange, and the divorce of the present from the past is assumed to be complete'.[47] It was, of course, Said's metaphorical language that attracted my attention to this statement because 'parsing', 'construing', 'grammars of exchange' are terms so intimately connected with the act of translation. Thus while we might view Lady Guest's translation as isolated to the cultural sphere, in practice her activity is as much a part of the political sphere as her husband's activities as a Whig member of parliament for the pocket borough of Honiton in Devonshire were.

As Janet Wolff shows in *Feminine Sentences*, women found a place in cultural production as 'artists, authors, patrons, and members of cultural institutions'.[48] Certainly Charlotte Guest's translation came about partly as a result of her sense of herself as a patron both of the Welsh and of Welsh National literature, for instance by attending the Eisteddfod in Cardiff and by appearing at the Cambrian Ball 'in my regular Welsh peasant's dress which I had worn at Abergavenny. Such a thing I believe had never been seen before in London and it caused quite a sensation' (*Journal*, 69). In a trip that same year to Scotland she records an ongoing antipathy 'to the Scotch' but adds that the highlander 'is a man of a different race and reminds me forcibly of my own Welsh' (*Journal*, 95). There is very little difference between such a statement and titles like *Our Maoris* by Lady Martin (1884) in which the possessives 'my' or 'our' are so significant, used much as parents would say 'my son' or 'our children'. This characteristic also occurs in the *Athenaeum* review of Guest's Part IV, 'Kilhwch and Olwen', which suggests that 'it would be difficult to find in the whole range of English fiction a tale of equal antiquity, and one which places the rude, warlike, and imaginative character of our Celtic aborigines so vividly before us'.[49]

Finally, and ironically for my reading of cultural appropriation, Charlotte Guest speculates that the Cymric nation may once have been invaders themselves who:

> driven out of their conquests by the later nations, the names and exploits of their heroes, and the compositions of their bards, spread far and wide among the invaders, and affected intimately their tastes and literature for many centuries. (*Mabinogion*, xxiii)

Certainly the *Monthly Review* could confidently assert in 1843 that while Charlotte Guest's collection of tales is a valuable gift to the Welsh, 'the Mabinogion is undoubtedly an acquisition to English literature'.[50] In the next chapter I consider

---

47   Said, *Culture and Imperialism*, 66–7.
48   Janet Wolff, *Feminine Sentences* (Cambridge, 1990), 13.
49   'Mabinogion, Part IV', *Athenaeum* (30 April 1842), 379.
50   'Welsh Fiction', 467.

a very different kind of 'acquisition' in the production of translated German travelogues that captured the imagination of the English readership they were designed for.

Chapter 6
Jane Sinnett
and the German Traveller

The acquisition of literatures, be they medieval or modern, as addressed in the last chapter, was not confined to Britain's colonial territories. Translation provided the British reading public with a vast range of various kinds of literature from Europe, with an inevitable focus on Germany and France, but which included Italian, Spanish and Portuguese translations of poetry, drama, novels and non-fiction of various kinds. This chapter explores the practice of the journalist and translator Jane Sinnett whose translations of various travellers offered the reading public different perspectives on a range of destinations, journeys which included British colonial possessions. In useful ways then, Sinnett's practice draws the two categories, travel and translation, quite tightly together. As not merely a traveller herself, but as someone domesticated within another culture – Germany – for eight years, Sinnett brings to her work both her language skills and an informed context. Sinnett takes her readers on a journey of some complexity because it includes the journey itself, the action which takes place outside the author's homeland, and the journey within the pages of the translated text that is inflected bi-culturally by the author's nationality and that of the translator. In Sinnett's work in particular it is noticeable how there are moments when, in James Clifford's terms, the two key cultures, those of Germany and England, come together, something he nominates 'cultural action' which takes place in 'contact zones' and along 'intercultural frontiers'.[1] Carmine G. Di Biase suggests that by translation, 'Clifford means what happens when two cultures come together'. Di Biase adds that there is an 'intriguing similarity' between Clifford's cultural translation and Venuti's linguistic translation, as has been discussed in more detail in Part I.[2] This concept has a particular relevance to Sinnett's German translations even if it is further complicated by the fact that she is translating travel narratives that take place outside Germany.

Mid-century is the high-water mark of Victorian colonialism and imperial ambitions, and the garnering of other perspectives and impressions made a necessary contribution to the home country's knowledge base. Such an outcome may well have been of real appeal to Sinnett whose article 'Colonization and Emigration', was published in the *Dublin Review* in 1849. Although four titles are listed as under review at the head of the article, they are virtually ignored in favour

---

[1]   Clifford, 7.

[2]   Di Biase, 24–5.

of a more specific opinion piece. Sinnett is very critical of British government practice in which colonization is viewed merely as a 'remedy, a mode of cure for certain chronic diseases of the body politic', and, to the proposition that any new community should be a facsimile of the old she asks: 'Is the parent country so perfect, that she can wish for nothing better than that the child shall be the exact copy of herself?'. In comparing the colonizing practices of ancient times (another perspective) she remarks that the Ancient Greeks 'had ... the natural and legitimate object of providing for the wants of an over-numerous population. Those of the moderns originated generally in the lust of gold or of enlarged empire, or, at best ... planted merely for the extension of trade and the accumulation of wealth'.[3] It is also worthwhile keeping in mind that Sinnett's profession was that of journalist and her choice of texts to translate was, I would argue, in part dictated by her profession, in part dictated by practicality, in that having reviewed most of her authors in their original language, her work of translation was already partly done.

Of all the British women authors and journalists discussed in this book, Jane Sinnett is the only one who does not make it into the *Oxford Dictionary of National Biography*. Widowed in 1844 when her children were still quite young, Sinnett continued to practice journalism and translation, with a focus on German, to earn a living as she had been doing since 1840. Biographical details are scarce although some information can be gleaned from an entry in the *Australian Dictionary of Biography* on her son, Frederick, who was born in Hamburg, Germany in 1830 and emigrated to South Australia at the age of 19, in an attempt to combat the tuberculosis which caused his early death in 1866. In 1851 Frederick had moved to Melbourne to work as an editor and later, a leader writer. Marjorie J. Tipping comments that 'with his knowledge of German language and literature he had many friends among the German artists, scientists and scholars living in Melbourne'.[4] His Obituary in the Adelaide *Register* notes that he 'was [the] son of Mrs. Percy Sinnett, a lady well known in the literary world'. Such a notice would more usually have included the profession of the late father rather than that of the mother, suggesting that Jane Sinnett had made an impact in the Victorian world of letters in her day.[5]

Cecil Hadgraft, in his 'Introduction' to Frederick Sinnett's 1856 essay, 'The Fiction Fields of Australia' notes that Edward William Percy Sinnett and Jane Fry, having married in 1825, moved to Hamburg in 1828 where Percy, as he was known, with C.F. Wurm, edited the *Hamburg Reporter* and the *Gleaner*, the latter consisting mostly of reprints from British and American journals. Both papers appeared three times a week. From 1831 to 1834 Percy Sinnett was sole editor of both. He also taught English at the Johanneum in Hamburg from 1833–1836. The

[3]   Jane Sinnett, 'Colonization and Emigration', *Dublin Review* 26(1849): 316, 317 and 319; 316–37.

[4]   Marjorie J. Tipping, 'Frederick Sinnett (1830–1866)', *Australian Dictionary of Biography*, ed. Geoffrey Searle and Russel Ward (Melbourne, 1976), VI: 131.

[5]   'Death of Mr. F. Sinnett', Adelaide *Register* (29 November 1866): 6.

family returned to England in 1836. These facts confirm a dominance of German language and culture in the family home, and the extensive period living in Germany.[6] The Sinnetts, like the Howitts, not only travelled to, but were domiciled for extensive periods in, Germany. There is also internal evidence in one of Jane Sinnett's essays published in the *Westminster Review* that she also travelled to Germany in 1847.[7] Unlike Anna Jameson, it seems safe to assume that Jane Sinnett's knowledge of German literature and language was superior and certainly sufficient to permit her to earn a living from her language and translation skills for 20 years. Like Jameson, she had noted, in 1841, the development of interest in German literature and culture, remarking that the 'principal literary names of Germany have, from some years past, been nearly as familiar to the educated classes in England, as those of native writers, and her language and literature have been made the objects, if not always of very assiduous study, at all events of zealous eulogy'.[8] Her position differs markedly from that of William Howitt whose residence in Germany is recorded in *German Experiences: addressed to The English; both Stayers at Home, and Goers Abroad* (1844), a follow up to an earlier published account. He declares that Germany 'has knowledge, practices, arts, or institutions, that we may copy, or introduce with good effect' and indeed goes on to list these, recommending in particular education which in Germany is free, 'within the reach of all'. However, he also warns against gathering up 'just what in these foreign practices is prejudicial to the public liberty and welfare', a possible reference to censorship. Jane Sinnett also notes the negative impact of censorship on German literary expression.[9] Notably, these various cultural encounters by journalists like Sinnett and Howitt are, despite Howitt's expressed anxiety, received as ultimately of benefit to the British national interest.

As a journalist writing irregularly for the *Athenaeum* Jane Sinnett reviewed mostly German publications, and predominantly travel narratives, between 1840 and 1860; from February 1848 to January 1849 she wrote a number of articles and produced several translations for *Bentley's Miscellany*; for the *Dublin Review* she produced a lengthy essay on Schiller in 1841, one of only two attributed contributions by her to that journal; for the *Foreign Quarterly Review* she produced seven review essays between 1842 and 1846, but the bulk of her journalistic work appears to have been done for the *Westminster Review*, from 1847 to 1855, and again, it is reviewing of travel writing which predominates. Of course she may have contributed to any number of other journals which existed in this time frame

---

[6]   Cecil Hadgraft, 'Introduction', *The Fiction Fields of Australia* by Frederick Sinnett (St. Lucia, 1966), 1. Hadgraft notes that Edward William Percy Sinnett married Jane Fry on 3 September 1825 and they had five children: Julia, Sophia, Frederick, Ellen Jane and Alfred Percy. The three middle children were all born in Hamburg.

[7]   Jane Sinnett, 'The Present Time', *Westminster Review* 50(1849): 583; 577–83.

[8]   Sinnett, 'Schiller', 477.

[9]   William Howitt, *German Experiences: addressed to The English; both Stayers at Home, and Goers Abroad* (London, 1844), 93–4 and Jane Sinnett, 'The Present Time', 581.

but whose contributors, because of the anonymity preferred in this period, are now mostly unknown.

When the new proprietor and editor of the *Westminster Review*, John Chapman, decided to divide the journal's book reviewing by country, focusing on English, American, German and French publications, he invited Jane Sinnett to write the 'Contemporary Literature of Germany' column, which she did from January 1852 until October 1853. Sinnett had been a regular contributor to the *Westminster* since 1847 and might therefore be considered a tried and experienced journalist capable of producing the requisite analyses. In confirmation of a growing readership and market for German literature, Sinnett remarks in the April 1852 column on the sheer quantity of books on Goethe 'throwing new light on his life or his writings, or of condensing his thoughts so as to render them accessible to the most general public'.[10] Chapman subsequently decided on specific categories for the reviewing: 'Theology and Philosophy'; 'Politics, Sociology, Voyages and Travels'; 'Science; History and Biography'; and 'Belles Lettres'. This last Sinnett also conducted, from January 1854 until April 1855.

Chapman's unpaid sub-editor, Marian Evans, later to become famous as the novelist George Eliot, complained to her friend Sara Hennell back in September 1852 'that tiresome Mrs. Sinnett pretends to correct her proof and leaves it as you see'.[11] Jane Sinnett has subsequently remained labelled with the epithet 'tiresome', frequently misinterpreted to impute the quality of her work. For instance, the *Wellesley Index* editor, in commenting on evidence for attributions to Sinnett for the *Westminster Review*, writes that Sinnett's 'wordy, banal style is exactly what made George Eliot call her "tiresome"', although subsequently it seems Sinnett's 'considerable knowledge of German literature' is the relevant evidence that Sinnett had written the column for April 1855.[12] However, Eliot does not appear to be dismissing Sinnett's ability as a German scholar, nor as a writer per se. In fact, Sinnett was 'tiresome' for not correcting her proofs properly. Again, the *Wellesley* editor, commenting on the success of the new reviews format in the *Westminster* under Chapman, also notes the 'surprising thing about these brief reviews was the reviewers. One would have expected run-of-the-mill journalists – and so they often were (even in the fifties the "tiresome" Mrs. Sinnett was a frequent contributor) – but often they were scholars of distinction'.[13] Rosemary Ashton states that in July 1855 on Eliot taking over the 'Belles Lettres' column, 'the literature round-up has a very different look from the usual mediocrity of the long-serving Jane Sinnett's contributions'.[14]

[10]   Jane Sinnett, 'Contemporary Literature of Germany', *Westminster Review* 57(1852): 686; 677–97.

[11]   George Eliot, *The George Eliot Letters*, ed. Gordon S. Haight, 9 vols (New Haven, 1954–78), II: 57.

[12]   Houghton, 'The Westminster Review', III: 623.

[13]   Houghton, 'Westminster Review', III: 551.

[14]   Ashton, 231.

However, Eliot's close friend Sara Hennell thought that Eliot herself had written the April 1854 'Belles Lettres' column when actually, as Eliot subsequently points out to Sara, 'Mrs. Sinnett did them as usual'.[15] Sara Hennell was very familiar with Eliot's writing style. They corresponded in this period very regularly and read each other's work. Moreover, the *Westminster* doubtless had its own particular house style, including a certain forthright tone, erudite reference, and a caustic humour, which their reviewers used. Sinnett begins her April 1854 column as follows, and incidentally it is interesting to note her use of metaphoric language that denotes these publications as so much merchandise with terms like 'wares', 'sustenance'; and a play on the old saying that 'bread is the staff of life':

> Someone has said of women, "*Je les hais en gros et je les adore en détail*," [I detest them en masse but I adore them individually] but we should be inclined to affirm the converse of the proposition concerning the works of fiction that make up so large a portion of the literature of modern Europe. If the importance of literary productions is to be estimated by the amount of their influence upon the world – and it is not easy to see how a better test could be applied – the scale would preponderate greatly in favour of the wares which, however slightingly spoken of, form, for better or for worse, the main article of mental sustenance, the staff of intellectual life, to the majority of readers, and against others assumed to be of higher dignity.[16]

Compare Sinnett's opening with the way in which Eliot begins her October 1855 column:

> We are inclined to think that when all the beasts of the field and fowls of the air were brought to Adam, "to see what he would call them", this large demand on his "organ of language" must have been rather embarrassing to him, and he would have found it much more convenient if the naming had been deferred until he could have the help of Eve, who doubtless was as ready as most of her daughters at telling her husband what to say. Something like this embarrassing position of Adam's is the case of that unfortunate son of Adam, a reviewer who sits surrounded with books on which he is required there and then to render an opinion – for is not all opinion, nay, all science, simply a *naming*? Of the genus *belles lettres*, novels are usually the most numerous species.[17]

For the most part both reviewers employ literary references or metaphors one remove from the eventual subjects of review; and both signal the lot of the

---

15   Eliot, *Letters*, II: 159.

16   Jane Sinnett, 'Belles Lettres', *Westminster Review* 61(April 1854): 619; 619–33.

17   George Eliot, 'Ashford Owen's *A Lost Love* and C.W.S. Brooks's *Aspen Court* (*Westminster Review* October 1855)', repr. *Selected Essays, Poems and Other Writings*, ed. A.S. Byatt (London, 1990), 329 (Eliot's emphasis).

reviewer and the vast number of publications sent for review in a wry, even comic, manner. Sinnett, for instance, begins the 'Belles Lettres' column of January 1854: 'In light literature our calendar, as the judges say, is unusually heavy; not that the offences are of a more serious nature, but that the offenders are more numerous'.[18] And in reviewing Coventry Patmore's tedious long poem *The Angel in the House* compares his love, that 'small, tranquil, pale flame' to 'hydrogen gas, which does burn, but does not give out much light or heat, because it has no solid stuff to take hold of'.[19]

I am not claiming that Jane Sinnett could ever have attained the literary distinction of a George Eliot, only that she was an intelligent, educated journalist, apparently well versed in modern languages, in particular German, and that it is too easy to dismiss her with terms like 'banal' or 'mediocre'. After all, why would the *Westminster Review* have continued with her if her journalism had been thought below average? There were more than enough budding authors ready to take her place, as George Eliot eventually did. Notably the change-over took place on the marriage of Jane Sinnett's daughter into a wealthy family. Eliot's own comment on this marriage seems, indirectly, to suggest that it enabled financial support for Jane Sinnett sufficient for her to retire, after a career of some 20 years, from the demands of journalism. In a letter to Sara Hennell of 3 June 1854 Eliot remarks of Sinnett that 'one of her daughters is engaged to young Ellis, only son of Mr. Ellis of Champion Hill. One likes to think of the rich and the poor coming together'. Haight notes that Edward Ellis and Ellen Jane Sinnett married on 6 June 1855.[20] Jane Sinnett did, however, produce at least two more translations, specifically from German travel writing, one in 1858 and another in 1861. The financial necessity to publish on a very regular basis does, however, appear to have lessened considerably.

In 1845 Elizabeth Rigby analyzed, for the *Quarterly Review*, that modern phenomenon, the lady traveller. The very fact that such a topic was considered good copy for the male-dominated, mandarin *Quarterly* indicates the degree to which women's travel writing had, in such a short period of time, become a highly significant component of a very popular genre. In a wry and often humorous assessment in which her own sex is carefully hidden from view, Rigby determines that travelling is a mode of life 'for which English nature and education alone seem adapted'. 'Foreign' women lack the English woman's 'four cardinal virtues of travelling – activity, punctuality, courage and independence'. Even if foreign women do travel, they do not publish their adventures. German ladies, she believes, do not 'excel in rapid observation, or lively delineation', a statement which the reception of Ida Pfeiffer's travels later dismantles. Travelling, Rigby decides, is an art form at which the English alone excel, maintaining nevertheless their talent for superior domestic practices wherever they happen to be, this last a careful shoring

18   Jane Sinnett, 'Belles Lettres', *Westminster Review* 61(1854): 301; 301–15.
19   Jane Sinnett, 'Belles Lettres', *Westminster Review* 63(1855): 283; 275–91.
20   Eliot, *Letters*, II: 159.

up of conservative domestic ideology. Rigby examples certain named English women travellers but not their publication titles. Named are Frances Trollope, Louisa Costello and Julia Pardoe. Rigby probably had in mind Trollope's *Belgium and Western Germany in 1833*; Costello's *A Summer amongst the Bocages and the Vines* (1840) and Pardoe's *The City of the Magyar, or Hungary and her Institutions in 1839–40* (1840).[21]

Despite such reservations regarding the foreign woman traveller, the journeys of various European women, as well as men were, as I have shown, translated for English popular consumption. Notably the bulk of Jane Sinnett's translations are predominantly German travelogues by mostly male travellers whose names are no longer, and may never have been, household words: Theodor Mügge's *Switzerland in 1847* (1848); August von Rochau's *Wanderings through the Cities of Italy in 1850 and 1851* (1853); *The Chinese Empire: forming a sequel to the work entitled "Recollections of a Journey through Tartary and Thibet"* by Eváriste Régis Huc (1855); Balduin Moellhausen's *Diary of a Journey from the Mississippi to the Coasts of the Pacific* (1858); and Johann Georg Kohl's *Travels in Canada, and through the States of New York and Pennsylvania* (1861). All of these titles were reviewed in the *Athenaeum*, but also more occasionally in other mainstream periodicals such as the *Spectator*, the *Dublin Review*, the *Saturday Review*, and, of course, the *Westminster Review*. Sinnett herself had previously reviewed a number of these authors' works, when they first appeared in print in their original languages, translating passages for her reviews where needed. These reviews were published in the *Athenaeum* and the *Westminster*, and she also produced a two-part translation from Mügge's *Switzerland* titled 'An Old Man's Recollections of the Pastoral Cantons of Switzerland' for *Bentley's Miscellany*.[22] Her ongoing familiarity with the style and politics of the various authors must have contributed significantly to her translating practice and confidence in her product. However, only the translation of Huc's *The Chinese Empire* went to a second edition in 1859, and was also reprinted by Kennikat Press, London, in 1970. The British Library catalogue notes on all the editions that Mrs. J. Sinnett is the translator. Moreover, her published translations of these authors' works received mixed reviews which often evinced, especially around mid-century, a certain weariness with the travel

21 Rigby, 101–103.

22 See by Jane Sinnett: 'Switzerland and its Condition' [Mügge], *Westminster Review* 48(1848): 531–52; 'Rambles in Schleswig-Holstein' [Mügge], *Westminster Review* 49(1848): 504–12 and 'An Old Man's Recollections of the Pastoral Cantons of Switzerland', edited by Mrs. Percy Sinnett, *Bentley's Miscellany* 23(1848): 25–30 and 366–74; 'Alpine Journeyings' Parts I and II [Kohl], *Westminster Review* 51(1849): 497–512 and 52(1850): 545–61; and 'Travels in the Netherlands' Parts I and II [Kohl], *Westminster Review* 53(1850): 243–48 and 507–16; 'Contemporary Literature of Germany' [von Rochau], *Westminster Review* 59(1853): 627–8; 617–34; 'Travels in the North-West of the United States' [Kohl], *Athenaeum* 1557(29 August 1857): 1081–2; and 'Travels in Canada' [Kohl], *Athenaeum* 1711(11 August 1860): 185–7.

genre generally. The anonymous reviewer of Sinnett's translation of Kohl's *Travels in Canada* begins the *Saturday Review* notice in just such a tone:

> As a general rule, travels on well-beaten tracks are a very dreary department of literature, of which the world is becoming thoroughly weary. There is a certain race of tourists whom our rapid locomotion ought to have improved off the face of the earth. It approaches to an impertinence to publish a pretentious book about scenes which have been described a hundred times before, and which a few days' luxurious travelling will enable anybody else to describe again.[23]

Despite this expressed weariness, even if her translations rarely ran to further editions, Sinnett did offer the British reading public travel literature which promised a different point of view, and often an openly politicised one. As the same weary *Saturday Review* journalist admitted, Kohl's book on Canada was redeemed by its author's 'peculiar qualifications', that is, his impartial observations which 'a foreigner can alone make'.[24] Impartiality is a quality to which Sinnett often returns both in her many reviews and her translator's prefaces to the travellers' works she translated. Kohl, for instance, in 'Alpine Journeys, II' 'carries with him no preconceived notions concerning any country he visits' and von Rochau in politics 'manifests the same impartial frankness'.[25] At this significant moment in British imperialism and politics, when acquisitions were being consolidated and new territories sought, the views of a nation not yet in serious colonial contention with Britain would prove useful, and accounts of societies both inside and outside Europe equally of interest.

Sinnett seldom produces translator's prefaces of any length, and does not always provide the kind of analysis of translating practice so prevalent in the prefaces of Sarah Austin for instance. She does address translation occasionally in her reviews and clearly understands instances where fidelity might be essential but also where a freer translation can work effectively. She remarks, for instance, on James Froude's translation of Goethe's *Elective Affinities* that while parts will be 'unpleasant, if not revolting, to English readers' Froude 'has wisely refrained from attempting to soften' Goethe's words. Goethe, she explains, writes to such plan and purpose that altering his prose would damage the content. Froude, however, has managed an essential 'perfect fidelity' united with a 'requisite grace and freedom'.[26] In addressing the needs of a very different readership, she praises John Edward Taylor's *Mouse and her Friends* which 'taken from Eastern sources' are 'freely translated into an easy form, so as to come easily within the comprehension of children. A work of this kind, freed from the prolixity and sentensiousness of

---

[23]   'Canada', *Saturday Review* 11(26 January 1861): 100; 100–101.

[24]   'Canada', 100.

[25]   Sinnett, 'Alpine Journeyings II', 545 and Sinnett, 'Contemporary Literature of Germany', 627.

[26]   Sinnett, 'Belles Lettres', 625.

Oriental phraseology, has long been wanting'.[27] In describing herself as 'Editor' of Mügge's *Switzerland in 1847*, she explains that the work is 'greatly abridged', in part because recent events had 'rendered obsolete many speculations'. The recent event in question was the Civil War of November 1847 in which the Sonderbund (Special Alliance) of Catholic Cantons was peacefully defeated, a popular victory, and a Federal Constitution instituted in 1848.[28] Like Sarah Austin, Sinnett maintains her own political position in spite of Mügge's opinions, denying responsibility for them: 'for instance the approbation he bestows on the celebrated expedition of the Free Corps to Lucerne',[29] an issue which is expanded on in her review of the German original for the *Westminster*.[30] The real value of Mügge's text rests in 'the picture it presents of a political and social condition' from an author who appears to be 'a most candid and honest observer and narrator of facts'.[31] The *Athenaeum* reviewer names Sinnett as the translator 'who has performed her office of introduction well' but complains that Mügge is a 'master in the facile art of book-making' and that his haste to publish has been detrimental to the work's impact because 'the striking consummation of the drama is omitted'.[32]

Similarly, as far as Sinnett is concerned, the Roman Catholic French missionary Evariste Huc, author of *The Chinese Empire* (1855), is believable because he resists the temptation to exaggerate the efficacy of his missionary labours and has been a keen observer of China's 'domestic life, and watched the working of the hidden mechanism of society in that mysterious empire'. Moreover, she comments politically on China's emergence into the world, remarking that 'the secluded population of China have come forth to mingle (in California and Australia) in some of the busiest haunts of men, and take part in the newest movements of the time'. To this sentence a footnote is added: 'Recent accounts from Melbourne mention the arrival of Chinese immigrants in such numbers as to cause some serious apprehension on the part of the English residents'.[33] Thus the importance of such a translation, as far as Britain's colonial interests are concerned, is highlighted here by the translator. C.W. Russell, for the Roman Catholic *Dublin Review*, who celebrates Sinnett's Huc translation as 'not, like the author's earlier work, a mere traveller's tale' but 'a learned, laborious and scholar-like description' of 'China and its institutions'.[34] As a direct counter to this praise, the *Spectator's*

---

27   Jane Sinnett, 'Belles Lettres', *Westminster Review* 63(1855): 597; 588–604.

28   Jane Sinnett, 'Editor's Preface', Theodore Mügge, *Switzerland in 1847: and its Condition, Political, Social, Moral, and Physical, Before the War*, 2 vols (London, 1848), I: iii. See also Ann G. Imlah, *Britain and Switzerland 1845–60* (London: Longmans, 1966), 40–41.

29   Sinnett, 'Editor's Preface', *Switzerland in 1847*, I: v.

30   Sinnett: 'Switzerland and its Condition', 533.

31   Sinnett, 'Editor's Preface', *Switzerland in 1847*, I: iii and v.

32   'Switzerland in 1847', *Athenaeum* No. 1060(19 February 1848): 181; 181–3.

33   Sinnett, 'Translator's Preface', *The Chinese Empire*, vi, v and viii.

34   C.W. Russell, 'Huc's Chinese Empire', *Dublin Review* 38(1855): 136; 134–69.

reviewer reveals a prejudice both against the French (Huc's nationality) and Roman Catholicism. Thus for this periodical, Huc's observations are as restricted as 'the European embassies of whose opportunities he speaks rather slightingly' and doubt is expressed 'as to the perfect fidelity of his pictures'.[35]

Sinnett's 'Preface by the Translator' to her translation of Kohl's *Travels in Canada* (1861) is centred primarily on Canada's place in the British Empire, addressed in the standard familial vernacular of the day, but is more acute in positing Canada as a political 'counterpoise to the immense and increasing power' of the United States through the claim that Canada offers its inhabitants equal, if not superior, freedoms to those enjoyed by its nearest neighbour. As with her other authors, Kohl is, states Sinnett, 'experienced, impartial, and eminently truthful': necessarily 'impartial', of course, because not British.[36] The *Saturday Review* rather unusually quotes from Sinnett's 'Preface' regarding Kohl's role as an 'impartial observer' to explain that the 'reason given by the translator for having undertaken his task indicates the title of the book to rank higher than as a mere circulating-library production'.[37] Misogynistic to the end, despite the incontrovertible evidence of the 'Preface' signature, 'Jane Sinnett', the *Saturday Review* insists on gendering the translator as male.

Sinnett's own review for the *Athenaeum* of Kohl's German original, *Reisen in Canada*, provides more detail than her 'Preface by the Translator'. Kohl was, it seems, interested in the French Canadians, a matter of political interest too in Britain in the period following the riots of the late 1830s, and an issue which Sinnett highlights at the start of her review by suggesting that French colonists are now on an equal footing with the British and have 'the same political rights'. This assessment is prompted by Kohl's discovery that after all the French Canadians are not 'horribly superstitious, stupid, and idle people, mere hindrances to the march of progress'. Sinnett remarks 'we may see in this ... cause for revising those rather hasty generalizations concerning the necessary connexion between Catholicism and dirt'. He is, she says, a 'model traveller', possessing the 'observant and reflective faculties in due proportions'.[38]

Jane Sinnett's only published foray into history, *Byways of History, from the Twelfth to the Sixteenth Century* (1847), indicates an intellectual journey, which she describes in the 'Preface' in these terms:

> It was in the first instance my intention merely to introduce to English readers the subject of the Peasant War of Germany, one of those interesting and important episodes which we sometimes meet with in rambling through what may be

[35]   'Huc's Chinese Empire', *Spectator* 28(1855): 54 and 55; 54–6.

[36]   Jane Sinnett, 'Preface by the Translator', *Travels in Canada, and Through the States of New York and Pennsylvania* by J.G. Kohl (trans. Mrs. Percy Sinnett, revised by the author. London, 1861), vii and viii.

[37]   'Canada', *Saturday Review*, 100.

[38]   Sinnett, 'Travels in Canada', 185–6.

called the "Byways of History," and which usually make us better acquainted with the true character of an epoch than a journey of greater extent along its beaten Highways.[39]

As she had observed in her review of Johanna Schopenhauer's *Jugendleen und Wanderbilder* [*Youthful Life and Rambling Sketches*] the traveller who keeps to the high road 'sees little thereof in comparison with the wanderer through its lanes and footpaths'. Moreover, Sinnett did not view an author's obscurity as a problem affecting reception of their observations, commenting that 'an obscure person will often afford a clearer insight into the state of a country at a given period than the most elaborate narrative of its public occurrences and legislative enactments'.[40]

Ida Pfeiffer, the 'lady' of Sinnett's only translation of a woman traveller's narrative, *A Lady's Voyage round the World: a Selected Translation* (1851), was just such a comparatively obscure figure who, however, firmly established a place for herself in the British reading imagination, confirming Sinnett's prescience that Pfeiffer was precisely the kind of writer who would be appreciated in England. Sinnett's decision to abridge Pfeiffer's narrative is explained in the 'Translator's Preface' as based on those portions of the narrative which are, to the English reader, 'familiar ground'; 'statistical notices' already published elsewhere; ship-board life and ship provisioning 'not without interest, perhaps, in Germany, where, as there are comparatively very few who "go down to the sea in ships" ... such things have more novelty, but too familiar to the English reader'. What she establishes here is a readership familiar with travel writing but not familiar with an author who presents as 'singular', to use Sinnett's term, and who displays a 'calm and unconscious heroism'.[41]

The German edition of *A Lady's Voyage round the World* [*Eine Frauenfahrt um die Welt*] was published in Vienna and London in 1850 and was reviewed in the *Athenaeum* in June 1851, and in the *Westminster*, possibly by Bayle St. John, in October 1851. I have been unable to locate any review of Sinnett's translation (the various translated passages in these two reviews do not match her translation of the same events) and I can only assume that having reviewed the original, it was not felt necessary to review an abridged translation following on so soon after. However, it is possible that Sinnett's 'selected' translation did prompt the publication of a separate, unabridged translation titled *A Woman's Journey round the World: from Vienna to Brazil, Chili, Tahiti, China, Hindostan, Persia and Asia Minor, an unabridged translation from the German* in London in 1852, by the Office of the National Illustrated Library, with no translator named. This too does not appear to have been reviewed. The appearance of this edition may have caused

---

[39]   Jane Sinnett, *Byways of History from the Twelfth to the Sixteenth Century*, 2 vols (London, 1847), iii.

[40]   Jane Sinnett, 'Youthful Life and Rambling Sketches', *Athenaeum* 1016 (17 April 1847): 409; 409–11.

[41]   Sinnett, 'Translator's Preface', *A Lady's Voyage round The World*, iii.

Sinnett's publishers, Longman, Brown, Green, and Longmans, to then issue a new edition of her selected translation the same year, 1852. This complicated publication and review history demonstrates how difficult it could be to succeed despite undertaking what appears to be a highly marketable enterprise, when competing products undercut success. In 1988 the publishers, Century, based their edition of Pfeiffer's journey on Sinnett's translation, confirming both the degree to which Pfeiffer retained a significant standing as a nineteenth-century woman traveller of note, but also that Sinnett's condensed version retained the essence of the travels, and was a sound commercial model. Other Victorian women's travels published by Century include *Life in Mexico* (1843) by Madame Calderón de la Barca; *A Pilgrimage to Nejd* (1881) by Lady Anne Blunt; and Kate Marsden's *On Sledge and Horseback to Outcast Siberian Lepers* (1892).

When it came to *A Lady's Second Journey round the World* (1855), Sinnett appears to have had the translating field to herself. A review in the *Literary Gazette*, 22 December 1855, is definitely a review of Sinnett's translation as quotations match precisely with her text. The reviewer is 'delighted again to meet with the adventurous Madame Ida Pfeiffer, whose former Journey round the World established for her a high name among modern travellers', and celebrates her as 'observant, intelligent, and trustworthy'. On the whole though the reviewer felt there was not 'much novelty' in parts of the narrative, but does note that the 'evils of slavery' in the United States 'are not passed lightly over, and the treatment of the free blacks, by the whites is spoken of in terms such as might have been expected in an Englishwoman'. The publication of Pfeiffer's first voyage round the world nevertheless remains the significant one.[42]

This raises the question as to what elements in Pfeiffer's account were sufficiently different from the general run of travellers' tales to capture the interest of publishers and readers and to sustain that interest across the decades? There had been other voyages around the world. The German Dr. F.J.F. Meyen's *Reise um die Erde* [*Voyage around the World*] attracted notices in both the *Quarterly Review* and the *Foreign Quarterly Review*.[43] As the *Quarterly's* reviewer Abraham Hayward claims:

> But a voyage round the world by a German differs materially from a voyage round the world by an Englishman: they see with different eyes, and refer to different standards of comparison, so that the same objects which have begun to

42   'A Lady's Second Journey round the World', *Literary Gazette* No. 2031(1855): 810, 811 and 812; 810–12.
43   See Abraham Hayward, 'Dr. Meyen's Voyage round the World', *Quarterly Review* 53(1835): 313–38 and [W.D. Cooley?], 'Meyen's Voyage Round the World', *Foreign Quarterly Review* 15(1835): 1–48.

grow wearisome in the descriptions of our own countrymen, may strike again with all the interest of novelty when placed in the point of view taken by a foreigner.[44]

Hayward naturally makes it clear that Englishmen have already achieved circumnavigation and draws the reader's attention to his earlier review of George Bennett's *Wanderings in New South Wales, Batavia, Pedir Coast, Singapore, and China* (1834), although at the same time maintaining his argument about seeing differently by favourably comparing Meyen's descriptions over those of Bennett. The reviewer for the *Foreign Quarterly* asks, less enthusiastically, 'what novelty can we expect from Brazil, Chili, Peru, or China?'[45]

Ida Pfeiffer, in *A Lady's Voyage Round the World*, could offer novelty on two counts, her sex, and her decisions about where to go and what to see, which were always dictated by her open admission of a lack of funds, 'my limited means'.[46] For instance, she seizes an opportunity to go to Canton in a Chinese junk because the fare is only three dollars, whereas the safer steamer is 12: 'The appearance and manner of the Chinese too was not such as to occasion me any fear, so I put my pistols in order and went quietly on board' (42). Landing at Canton she only learns afterwards that she had taken a great risk in seeking her accommodation on foot:

> I had certainly remarked that on my way from the ship to the factory, that old and young had called and hooted after me … But there was nothing to be done but to put a good face on the matter, and I therefore marched fearlessly on; and it may be that precisely because I showed no fear, no harm happened to me. Since the last war with the English the hatred against Europeans has been on the increase, and it has been embittered against the women by a Chinese prophecy, which declares that a woman shall one day conquer the Celestial Empire. (44–5)

This is a reference to the 1839–41 'Opium War'. Settlement included the ceding of Hong Kong to Britain.[47] Compare Pfeiffer's cheerfully insouciant account to Isabella Bird's arrival in Canton in 1878, under the protection of Mr. Mackrill Smith and taken 'in a bamboo chair, carried by two coolies' to a house owned by Jardine, Matheson & Co.[48] Such careful custodial practice must inevitably have limited Bird's ability to freely comment on British politics. Ida Pfeiffer, on the other hand, is readily able to comment on pointed historical political issues connected to Britain in a way that an English traveller might not, although Pfeiffer herself often depended upon the goodwill of various trade and government agents

---

44   Hayward, 'Dr. Meyen's Voyage round the World', 313.

45   [Cooley?], 1.

46   Pfeiffer, *A Lady's Voyage Round the World*, 42.

47   See Norman McCord, *British History 1815–1906* (Oxford, 1991), 204–205.

48   Isabella Bird, *The Golden Chersonese* (1883; Köln, 2000), 59.

for free accommodation and transport. Pfeiffer is also openly scathing about the conditions on board the English steamer which takes her to Singapore:

> This description of our style of living will perhaps be thought exaggerated, as every thing connected with the English is supposed to be in the highest degree comfortable and orderly; I can only say, that I have spoken the strict truth, and I may add that ... I never, before or since, paid so high a price for such miserable accommodation, never in my life have I been subject to a more infamous extortion. (69)

A Lady's Second Journey revisits the political issue of China and opium, Pfeiffer asking:

> What shall we say to the war declared by the English against the Emperor of China, who was doing his best to guard his subjects from this poison, by prohibiting the importation of opium? How can we ask uncivilized nations to respect our religion, when we let them see that it does not restrain us from the most unprincipled and shameful grasping, and that a sufficient amount of profit will reconcile us to any proceeding however flagitious?[49]

In part this quite aggressive questioning sounds like Sinnett and certainly reflects her own political position as located in 'Colonization and Emigration' that Britain as a modern colonizing empire does not seek to 'raise up a community that should be prosperous in itself' but rather only colonies 'that should be profitable to the parent state'.[50]

If journeys round the world were standard fare by the mid 1830s, it must be assumed that Pfeiffer's sex alone was sufficient to give some novelty to her *Voyage* and to encourage both translators and publishers to invest in its publication. Her journey to Iceland (*Reise nach dem skandinavischen Norden und der Isel Island im Jahre 1845*) had been published in 1846 as had her visit to the Holy Land (*Reise einer Wienerin in das heilige Land*), so that she was not completely unknown to an English readership skilled in the German language. English translations of these two earlier works did not, however, appear until 1852 (and *Visit to Iceland* again in 1853) that is, *after* her voyage round the world had been published, suggesting that it is this work and Sinnett's ground-breaking translation of it that suddenly made Pfeiffer worth investing time and money in.[51]

---

[49]   Ida Pfeiffer, *A Lady's Second Journey round The World* (2 vols; London, 1855), I: 154.

[50]   Sinnett, 'Colonization and Emigration', 319.

[51]   *Journey to Iceland* was first translated by Charlotte Fenimore Cooper and published by Bentley, and *Visit to the Holy Land* was translated by H.W. Dulcken, and published by Ingram Cooke.

The *Athenaeum* and *Westminster* reviews of *Eine Frauenfahrt um die Welt* [*A Woman's Journey round the World*] may have contributed at the outset to public interest in Pfeiffer. Both make much of Pfeiffer's sex and her status as an 'unprotected female', an epithet I have addressed in Part I: Travel, Translation and Culture. The *Athenaeum* at first warily categorizes her expedition as a 'strange' enterprise, and claims that her sex doubles the danger. This statement is then unsettled by the claim that her travels should not be regarded as a mere curiosity based on her sex, but valued for her different way of viewing even well-travelled scenes.[52] This again accords with the general argument that the European traveller will see things differently, may indeed re-orient British perspectives and practices. In Bengal, for instance, Pfeiffer remarks:

> We Germans have no conception of what the housekeeping of Europeans in India is. Every family inhabits a palace, and keeps from twenty-five to thirty servants ... In my opinion, all this inordinate expenditure is, in a great measure, the fault of the Europeans themselves. They see the rajahs and great people of the country with these swarms of idle attendants, and they will not be outdone by them; by degrees the custom becomes established, and now, I believe, it would be difficult to break through it. (94–55)

Critics appear to have been willing to accept such reprimands, the reviewer for the *Athenaeum*, for instance, declares Pfeiffer to be a 'perfectly sincere journalist of her actual impressions'. On the down side, however, Pfeiffer is 'not learned', 'seldom accurate', lacks 'historical knowledge', is 'superficial' and depends too much on hearsay. Her exploits are, however, summed up as 'the boldest adventure of its kind that woman ever accomplished' and from then on it seems that what most impresses this reviewer is Ida Pfeiffer's strength of character. The rest of the review is scattered with terms like 'resolution', 'tenacity', 'energy', 'endurance', 'courage', 'fortitude' and 'self-reliance': all the characteristics which, for Elizabeth Rigby, summed up the intrepid English woman traveller.[53] Similarly, the *Westminster* praises her 'prudence, patience and courage' ('the chief point of interest in her book') and remarks that Pfeiffer 'has been accused of pursuing her singular course merely for the sake of notoriety', an accusation the reviewer (possibly Bayle St. John) disputes. Like the *Athenaeum*, this notice too remarks that her 'intellectual endowments' are mediocre but that her adventures, related in a tone of 'plain and housewifely sobriety', are striking. The emphasis on a domestic perspective is interesting, because it demonstrates that Pfeiffer is being read as a woman who, while undertaking unusual exploits, has nevertheless not overstepped the gendered boundaries so dear at this time to English sensibilities. Clearly, the thrust of both reviews is that Pfeiffer's journey is remarkable because

---

[52]   'A Lady's Voyage round the World – [Eine Frauenfahrt um die Welt]', *Athenaeum* No. 1232(7 June 1851), 602; 602–604.

[53]   'A Lady's Voyage round the World', *Athenaeum*, 602.

performed by a very ordinary, plain, mature woman from a country where women rarely stray 'beyond the domestic circle' as the *Westminster* puts it.[54]

There is no mention whatsoever in the reviews of the supposed scientific researches so praised later in the century by W.H. Davenport Adams. Pfeiffer's British reputation became such that she was included in Adams's *Celebrated Women Travellers of the Nineteenth Century* (1883) by which time Elizabeth Rigby's contempt for the 'foreign' woman traveller had seemingly disappeared from view. Adams begins his account of Pfeiffer with the gendered statement below, in which Pfeiffer is, however, accorded both masculine status and vindication with the assertion that her travels yielded 'scientific results'. For Adams, travellers, it seems, fall into two classes:

> [t]hose who discover and those who observe – that is, those who penetrate into regions hitherto untrodden by civilized men, and add new lands to the maps of the geographer; and those who simply follow in the track of their bolder or more fortunate predecessors ... To the latter class ... belong our female travellers ... Unless, indeed, we regard as an exception the wonderful woman to whose adventures and experiences the following chapter will be devoted. Of Madame Pfeiffer we think it may justly be said that she stands in the front ranks of the great travellers, and that the scientific results of her enterprise were both valuable and interesting.[55]

This is said despite Pfeiffer's own assertion, in *A Lady's Voyage round the World* at least, that she was mistaken for a naturalist by her guide in Brazil because she had been seen collecting flowers and insects and so it was assumed 'the object of my journey was a scientific one' (21), and the comment in the *Athenaeum*, which followed Pfeiffer's second world journey, by publishing occasional sightings from correspondents, that she was 'not a scientific traveller'.[56]

Jane Sinnett, in her 'Translator's Preface' to *A Lady's Voyage round the World: A Selected Translation*, bases the work's interest around the personal narrative of a 'singular' woman as noted earlier, but goes considerably further than the two reviewers while at the same time treading the inevitable careful discursive line, and in this regard Sinnett's choice of 'lady' for her title over 'woman' is suggestive. Sinnet is so conscious of the prevailing gender ideology, that she appears almost to be denying what she is actually stating:

[54]   [Bayle St. John?], 'A Woman's Voyage round the World', *Westminster Review* 56(1851): 249 and 250; 249–57.

[55]   W.H. Davenport Adams, *Celebrated Women Travellers of the Nineteenth Century* (1883; London, 1889), 215.

[56]   Augustus Petermann, 'Madame Pfeiffer in Africa', *Athenaeum* 1258(6 December 1851): 1281.

We have often heard of late years of a certain, probably fabulous, creature supposed to exist in the latitude of Berlin, and elsewhere, and denominated an "emancipated woman": nothing can be less like Madame Pfeiffer: yet truly she has emancipated herself in earnest – ... from indolence, and vanity, and fear – ... There is no country in the world where such a writer is likely to meet with more cordial appreciation than in England; and this feeling has greatly lightened the labour of clothing the original in an English dress.[57]

Sinnett's metaphor for her translation, that Pfeiffer has been clothed in 'English dress' works to reinforce the domestic. Sinnett cleverly chose to translate and include Pfeiffer's 'Preface', written for *A Visit to Iceland*, in place of the shorter, less explanatory preface Pfeiffer provided for *A Woman's Journey round the World*. The *Iceland* 'Preface' offers the reader a modest woman, religious in temperament, who explains away charges of eccentricity by detailing the powerful desire she had always felt to experience 'distant lands and strange customs'. Indeed where the *Iceland* translator had expressed this as: 'I thought of strange manners and customs, of distant regions, where a new sky would be above me, and new ground beneath my feet', Sinnett translates the last clause by quoting from Milton's *Paradise Lost*: 'My imagination dwelt on distant lands and strange customs – a new heaven and a new earth'. English dress indeed.[58]

Throughout her travels, however, Ida Pfeiffer is very conscious of the relations between Europeans and the citizens of the various lands she journeys across. Witnessing an incident in Benares she remarks: '[H]ow many similar instances have I seen, and how little is it to be wondered at, if these barbarous and heathen nations often hate us! Wherever the European comes he will reign supreme; and his rule is often more oppressive than that of the natives' (107). This statement must have resonated with Sinnett who questions in her essay 'Colonization and Emigration' why so-called successful colonization must include the 'unavoidable decay of an aboriginal wild race' and 'the necessity of driving away or exterminating the native owners of the soil'.[59] While in Benares Pfeiffer noted that all 'the land belongs either to the English government or the native princes, and they let it in large estates to the chief farmers' (116). Sinnett omitted a third landowner originally included in Pfeiffer's text, namely the East India Company.[60] Nowhere in Pfeiffer's narrative is there any celebration of European dominance, although she readily remarks on what she perceives as a lack of cleanliness, lack of

---

[57]   Jane Sinnett, 'Translator's Preface', *A Lady's Voyage round the World*, iii–iv.

[58]   Ida Pfeiffer, 'Author's Preface', *Visit to Iceland and the Scandinavian North* (2nd edn; London, 1853), ix and Ida Pfeiffer, 'Introduction', *A Lady's Voyage round the World*, I: x.

[59]   Sinnett, 'Colonization and Emigration', 318.

[60]   Ida Pfeiffer, *A Woman's Journey Round the World*, trans. Anon (London, 1852), 172.

morality, lack of modesty, lack of honesty, unaware that she reveals an ideological 'belief in the intrinsic superiority of European culture' as Ian Saunders puts it.[61]

Jane Sinnett, the first of many translators of Ida Pfeiffer's journeys, had quickly recognized the value of her narrative, not for mere gendered difference, the source of Adams's enthusiasm, but for her keen social observations untrammelled by the politics of colonization and nationalism, and therefore capable of re-orienting the perspectives of her British readers. Finally, Sinnett's use of the word 'emancipation' has specific connotations when it comes to Pfeiffer's references to the condition of the various women she encounters on her travels and her occasional references to slavery. In her own embracing of the freedom to travel and discover 'what lay beyond',[62] Pfeiffer makes no personal connection between her own condition and the enslaved state of others, even as she declares herself to be an 'enemy to slavery' and an abolitionist (22). In Brazil, she observes, at least 'the negro slave, under the protection of the law, has a better lot than the free fellah in Egypt, or than many peasants in Europe' (22). In this type of witnessing of the prevailing culture she could be likened to my next traveller, Fredrika Bremer, except that for Bremer, despite any such observed apparent ameliorating circumstances, the politics of slavery remains always the embarrassing issue for a woman conscious for the first time of her own personal quest for freedom.

---

[61]   Ian Saunders, *Open Texts, Partial Maps. A Literary Theory Handbook* (Nedlands, WA, 1993), 49.

[62]   Pfeiffer, 'Introduction', *A Lady's Voyage*, ix.

Chapter 7
Emancipatory Politics:
Mary Howitt translates Fredrika Bremer

The Swedish author Fredrika Bremer travelled to England and then on to the United States and Cuba in the years 1849 to 1851. She travelled as the celebrated Miss Bremer whose novels, centering on home and family life, on the social and cultural domestic life of Sweden, had enjoyed unprecedented popularity, in both England and the United States, throughout the 1840s, primarily via the translations of Mary Howitt. Bremer stayed with the Howitts in London on both the outward and return journeys. Between 1842 and 1850 Mary Howitt translated various novels and novellas by Fredrika Bremer. In the 1850s she translated several more of Bremer's novels; and in the 1860s four of Bremer's five travel books. Most of these publications ran to a number of editions although the novels were far more popular and widely reviewed than the travel books.[1] William and Mary Howitt, with their children, had moved to Heidelberg in Germany in 1840 where they lived until 1843 and it is there, according to Mary Howitt's *Autobiography*, that they began to learn Swedish, an activity Howitt terms 'a delightful employment ... for here were no puzzling terminations as in German, but a similarity of construction with the English'. She then recalls encountering Fredrika Bremer's novels in the German versions, delighted, she says, 'by their originality, freshness, and delicate humour'.[2] The Howitts were unusual in maintaining a long joint working life as writers, publishing books, poetry, and journalism, as well as stints as editors and translators, across many decades of the nineteenth century. In the 1840s and 1850s particularly, the Howitt name was an imprimatur for respectable, moral writings suitable for family reading.

---

[1]   Publications translated by Mary Howitt in chronological order include: *The Neighbours: A Story of Every-Day Life* (1842); *The Home: or, Family Cares and Family Joys* (1843); *The President's Daughters*; including *Nina* (1843); *New Sketches of Every-day Life: A Diary.* Together with *Strife and Peace* (1844); *Domestic Life or The H – Family* (1844); *Brothers and Sisters. A Tale of Domestic Life* (1848); *The Midnight Sun; a Pilgrimage* (1849); *An Easter Offering* (1850); *The Homes of the New World; Impressions of America* (1853); *Hertha* (1856); *Father and Daughter: Portraiture from the Life* (1859); *Two Years in Switzerland and Italy [Life in the Old World]* (1862); *Travels in the Holy Land* (1862); *Greece and the Greeks. The Narrative of a Winter Residence and Summer Travel in Greece and its Islands* (1863).

[2]   Mary Howitt, *Mary Howitt. An Autobiography*, ed. Margaret Howitt (1889; London, n.d.), 179.

The very titles of the early Bremer novels signal such suitable family subject matter, Howitt producing, with her husband William, *The Neighbours; a Story of Every-Day Life* (1842) and *Home; or Family Cares* (1843); and *The President's Daughters* (1843) in quick succession. These early translations were received with little comment on Mary Howitt's translating practice (hers was the only name to appear as translator on the publications) although in later years her work was subjected to far more severe scrutiny. In part such criticism fed into a current debate from the late 1840s about translating practice as discussed in Chapter I, as people with better skills and training came into the field. Her original translating process is described in her *Autobiography* thus: 'My husband and I translated "The Neighbours" and "The Home" from the German versions, but in the new editions which speedily followed we compared and revised them with the Swedish'.[3] Their first Bremer translations were published at their own risk but the novels proved instantly popular and by the end of 1843 were being pirated both in England and America. Bremer had written to Mary Howitt in appreciation of the English translation in February 1843 and when her new novel was ready sent it direct to the Howitts for them to translate. Mary Howitt tells her sister: 'We began its translation this week and hope by beginning translating immediately to be able to publish it at the beginning of the year about the time when it is published in Sweden and Germany and then we shall have a good advantage with a fair field to ourselves.'[4]

One of the earliest reviews of *The Neighbours*, the first of Bremer's novels to be published in England, is by Christian Isobel Johnstone writing for *Tait's Edinburgh Magazine*. Notably, Johnstone's review never mentions translation practice at all. Rather, the review is focused on the idea of cultural exchange. In conclusion Johnstone congratulates Howitt for her 'useful labours' and states her belief that British readers, 'us', still have sufficient taste, nature and goodness to appreciate the work. Johnstone celebrates the publication above all because it is domestic, because it explores what she terms 'every-day life' and 'everyday men and women'. In determining on a politics of the domestic informed by fairly recent and popularized ideas on political economy as the basis for her critique, Johnstone also has in mind the condition or state of the nation, writing:

> it is of the essence of real life among a people whom we, in past times more closely resembled, and by whose example we might, perhaps, in some things profit still. If the sunshine of England's prosperity is really on the decline; if every class is waxing poorer; and if many, once comfortable, are *uneasy*, or

3   Howitt, *Autobiography*, 179.
4   University of Nottingham, Manuscripts and Special Collections. Howitt Collection (ACC 1280), Box 1: Mary Howitt to Anna Harrison Ht/1/1/1-196, Ht/1/1/153.

actually impoverished, lessons of economy, of prudence and order in domestic affairs, were never more required than now.[5]

Also in 1842, a critic for the *Monthly Review* remarks of Bremer's *The Neighbours*, it 'is, in truth, "a story of every-day life" – a fiction of reality, so far as we can judge of verisimilitude, and of Swedish scenes, character and incident', another unexpected neighbourhood.[6]

Johnstone's invoking of 'domestic affairs' is echoed in Samuel Laing's review with its extended analogy based on a market economy to introduce the Howitt translations of Bremer's novels as 'food for the mind'. Laing then claims:

> we cannot be blind to the fact, that the literary interests of the country have thriven remarkably well with this free trade in ideas. We produce enough for our own use and consumpt [sic] at home, import very little, and export large quantities to foreign parts in the various marketable forms of history, philosophy, political economy, poetry, and romance.

Laing's words conjure very precisely the idea of an intellectual empire, in particular one based not only on an economy of agriculture and mining, but as Laing puts it a 'free trade in ideas'. He evaluates Bremer's productions as restoring the balance to the exchange of ideas, and overturning the 'monopoly of the supply of the home-market', equating 'our growers of poetry and romance' with 'our growers of wheat and barley'.[7]

Laurie Langbauer reminds us that the everyday is 'the very medium of culture', and Howitt's translation serves as an essential contribution to the knowledge industry of the day. Langbauer argues for the everyday as a site of political struggle, especially for women.[8] While Mary Howitt's translating process and practice may have been basic, she nevertheless remains an important contributor to the exchange of ideas whose work on Scandinavian domestic texts (she was also an early translator of Hans Christian Andersen) comes at a significant moment socially and culturally for British women and empire. A critic for the *Athenaeum* reviewing '*The Home; or Family Cares*' actually begins by celebrating the fact that the translation is 'by an English wife and English mother' and is therefore 'good service done to her country',[9] interpreting reception of the work in nationalistic terms as a contribution to domestic politics and thereby, I would argue, signalling appropriation in colonizing terms. In considering Bremer's transformation for an

---

[5] Christian Isobel Johnstone, 'New Novels. The Neighbours, – Evelyn Howard', *Tait's Edinburgh Magazine* 13(1842): 796, 779 and 784; 779–99.

[6] 'Novels', *Monthly Review* 159(1842): 513; 507–23.

[7] Samuel Laing, 'Frederika (sic) Bremer's Novels', *North British Review* 1(1844): 168; 168–83.

[8] Laurie Langbauer, *Novels of Everyday Life*, 15 and 4–5.

[9] 'The Home: or, Family Cares and Family Joys', *Athenaeum* 811(1843): 457; 457–8.

English readership I want to link this political concept of the everyday to both domestic ideology and the politics of home because they proved essential with regard to successful colonization and consolidation of the empire.

By 1856 George Eliot was readily dismissing Bremer's novels: '[N]o one quotes them, no one alludes to them: and grave people … remember their enthusiasm for the Swedish novels among those intellectual "wild oats" to which their mature wisdom can afford to give a pitying smile'. Even if the impact of Bremer's writing was short-lived, as Eliot suggests, nevertheless she acknowledges that the novels described manners that 'were fresh to the English public', conveying the 'humour, of that easy, domestic kind which throws a pleasant light on every-day things'.[10] Fredrika Bremer's work focuses on women, often single women, and what they do with their lives. To this end then her writing revolves around a gendered politics of home in which women's ordinary lives are privileged over other narrative forms. Her writings enabled British women readers to discover that the 'Woman Question' was not an isolated circumstance within their own world, but a debate engaging minds in other countries, as Bessie Parkes's significant feminist reaction to Howitt's transformation of *The H.– Family* (1844) demonstrates. Parkes, in a letter to Kate Jeavons, in 1854, a decade after the novel's first publication in English, writes: 'But oh how natural Emily seems to me in the H. Family, don't you remember the admirable description of her total reluctance actually to marry, however willing to be betrothed. All very independent women must feel this at times, till – the marriage laws are altered –'.[11] Significantly, this particular novel had been reprinted three times by 1854, suggesting an ongoing enthusiasm for Bremer's writings, as transformed by Howitt (and often dismissed as minor precisely because they record the everyday) which served both the nascent British women's movement and the imperial project. Mary Howitt's translation of Bremer's novels had thus produced for the Swedish author an extensive and enthusiastic anglolexic audience.[12]

Although Bremer journeyed widely in her later years, and produced five travel books in her native language, four of which Mary Howitt translated, the main focus of the remainder of this chapter will be on Bremer's first travel book, *The Homes of the New World; Impressions of America*, in part because, as Mary Howitt said of this journey, Bremer's 'religious and social views had, in America, been materially influenced. An intense desire animated her to aid in the liberation

---

[10]   George Eliot, 'Dred, Never Too Late to Mend and Hertha', repr. in *Selected Essays, Poems and Other Writings*, ed. A.S. Byatt and Nicholas Warren (London, 1990), 384 and 384–5.

[11]   Girton College, University of Cambridge, GCPP Parkes 6/59/1 and 2 and 3.

[12]   A version of this foregoing information appears in Johnston, 'Britain's Intellectual Empire and the Transformation of Culture: The Case of Mary Howitt and Fredrika Bremer', *Australasian Victorian Studies Journal* 11(2005): 54–64. The article is, however, about the reception of the novels alone.

of every oppressed soul'.[13] This emancipatory drive accorded with Howitt's own politics. However, Howitt herself, as translator, came in for some rebuke from most reviewers of *Homes of the New World* with regard to her failure to edit Bremer's text. The *Athenaeum* notes, for instance, 'there are but few signs of an editor's care'.[14] Notably the critic for the *Spectator* is even more severe regarding this failure:

> Miss Bremer's *Impressions of America* must be ranked among remarkable specimens of bookmaking. The translation is in this respect more censurable than the original. The historical summaries, suggested by particular provinces and places, may be wanted for Scandinavian readers; the descriptions of well-known natural curiosities or town sights may be new to them; and the long quotations from printed authors may not be out of place. For the English public none of these were needed; they already know all that Miss Bremer tells them on such points.[15]

It is worth comparing this to Jane Sinnett's practice. She readily edited such material out of texts for her English readership (as she states with regard to Ida Pfeiffer's world journey) and this suggests, I think, Sinnett's more professional ability, both linguistically and as a translator. Indeed Howitt's failure to edit some of the more personal commentary resulted in a considerable contretemps.

Late in December 1853 an announcement appeared in the Washington *Daily National Intelligencer* and in the London *Times*. The *Times* announcement was headed 'To the Editor of the Times', followed by a statement titled 'A Card' and signed 'Fredrika Bremer'. In it Bremer states that the English translation of *Homes of the New World* contains 'misconceptions as to the words and meanings of the Swedish original'.[16] As a popular author Bremer received many invitations to stay in private homes during her journey through America. With the publication of *Homes of the New World* there, her various hosts were dismayed to discover accounts of their domestic lives exposed to the public gaze. Bremer, perhaps ingeniously or ingenuously, blamed her translator, Mary Howitt, and placed announcements in the main newspapers of the capital cities of Britain and America to that effect, indirectly intimating that embarrassing personal details had been retained against her strict instructions. Howitt countered almost immediately (three days later in fact) quoting a letter from Bremer which refers to the translation as 'truly good and excellent work, and quite wonderful when I think of the circumstances under which it has been achieved', referring here to the translation from manuscript

---

13   Mary Howitt, *Autobiography*, 211.

14   'The Homes of the New World', *Athenaeum* No. 1353(1 October 1853): 1153; 1153–4.

15   'Frederika [sic] Bremer's Impressions of America', *Spectator* 26(1853): 898; 898–9.

16   Fredrika Bremer, 'A Card', *The Times* (23 December 1853), 7.

rather than print, and the speed with which the task had to be undertaken.[17] Bremer published a rejoinder, in the *Times* on 24 January 1854 and as in 'A Card' it is clear that she is trying to suggest, speciously, that minor infelicities in the translation of single words are errors that 'reflect on, and thereby ... give pain to, very dear friends and their friends'.[18]

Back in October the reviewer of the English version of Bremer's book in the *Athenaeum* had taken Bremer to task at some length for making public characters of private persons, a practice it states sententiously that 'is becoming prevalent and offensive'.[19] In the interim doubtless letters of protest from American friends had begun to arrive. The day after the *Times* announcement by Bremer, the *Athenaeum* published what it called 'a note of rectification' offering Bremer's version that mistranslation was the problem.[20] In fact, critically, as Laurel Ann Lofsvold points out, the book was condemned in the press for its 'gossipy indiscretions and breaches of confidence'.[21] This very public dispute must have been a blow to Howitt, personally, professionally and financially. Subsequently commentators have blamed this reputedly poor translation for the book's unenthusiastic reception in the United States. Only in 1996 has a complete exploration of the translation itself, and the instructions Bremer claimed to have given to Howitt, been undertaken by Laurel Ann Lofsvold. She reveals that if 'the extant collection of letters from author to translator is complete, Bremer did *not* make many of the specific requests she claimed to have made' and that Howitt followed those specific instructions she did give 'in all but three cases'.[22] Moreover, it seems that Bremer placed what Lofsvold terms a well-founded implicit trust in the judgment and taste of her translator, noticeable when the Swedish version is compared to the English one.

What this dispute tells us, however, is the importance Bremer placed on the English versions of her work, and her recognition of the power of her English language readership and the viability of her English language market. If she wished to make a political impact, and it seems that she did, it was through English as her lingua franca rather than confining herself to Sweden and a Swedish readership. In January 1854 she describes her account of slavery in America in a letter to her American friends the Springs as 'the chief work of my work' and that her journey to America on that account was 'God[']s special will'.[23] The English word 'work' in Bremer's parlance suggests the desire to effect, intellectually at least, changes to social policy.

[17]   Mary Howitt, 'To the Editor of The Times', *The Times* (26 December 1853), 9.

[18]   Fredrika Bremer, 'A Word in Reply to Mrs. Howitt', *The Times* (24 January 1854), 8.

[19]   'Homes of the New World', *Athenaeum*, 1153.

[20]   [Note of Rectification], *Athenaeum* No.1365 (24 December 1853), 1557–8.

[21]   Laurel Ann Lofsvold, 'Blaming the Messenger: Mary Howitt's Translation of Fredrika Bremer's *Hemmen i den Nya verlden*', *Scandinavica* 35(1996): 215; 213–31.

[22]   Lofsvold, 'Blaming the Messenger', 216–17.

[23]   Rooth, 231.

Lofsvold observes of Bremer's first foray into travel writing, *The Homes of the New World*, that it is 'in terms of style a typical Fredrika Bremer text. It bears the same sentimentality as her novels, and the same concern with home, family relations, moral and charitable living, and the need and right of each individual to realize her or his potential'.[24] Bremer anticipated the journey as a translation both of her female and of her European self: a transformation that will produce a new identity. She desired to travel, she said, 'in order that the new human being in me, in thoughts, in will, may develop its wings more freely, come to a consciousness which it cannot win under the old conditions at home'.[25] This statement suggests that Bremer's polemic appears to be solely concerned with gender ideology, and at a personal level she merely seeks to develop her own potential as an individual. Her travel narrative insists on the traveller herself being centre stage, a positioning Bremer consistently disclaims and then reclaims as she confronts her desire for personal transformation. The two prefaces to *The Homes of the New World*, 'To the Reader' and 'To My American Friends' both confirm this. In 'To the Reader', Bremer states that the work suffers from 'egotism – the offense of all autobiography'.[26] Indeed one reviewer, writing for the *Athenaeum*, remarks sternly that the work 'is certainly tedious. The subjects are overdone – there is neither narrative nor adventure – and there is a great deal too much of the author's own self'.[27] Ironically however, this very quest for individual personal freedom from Old Europe's gender ideology comes into diametric collision with the key political debate of the day in the United States: slavery. Furthermore, Bremer's text reveals that politically slavery cannot be contained solely within the public sphere, that its impact is realized in both the public and the domestic worlds, despite their ideological separation via gender. However, the concerns of Bremer's fictions, Lofsvold's 'home, family relations, moral and charitable living', are politicized not only through gender in her American travelogue, or only through race, but through her choice of English as the medium through which she voices her concerns to the world.

For this reason, English, I would like to argue here, is Bremer's lingua franca and England too may well be a cultural touchstone. The English versions of her work offered her a place on the world stage and English as lingua franca is important with regard to this, her first foray into published travel writing as opposed to fiction writing, both as the medium through which she obtains information, in particular

---

[24]   Laurel Ann Lofsvold, *Fredrika Bremer and the Writing of America* (Lund, Sweden, 1999), 13. I wish to acknowledge here my indebtedness to the work of Laurel Ann Lofsvold whose investigation of the Swedish originals and Bremer's manuscript material has proved invaluable in preparing this chapter.

[25]   Quoted in Rooth, 5–6.

[26]   Fredrika Bremer, *The Homes of the New World; Impressions of America*, trans. Mary Howitt (1853; 2 vols; London, 1968), I:iii. All subsequent references are to this edition.

[27]   'The Homes of the New World', *Athenaeum*, 1153.

about slavery, and the medium through which her journey is first presented to a broad reading public. The slave trade, in this period, was generally viewed by abolitionists, both in America and Britain, as an illicit trafficking in human lives. But Bremer's translated account also forms part of a commercial traffic predicated on the politics of slavery in the shape of publications: in particular publications by women through the lens of the domestic. It is probably no co-incidence that Harriet Beecher Stowe's polemical novel is titled *Uncle Tom's Cabin*. Through this title, slavery and the politics of home are imbricated, one with the other. Catherine Sedgwick, noted early American novelist whose popular work focused on the domestic, published in this same period 'Slavery in New England' for *Bentley's Miscellany*. These are just two examples from a wide range of other writings on the same theme. Mary Howitt too was politically a long-time opponent of slavery and an advocate of women's rights. This is evidenced in both her personal correspondence, as early as 1830, and in her public journalism for the *People's Journal*, and later *Howitt's Journal of Literature and Popular Progress*, which she ran with her husband from 1847–8. In a letter to her sister around 1845 she writes 'I am just now most deeply interested in the Antislavery question' and goes on to discuss William Lloyd Garrison and Frederick Douglass, both of whom are the subjects of articles in the *People's Journal*. William Lloyd Garrison was an abolitionist and founder of the American Anti-Slavery Movement. Frederick Douglass was an escaped slave who became a leading figure in the abolitionist movement. He travelled to the United Kingdom in 1845–6. In the same letter she also addresses female education, stating the 'fault of girls' education always is that independence and firmness of character is not sufficiently cultivated'.[28] Politically, therefore, Mary Howitt was an informed and committed translator for a work which ultimately engages with both these emancipatory movements. Enthusiastically and in hopeful vein, Mary Howitt records in February 1853: 'Miss Bremer writes beautifully on slavery. She seems to think that a spirit of emancipation is growing up in the South itself.'[29]

Bremer's journey begins and ends in England, and she published, again in 1853, a brief account of her time there titled *England in 1851, or Sketches of a Tour in England* (not translated by Howitt, given the currency of their dispute), which in some ways is a companion volume to her American journey. This publication confirms my reading of England as a social, political and cultural touchstone for Bremer. For instance, she writes in almost rapturous tones:

And this is England! The little Island which can be traversed, from end to end
by rail, in any direction, in four and twenty hours; this little isle, Britain, has

---

[28]   University of Nottingham, Howitt Collection, Mary Howitt to Anna Harrison, Ht/1/1/168/1, 2, and 3. Mary Howitt's article, 'Memoir of Frederick Douglass' and her four-part series 'William Lloyd Garrison' appeared in the *People's Journal* 2(1847): 302–305; and 141–4; 166–8; 179–80; 185–6.

[29]   Mary Howitt, *Autobiography*, 217.

accomplished all this. This little land, sits, like a Queen Victoria, on the sea and stretches her sceptre from Pole to Pole, from East to West. This little Island peopled North America and by these, her children, stamps her character on the States and nations of the new world. (64)[30]

Compare this to the opening pages of *The Homes of the New World*:

> it was requisite to see a little of England ... before I saw America and New York. I did not wish to be too much overcome by New York, therefore I would know something of the mother before I made acquaintance with the daughter, in order to have a point and rule of comparison, that I might correctly understand the type ... England had in the first place given population, laws, and tone of mind to the people of the New World. It was the Old World in England which must become my standard of judgment as regarded the New. (I: 1–2)

For Bremer, England is the mother, the United States the daughter, which substantiates my assertion that both English (the voices she hears) and England (socially, politically and culturally) forms the basis of Bremer's lingua franca. At the end of *England in 1851* Bremer thanks England 'for the view of the people raising itself up in the consciousness of its own powers ... for new hope, as regards the future of Europe ... the English race is the finest on earth'.[31]

Bremer's private letters to her sister describing her American travels were actually first published in English as *The Homes of the New World* (1853) for the British and American markets (translated with some difficulty from the manuscripts of the correspondence by Mary Howitt). Each chapter is designated 'Letter I', 'Letter II', etc. reflecting the manuscript origin as a set of private letters. Although simultaneous publication in England, Sweden and the United States was aimed for, as it turns out, the English publication appeared before the Swedish, *Hemmen i den nya Verlden* (1853), as Laurel Ann Lofsvold has shown. Lofsvold describes in some detail the problems that Mary Howitt encountered in producing the English translation. As Bremer edited the letters, copies were sent to Howitt via friends and relatives who happened to be travelling between Sweden and England, but apparently Bremer often requested changes long after these manuscripts had been received and translated.[32] This work took 18 months in all. The American edition went through five printings in the first month and the 'book was also translated into Danish, Dutch, French, and German, receiving numerous reviews in Europe'.[33] While Rooth offers one or two quotations from French and

---

[30]   Fredrika Bremer, *England in 1851. Sketches of a Tour of England*, trans. From the German by L.A.H. (Boulogne, 1853), 64.

[31]   Bremer, *England in 1851*, 138.

[32]   Lofsvold, 'Blaming the Messenger', 216.

[33]   Rooth, 126.

German critics, I have not located any information on the critical reception of the Swedish edition.

To reinforce my argument regarding the importance of English as a lingua franca to Bremer's publications, in the translator's 'Preface' to Bremer's *New Sketches of Every-Day Life: A Diary* (1844) Mary Howitt writes of the 'intellectual intercourse' Bremer's novels have opened up between England and Sweden, adding:

> I regard it as one of the happiest and most honourable events of my life – of which nothing can deprive me – that I have introduced her beautiful and ennobling writings, not only to these islands, but to the whole vast English family. I have sent them expressly to Australia; and in America, in India, at the Cape as well as in Australasia, MISS BREMER is now a household word – nay, more – a household possession and blessing.[34]

And in confirmation of this sense of a world opening up, in a letter to Rebecca Spring of 12 June 1852 Bremer herself writes that:

> the earth is all alive ... the great hive is swarming, and all the ends of the earth are filling with – especially the Anglosaxon race. 60,000 emigrants are next going out to Australia to dig Gold (Mr. Howitt his two sons and intended son in law are already there in quest of gold) ... so the far east and the West are through gold mines and Anglosaxon-Norman homes preparing for the golden age ... My land is out of the great thoroughfare, and is comparatively quiet, but still the movement is felt even here.[35]

Having her work published in English gave Bremer access to 'the great thoroughfare' of modern life.

On 29 September 1853, just after *The Homes of the New World* was published, Fredrika Bremer wrote from Stockholm to the novelist Elizabeth Gaskell about Gaskell's novel *Mary Barton* (1848) which she celebrates as a work 'only an English woman could write', in which the working classes are presented in the form of a 'new romance' to use Bremer's words. Gaskell's novels, Bremer tells her, 'have opened many an eye, many a mind in Sweden as well as in England'. Bremer also admits that she has been provoked by Gaskell's success to consider what political work (although she does not use the term) she ought to do and informs Gaskell she has sent her a copy of her newly published book, *The Homes of the New World*. Bremer claims the book stresses 'the necessity of the full development of woman's mind and sphere' but surprisingly this is her only direct comment on its content. She adds that 'the problems of society are working in Sweden as

---

[34] Mary Howitt, 'Preface', *New Sketches of Every-Day Life: A Diary* (London, 1844), xvii.

[35] Quoted in Rooth, 206.

every where among free nations' and she expresses the hope that England will 'raise the position of women to give them [,] through education, and ... enlarged opportunities for work – employment for their minds and hands'.[36] In *England in 1851* Bremer writes 'Through many sad appearances and dark experiences I live on, still hoping for the future, which must be coming for society, when fettered woman shall become perfectly free'.[37] About slavery, however, the letter to Gaskell is silent. In this brief retrospect of her American travels and experiences in the letter to Gaskell, Bremer's silence is difficult to read. It is as if she returns to the 'Woman Question' as a more straightforward and manageable issue because her own desire for freedom as a woman has quite evidently come into direct conflict with the contradiction slavery presented to her mind. The phrase 'fettered woman' above has a particular resonance here.

In obvious contrast, the published account of her journey, *The Homes of the New World*, is definitely not silent about slavery. Lofsvold in *Fredrika Bremer* calculates that all but eight of the 43 letters which comprise the Swedish version of *Homes of the New World* mention slavery. The proportion is similar in the English version. As Lofsvold so astutely puts it, Bremer engages in an 'ongoing conversation' not only with the addressees of these letters, but also with herself.[38] It's a conversation which, via Howitt's sympathetic and engaged translation, is continued with her English-language readers of the work, both in Great Britain and in the United States and to a wide middle-class reception through reviews in the influential journals the *Athenaeum*, the *Spectator*, the *Literary Gazette* and the *British Quarterly*. The *Athenaeum* was regarded as 'one of the most influential papers of its day'; the *Spectator*'s profile 'was measured not in sales but in its level of political influence and the stature of its readership'; the *Literary Gazette*'s reviewer William Jerdan 'could make or break a novel's fortune'; and the *British Quarterly* had a respectable circulation in this timeframe.[39] While these four journals may have expressed negative issues with regard to the book as a whole, all respond pointedly and positively to her accounts of slavery and the slavery debates current at the time of Bremer's travels, by reproducing extracts that describe them. As a sample the *Spectator* reviewer states unequivocally:

> The parts relating to the South and its slavery are among the most interesting in the book. The writer does not indeed tell many stories, or delight in recounting the horrible: with almost over-sensitiveness she refrained from questioning,

---

[36] Fredrika Bremer, 'Autograph 4-page Letter to Elizabeth Gaskell 29 September 1853', in *Gaskell and the Brontës. Literary Manuscripts of Elizabeth Gaskell (1810–65) and the Brontës* from the Brotherton Library, University of Leeds [seven reels of 35mm silver-halide microfilm and guide], (Marlborough, 2003).

[37] Bremer, *England in 1851*, 121.

[38] Lofsvold, *Fredrika Bremer*, 179.

[39] See *Dictionary of Nineteenth-Century Journalism*, ed. Laurel Brake and Marysa Demoor (Gent and London, 2009), 26; 589; 366 and 79.

especially slaves, that she might not appear as a spy. What she tells and what she says confirm the view that has often been held in this journal – ... the great evil is more moral than physical ... It is the human degradation which is the dark feature of the case; and all the concomitants of slavery partake of this idea.[40]

Lofsvold remarks that while Bremer read and understood English well, pronunciation was a problem.[41] However making herself understood appears not to have impeded Bremer in her journeyings through the United States and her questing after information because she records both the voices of slave owners and the voices of slaves themselves, despite the *Spectator's* claim that she refrained from questioning. Indeed, Eugene D. Genovese makes excellent use of Bremer's voiced accounts as a means to explore the existing conditions of slavery in the decade prior to the American Civil War. Genovese says of Bremer's accounts that she 'heard', she 'questioned', she 'thought', she 'noted' and she 'reported'. He describes her as 'astute' and regarding her description of the words of a black preacher, writes 'Miss Bremer was right to call the preacher's message one of "spiritual freedom". She had heard an old theme among the slaves'. Bremer also records a black preacher invoking, in Genovese's words, 'blunt black nationalism'.[42] While she is consistently racist in the unthinking terms of her own day (a racism continually encountered in anti-slavery treatises from the 1790s on), and while she meets and enjoys the hospitality of charming slave owners, to the extent that her position seems at times irredeemably compromised, Bremer nevertheless continually reasserts her position that slavery is wrong, most commonly invoking Christianity as the basis for her position. She witnesses its ill effects on both slaves and slave-owning families, and she offers accounts of the debates of the day, dominated by the slavery issue, both in the American Senate, and at various abolitionist rallies and other public meetings she attends. In this more thoughtful approach her position seems notably different to that of other European women travellers, in particular Ida Hahn-Hahn's *Letters from the Orient* (1845), translated by Samuel Phillips, and Ida Pfeiffer's *Visit to the Holy Land, Egypt and Italy* (1853), translated by H.W. Dulcken, both of whom were travelling and writing in Bremer's identical timeframe. Both women encounter slavery in the east and their reactions may well be in part dictated by an inherent orientalism that is locked into an unhistoricized past whereas Bremer is clearly engaged with the concept of the possibilities of modernity and change in the 'New' world.[43]

---

[40] 'Fredrika Bremer's Impressions of America', 899.

[41] Lofsvold, *Fredrika Bremer*, 11.

[42] Eugene D. Genovese, *Roll, Jordan, Roll. The World the Slaves Made* (London, 1975), 41–2; 128; 256; 265; 266.

[43] See also Tamara Felden, 'The Different Faces of Slavery. German-Speaking Women Authors of the 19th Century Discuss Race, Gender, and Culture', *Schatzkammer der Deutschen Sprache, Dichtung und Geschichte* 23(1997): 31–48.

What underlies Bremer's journey is her reiterated hope and belief that in the so-called 'New World' there is an opportunity for society to be differently structured and to grasp the opportunity to embrace what she terms 'civil liberty' (I: 179), a concept which the reality of slavery continually damages and overturns. In 'Letter X' Bremer recounts to her sister the story of the pilgrims of the *Mayflower*. For Bremer the pilgrims represent a quest for political freedom contained in her description of their founding 'a new civil community which should be a home and a community for all people of the earth' (I: 184). Bremer remarks that wherever she goes: 'I see ... the empire founded by a people composed of all ... who ... sought freedom of conscience and peace on a new free soil' (I: 187). This is her idealized vision of the New World, the vision she seeks, and which her encounter with slavery disrupts and then perverts. The word *freedom* recurs over and over again in *The Homes of the New World*. In part this focus may well be attributable to the social conditions existing in Sweden at this time. As J.R. Lowell had noted in 1844, Bremer's characters must of necessity come from the upper classes and that she never portrays what he terms 'humble life'. Lowell accounts for this by explaining that the Swedish population is divided 'strictly into two classes ... and the mass of the people are in a state scarcely better than degraded ... from which there is but a bare possibility of rising'.[44] Perhaps Bremer was making such home comparisons in her own mind, even if she does not articulate them here. She does articulate them, however, in *England in 1851*. There she writes of Sweden: 'we are deficient in much of what constitutes the greatness of other nations ... We still sigh for religious freedom of thought, liberty of conscience to the fullest extent'.[45]

Metaphorically, back in 'Letter III', Bremer equates the vastness of America with the expectations, demands and hopes of life, 'a something which makes me draw a deeper breath, and, as it were, in a larger, freer world' (I: 41). The expectation of a transformative freedom then is apparent from the outset, although her stated purpose for her journey is little different from those of the many other travellers (in particular English ones) also embarking for the States in the 1830s and 1840s, including celebrated writers like Harriet Martineau and Charles Dickens. Bremer's stated purpose is:

> to observe the popular life, institutions, and circumstances of a new country; to become clearer in my own mind on certain questions connected with the development of nations and people; and in particular, to study the women and the homes of the New World. (I: 53)

However, she then admits that although theoretically she had intended to report on what she terms 'public affairs' (I: 53) she confesses that in fact it is the private, the individual 'which seizes upon my interest, my feelings, my thoughts', the very

---

[44]   J.R. Lowell, 'New Translations of the Writings of Miss Bremer', *North American Review* 58(1844): 486–7; 480–508.

[45]   Bremer, *England in 1851*, 46.

material on which her fictions are based. She had thought she could break loose, as she puts it, from fiction and fiction writing, only to discover that she is drawn to fiction 'more forcibly than ever' (I: 53) because she is so drawn to the world of 'private life' (I: 54). This is the element which makes Bremer's travelogue unique: her focus on the private world of those she encounters. As Vaughan and Allon remark: 'We know of no book that does really give you so much of the "homes" – that is of the home manners, talkings, and feelings of the people in the New World.'[46] Yet at the same time what the reader discovers is the way in which the public affair of most moment in the period – slavery – necessarily cannot be separated from the domestic lives Bremer recounts nor from its impact on the individual mind, her own in particular.

Bremer's first encounter with slavery is a meeting with the noted abolitionist William Lloyd Garrison at which she tells him she thinks that abolitionist 'want of moderation' and the violence of their language damages their cause (I: 123). She also conducts an interview with two escaped slaves, William and Ellen Craft. Ellen Craft apparently chose to escape not because of physical mistreatment but, so Bremer records in Ellen's own words, 'because they would not give me my rights as a human being. I could never learn any thing, neither to read nor to write'. Bremer's only comment is a racist one, 'I remarked in her the desire for learning peculiar to the white race' (I: 124). Notably, however, what Ellen Craft desires is education and thereby greater opportunities for meaningful work. Her ambitions are therefore identical to those of women generally in this period, and identical to Bremer's own statement to Elizabeth Gaskell that *Homes of the New World* focuses on the need for women's minds and spheres to be more fully developed.

Through her close connection to her translator, Mary Howitt, Bremer must also have been keenly aware of the degree to which the Howitts published anti-slavery material in both the *People's Journal* and *Howitt's Journal*, and the connection made continually between the condition of women and slavery in the various and long-running discourses on the 'Woman Question'. For instance, the Howitts published a poem titled 'Offerings from the Old World to the New, by Englishwomen', which is signed 'M.C.' Investigation suggests this is Mary Carpenter. A note beneath the poem states 'The above excellent poem accompanied the contributions sent from Bristol to the Anti-Slavery Bazaar now holding in Boston'. Mary Carpenter resided in Bristol and contributed to the fund-raising Abolition Fair. In part this poem reads:

> – And shall we now
> Be silent, when we see our sisters bound in chains,
> Heaven's holiest ties polluted, – their souls sunk
> In ignorance, – degraded to the brutes? –
> Shall we behold them on the hated block,

---

[46]   Robert Vaughan and Henry Allon, 'Our Epilogue on Books', *British Quarterly Review* 18(1853): 570; 569–70.

Sold to the highest bidder, – and not speak?
America! Thy country, – glorious, great,
As ever it should be, – is sinking down
To be the scorn of nations.[47]

Nevertheless, Bremer is unlikely to have made the necessary connection between her own feminist agenda and Ellen Craft's similar ambitions, because of her innate racism, for instance her stated belief that 'the negro race ... have a natural tendency to subordination to the white race' (I: 277–8). It is also her reiterated stance that the curse of slavery warps and degrades the white slave-owners more than it does their black slaves (I: 279).

Bremer subsequently travels to South Carolina, 'merely seeking', she claims, 'the truth in every thing, and ready to do justice to the good in all, even in slavery ... I am come hither to see and to learn, not as a spy' (I: 266). Her writing often belies such statements. For instance, South Carolina is initially characterized by her as a 'feeble Southern beauty reposing upon a luxurious bed of flowers in a nectarine grove, surrounded by willing slaves' (I: 268) in the commonplace language of the anti-slavery productions of the late eighteenth century. I am thinking for instance of Anna Barbauld's 'Epistle to William Wilberforce' (1792):

Lo! where reclined, pale beauty courts the breeze,
Diffused on sofas of voluptuous ease. (lines 57–8)[48]

Despite the loaded metaphorical language, Bremer confesses that South Carolina is beautiful and admits 'I have inexpressibly enjoyed her peculiar charm, so delightful, so rich, and to me so novel' (I: 268). This kind of conflict manifests itself many times throughout Bremer's narrative as a form of tension which is never actually resolved. Yet it is in South Carolina that she encounters more significantly for the first time the actual impact of slavery. She comments 'I scarcely ever meet with a man, or a woman either, who can openly and honestly look the thing in the face' (I: 275). She is shocked by what she terms the 'obstinate blindness' of educated people, and even more by the short-sightedness of the women she meets. Bremer endorses the long-held ideological view of women: that they have an innate sense of moral right and, as she puts it, 'inborn feeling for the true and the good' (I: 276). Slavery, Bremer writes, is both immoral and impure, not least because it breaks up families, separating 'husband and wife, mother and child' (I: 276). She sees that slavery prevents the 'free-will attachment of one rational being

---

[47]   M.C. [Mary Carpenter], 'Offerings from the Old World to the New, by Englishwomen', *Howitt's Journal* 3(1848): 26. See also Jo Manton, *Mary Carpenter and the Children of the Streets* (London, 1976), 76.

[48]   Anna Laetitia Barbauld, 'Epistle to William Wilberforce, Esq., on the Rejection of the Bill for Abolishing the Slave Trade' (1792), *Romanticism: an Anthology*, ed. Duncan Wu (Oxford, 1994), 22.

to another' (I: 277). She continues her journey by steamboat to Savannah and on this leg of the journey takes every opportunity to interview whoever she comes across. After each conversation in which defences of slavery are often recounted, she nevertheless reasserts her own implacable position: 'the institution is – a great lie in the life of human freedom, and especially in the New World' (I: 318).

A train journey brings Bremer to Macon. She awakes to a glorious day and in what can only be described as an epiphany, revels in her sense of personal freedom despite the 'great lie' that is the public life around her. As in the letter to Gaskell, Bremer's silence regarding slavery when she expresses her own sense of personal freedom might be construed as either a failure to recognize the irony of celebrating her own freedom in the face of the fettered lives confronting her on every side or, a wish to keep gender and race quite separate as categories in her narrative, despite the imbrication of both throughout her book. A third construction might be that by offering a personalized account of the joy freedom brings, a moral lesson may thereby be inculcated. I have only slim evidence for such a reading, but am tempted to make it nevertheless. This is Bremer's moment of epiphany:

> Did I not wander free – free as few could be, in the great, free New World, free
> to see and to become acquainted with whatever I chose? Was I not free and
> unfettered as a bird? My soul had wings, and the whole world was mine! (I: 323)

This was written on 7th May 1850. A week later she brings all of the issues together: 'I have watered with tears of joy the flowers of freedom on the soil of slavery' (I: 340). Physically Bremer finds the South alluring, but discovers that slavery fetters 'more or less, all and every one'. She then adds:

> Yet I love the South ... I have in the South felt myself to have a Southern
> tendency; and having entered into the peculiar life of the South ... I have
> perfectly understood that bitter feeling which ferments ... towards the despotic
> and unreasonable North ... What would I not give if the South ... would ...
> allow the slaves to purchase their own freedom ... as an act of justice to their
> posterity, to the people whom they have enslaved, and for whom they thereby
> would open a future, a new existence in a life of freedom. (I: 383)

As Lofsvold points out Bremer never asks why it should be necessary for any one to purchase him or herself and argues that for Bremer white people are 'slavery's principle (sic) victims', although this does not quite take into account the degree to which Bremer wrestles with the issue throughout her book.[49]

Journeying back up to Philadelphia Bremer decides to read the American Declaration of Independence (I: 427) and quotes the famous Enlightenment passage: 'We hold these truths to be self-evident, that *all men are created equal*' (I: 428). She describes the document as splendid but specifically notes that as

---

[49]   Lofsvold, *Fredrika Bremer*, 227 and 241.

a 'declaration of the inalienable freedom and rights of humanity [it] is now, however, opposed to many things in this country' (I: 429). In Washington, as the capital of the New World, she apparently abandons the domestic and the private to experience the public affairs with which she had originally intended only to deal. She sees for the first time in Washington a slave-pen where slaves are sold noting that Washington is located in Maryland, a slave state. It is these passages which the *Spectator* reviewer extracts. This encounter produces a rare ironic comment from Bremer, that Southerners, 'are anxious to maintain, even here, their beloved domestic institutions, as the phrase is' (I: 459). The words 'even here' refer of course to Washington as the nation's capital. For a woman whose published work has been celebrated most for its domestic qualities – J.R. Lowell, for instance, lauds her 'sweet, domestic, fireside style'[50] – the irony contained in referring to slavery as a 'beloved domestic institution' seems palpable.

In Washington during July 1850 Bremer visits the Senate and the House of Representatives nearly every day and listens attentively to the speeches, which are then fully recorded in her work. Her accounts of the slavery debates are praised in the English press, by the anonymous *Athenaeum* reviewer, for instance, for their vigour, and indeed this journal selects one of these accounts as the only printed extract in the review, making it the centre-piece and privileging after all public affairs over the private. The *Literary Gazette* published two lengthy reviews, and in the second extracts both a long account of slavery in Cuba, and an interview in St. Louis, Missouri with a woman who, on being asked if she is a Christian, says no. She had been separated from her husband, and her three living children had been sold (II: 93–4). Bremer's anger erupts here and slavery is denounced as a 'pagan institution' (II: 94) and an offence in a country which claims to be both Christian and liberal. On board a steamboat on the Mississippi travelling through Louisiana Bremer meets a planter who tells her in precise detail of the violence and suffering in the region. Her reaction is written in the strongest possible terms:

> I seemed to hate my own kind who could perpetrate such cruelties and such injustice. I hated those who could gloss all this over for the interests of trade. I was indignant with myself for having wished to spare myself, to blind myself, to what I must have known would be the inevitable consequences of the institution of slavery. Yes, I ought to have known it; but I thought that it now no longer could be so! (II: 193)

Despite their quite trenchant criticisms of portions of her book, the English reviews must inevitably have fed into Britain's own anti-slavery debates. As Vaughan and Allon state in the *British Quarterly*, 'We accompany Miss Bremer through North and South, through free states and slave states ... In politics, Miss Bremer's sympathies are strongly on the side of freedom and humanity'.[51] The *Athenaeum*

---

50 Lowell, 491.
51 Vaughan and Allon, 570.

reviewer indeed, having noted the numerous references to slavery throughout the book, adds that the tone of Bremer's accounts 'may be readily inferred'.[52] The journal is clearly assuming here that anti-slavery is naturally Bremer's political and personal position on the debate, in common with other popular women writers of the day, and in common with the majority of its readers.

There were counter-narratives to that of Bremer. The American Julia Ward Howe published *A Trip to Cuba* in 1860. It is evident that she had read the previous American travel writings of various noted authors, stating 'I do not know why all celebrated people who write books of travels begin by describing their days of sea-sickness. Dickens, George Combe, Fanny Kemble, Mrs. Stowe, Miss Bremer, and many others, have opened in like manner their valuable remarks on foreign countries'.[53] Howe is also clearly very conscious of the current criticism regarding the naming of private individuals in print, boasting 'I will not, I, give names, to make good-natured people regret the hospitality they have afforded. If they have entertained unawares angels and correspondents of the press, (I use the two terms as synonymous,) they shall not be made aware of it by the sacrifice of their domestic privacy. All celebrated people do this' (52–3). Howe also refers several times to R.H. Dana's *To Cuba and Back, a Vacation Voyage* (1859) only mentioning the author by name; wondering at one point if he also describes the Dominica, 'Well, if he has, I cannot help it' (99) and at another noting that he 'recounts his shopping in Havana' (116). In spite of the flippancy she is, nevertheless, troubled by the issue of slavery, using as a euphemism the term 'compulsory labour' (13), commenting often on miscegenation in far more open terms than are usually encountered in this timeframe, and in the end merely hopes that slavery 'must gradually ameliorate, and slowly die out' (214). Incidentally, her book contains far more offensive physical descriptions of enslaved peoples than anything which might be construed as racist stated by Bremer.

Howe does at one point attempt to link herself to a form of investigative reportage:

> The writer ... came abroad prepared for microscopic, telescopic, and stereoscopic investigation, – but, hedged in on all sides by custom and convenience, she often observed only four very bare walls ... What could she see? Prisons? No ... She invoked the memory of Mrs. Fry and the example of Miss Dix. "Oh, they were saints, you know." ... Bull-fight? No ... Negro ball? "Not exactly the place for a lady." "Miss Bremer went." "Very differently behaved woman from you." (126)

This is supposedly a conversation between the author and her husband, a reference to the local practice that ladies should not go out unaccompanied by a male relative or friend. If the conversation is true, it confirms my overall impression

[52]   'The Homes of the New World', *Athenaeum*, 1153.
[53]   Julia Ward Howe, *A Trip to Cuba* (Boston, 1860), 3. All subsequent references are to this edition.

that women accompanied by male relatives saw far less of the countries they visited than did so-called 'unprotected females'. What the remark about Bremer in this conversation confirms, however, is that this publication is a rebuttal in part to Bremer's account of both the New World and of slavery. Howe's work is very light in tone and often anecdotal, making it a very different production to that of Bremer and lacking Bremer's serious engagement with the topic as the above conversation suggests. Most noticeably, and in clear political terms, Howe remarks a number of times on the English position on slavery towards the end of her book, stating at one point 'The far-off English, in their cool island, could emancipate the slaves in their own Indies, but the English dwelling among them would never have relinquished the welcome service' (233) and finally states that all 'the white handkerchiefs in Exeter Hall will not force the general Congress of Nations to decide questions otherwise than by the laws of convenience and advantage. England as a power has never lifted a finger nor a breath against Russian serfdom or Austrian oppression' (255).[54]

Co-incidentally with Bremer's journey to America, the first instalment of Harriet Beecher Stowe's *Uncle Tom's Cabin* was published in the anti-slavery journal *National Era* in June 1851, just as Fredrika Bremer's journey was coming to its end.[55] Bremer significantly connects her own work to Stowe's by producing a brief *Appendix* with which she concludes her work, announcing that the publication of *Uncle Tom's Cabin* and *A Key to Uncle Tom's Cabin Presenting the Original Facts and Documents upon which the Story is Founded* obviates the necessity for her to produce an Appendix containing 'such of the scenes which I had witnessed, and my own experience in the slave states of America and in Cuba' (II: 653). In a letter to Mary Howitt dated 25 May 1853, Bremer writes: 'The Key is a capital Key to the *hell of slavery*, but it does not open all apartments to the slave-Cabin. *That* I have attempted to do. May God bless her work and mine. I cannot help to think them providentially connected'.[56] The 'Appendix' ends with a hopeful statement on the emancipation issue which several reviewers questioned:

> The South alone knows the burden, the danger, the responsibility, all the great difficulties; it alone has the labour and the sorrows. If it succeed in unloosing the fetters of the slave, and freeing its glorious, grand country from slavery, it will achieve for itself unfading glory. (II: 654)

The reviewer Samuel Warren remarks of Stowe's novel, 'No English man or woman, again, could have written it – no one, but an actual spectator of the scenes described, or one whose life is spent with those moving among them; scenes scarce appreciable by FREE English readers – fathers, mothers, husbands, wives,

---

[54]   Anti-slavery meetings were held in Exeter Hall, The Strand, London.

[55]   Lofsvold, *Fredrika Bremer*, 181.

[56]   Quoted in Lofsvold, *Fredrika Bremer*, 184–5.

brothers and sisters'.[57] Stowe's novel sold approximately 1.5 million copies in Britain and its colonies.[58] As Andrew King observes, sympathy 'provided women with a role and status in society ... There is ample evidence that *Uncle Tom's Cabin* empowered women'.[59] Bremer obviously believed that like Stowe she had produced a work in *The Homes of the New World* that would open eyes and minds in the same way that Gaskell's *Mary Barton* had done five years earlier. And in the heightened atmosphere generated by the appearance of Stowe's novel, Bremer clearly felt empowered by her experiences and her publishing success. She tells the American, Marcus Spring, in her idiosyncratic English that her book is 'exceptional. It is written to the homes of earth and *of* the homes'. In January 1854 she again writes to the Springs claiming her book's enormous success in Sweden but more importantly, that 'letters and papers from England every week now tell me of its full success even there. The sale in England has been so rapid, that in two months ... the book had wholly repaid its outlay'.[60] And this despite the very public row with her translator. Bremer was a novelist who found the new world before her too vast a canvas for fiction but her excitement is palpable when she tells the Springs that 'My treatment of the Slavery question seems to rise in favour both in America and in England', and adds that it seems as if this was the outcome intended by God of her journey to America: 'certainly I had not myself plans or any intentions to work in that directions [sic]'.[61] Reception of her work in the English-speaking world suggests that through Mary Howitt's translation, Bremer did in measurable ways contribute to the discourse of slave emancipation, and that she then reconfigured that discourse, her new messianic identity giving her the courage to work towards facilitating change for the women in Sweden. She was indeed translated.

[57]   Samuel Warren, 'Uncle Tom's Cabin', *Blackwood's Edinburgh Magazine* 74(1853): 395; 393–423.

[58]   See Nicholas Daly, *Sensation and Modernity in the 1860s* (Cambridge, 2009), 15.

[59]   Andrew King, 'Sympathy as Subversion? Reading Lady Audley's Secret in the Kitchen', *Journal of Victorian Culture* 7/1(2002), 76; 60–85.

[60]   Quoted in Rooth, 209 and 231.

[61]   Quoted in Rooth, 231.

Bibliography

Abbeele, Georges Van Den. *Travel as Metaphor from Montaigne to Rousseau.* Minneapolis: University of Minnesota Press, 1992.

Adams, Percy G. *Travel Literature and the Evolution of the Novel.* Lexington, KY: University Press of Kentucky, 1983.

Adams, W.H. Davenport. *Celebrated Women Travellers of the Nineteenth Century.* 1883. London: Swann Sonnenschein, 1889.

Anster, John. 'Goethe'. *Dublin University Magazine* 8 (1836): 350–66.

Arnold, Matthew. 'Preface to Poems (1853)'. *Poetry and Criticism of Matthew Arnold.* Boston: Houghton Mifflin, 1961.

Ashcroft, Bill, Gareth Griffiths and Helen Tiffin. *The Empire Writes Back.* London: Routledge, 1989.

Ashton, Rosemary. *142 Strand. A Radical Address in Victorian London.* London: Chatto & Windus, 2006.

Auden, W.H. *W.H. Auden. Collected Poems.* Ed. Edward Mendelson. London: Faber & Faber, 1976.

Austin, Sarah. 'Specimens of German Genius'. *New Monthly Magazine* 28 (1830): 311–17; 444–50; 519–26; and 29 (1830): 34–42 and 180–89.

Austin, Sarah. 'Translator's Preface'. *Tour in England, Ireland, and France, in the Years 1828 and 1829; with remarks on the Manners and Customs of the Inhabitants, and Anecdotes of Distinguished Public Characters. In a Series of Letters.* By a German Prince. 2 Vols (1.2 and 3.4). London: Effingham Wilson, 1832.

Austin, Sarah, trans. *Characteristics of Goethe. From the German of Falk, von Müller, etc. with Notes, Original and Translated, illustrative of German Literature.* 1833. Philadelphia: Lea & Blanchard, 1841.

Austin, Sarah. 'Translator's Preface'. *England in 1835: Being a Series of Letters written to Friends in Germany, During a Residence in London and Excursions into the Provinces* by Frederick Von Raumer. London: John Murray, 1836.

Austin, Sarah. 'Travels and Travellers in Italy'. *Bentley's Miscellany* 20 (1846): 244–52.

'Austin's German Prose Writers'. *North American Review* 54 (1842): 504–506.

Barbauld, Anna Laetitia. 'Epistle to William Wilberforce, Esq., on the Rejection of the Bill for Abolishing the Slave Trade'. 1792. *Romanticism: An Anthology.* Ed. Duncan Wu. Oxford: Blackwell, 1994.

Basini, Mario. *Real Merthyr.* Bridgend, Wales: Seren, 2008.

Bassnett, Susan. *Comparative Literature. A Critical Introduction*. Oxford: Blackwell, 1993.

Bassnett, Susan. 'Travel Writing and Gender'. *The Cambridge Companion to Travel Writing*. Ed. Peter Hulme and Tim Youngs. Cambridge: Cambridge University Press, 2002.

Bassnett, Susan and André Lefevere. *Translation, History and Culture*. London: Pinter, 1990.

Beaumont, T.W. 'Prospectus'. *British and Foreign Review* 1 (1835): 1–4.

Beer, Gillian. *Open Fields: Science in Cultural Encounter*. Oxford: Clarendon Press, 1996.

Beetham, Margaret. 'Women and the Consumption of Print'. *Women and Literature in Britain, 1800–1900*. Ed. Joanne Shattock. Cambridge: Cambridge University Press, 2001.

Behdad, Ali. *Belated Travelers. Orientalism in the Age of Colonial Dissolution*. Durham and London; Duke University Press, 1994.

Beinecke Rare Book and Manuscript Library, Yale University. Speck Collection, MS J23b M833 7:30. Anna Jameson, Manuscript Letters.

Beinecke Rare Book and Manuscript Library, Yale University. Osborn Files. Sarah Austin to Anna Jameson, 26–28 September 1835. No accession number.

'Belgium and Western Germany by Mrs. Trollope and Sir A. B. Faulkner'. *Quarterly Review* 52 (1834): 203–33.

Bellairs, Nona. *Going Abroad; or, Glimpses of Art and Character in France and Italy*. London: Charles J. Skeet, 1857.

Berman, Antoine. *The Experience of the Foreign. Culture and Translation in Romantic Germany*. Trans. S. Heyvaert. Albany, NY: State University of New York, 1992.

Bird, Christopher. 'Introduction'. *British and Foreign Review* 1 (1835): 5–16.

Bird, Isabella. *The Englishwoman in America*. 1856. Köln: Könemann, 2000.

Bird, Isabella. *The Golden Chersonese*. 1883. Köln: Könemann, 2000.

Blackie, J.S. 'Eckermann's *Conversations with Göthe*'. *Foreign Quarterly Review* 18 (1836): 1–30.

Bledsoe, Robert. 'Henry Fothergill Chorley'. *Oxford Dictionary of National Biography*. Oxford: Oxford University Press, 2004.

Brake, Laurel. *Print in Transition, 1850–1910. Studies in Media and Book History*. Basingstoke: Palgrave, 2001.

Brake, Laurel and Marysa Demoor, Eds. *Dictionary of Nineteenth-Century Journalism*. Gent and London, Academia Press and The British Library, 2009.

Bremer, Fredrika. *The Neighbours: A Story of Every-Day Life*. Trans. Mary Howitt. 2 Vols. London: Longman, Brown, Green & Longmans, 1842.

Bremer, Fredrika. *The Home: or, Family Cares and Family Joys*. Trans. Mary Howitt. 2 Vols. London: Longman, Brown, Green & Longmans, 1843.

Bremer, Fredrika. *The President's Daughters; including Nina*. Trans. Mary Howitt. 3 Vols. London: Longman, Brown, Green & Longmans, 1843.

Bremer, Fredrika. *Domestic Life or The H— Family*. Trans. Mary Howitt. 2 Vols. London: Thomas Allman, 1844.

Bremer, Fredrika. *New Sketches of Every-Day Life: A Diary*. Together with *Strife and Peace*. Trans. Mary Howitt. London: Longman, Brown, Green & Longmans, 1844.

Bremer, Frederika [sic]. *England in 1851. Sketches of a Tour in England*. Trans. from the German by L.A.H. Boulogne: Merridew, 1853.

Bremer, Fredrika. 'Autograph Letter to Elizabeth Gaskell 29 September 1853'. *Gaskell and the Brontës. Literary Manuscripts of Elizabeth Gaskell (1810–65) and the Brontës from the Brotherton Library, University of Leeds*. 7 reels of 35mm silver-halide microfilm and guide. Marlborough: Adam Matthew, 2003.

Bremer, Fredrika. *The Homes of the New World; Impressions of America*. Trans. Mary Howitt. 1853. Two Volumes. London: Johnson Reprint, 1968.

Bremer, Fredrika. 'A Card'. *The Times* (23 December 1853): 7.

Bremer, Fredrika. 'A Word in Reply to Mrs. Howitt'. *The Times* (24 January, 1854): 8.

Bremer, Fredrika. *Two Years in Switzerland and Italy*. 1860. Trans. Mary Howitt. 2 Vols. London: Hurst & Blackett, 1861.

'Brief Notices'. *Eclectic Review* NS4 (1852): 375.

'Briefe eines Verstorbenen'. *Athenaeum* (18 February 1832): 105–107; (25 February 1832): 122–3 and (3 March 1832): 141–2.

Bromwich, Rachel and D. Simon Evans, *Culhwch and Olwen. An Edition and Study of the Oldest Arthurian Tale*. Cardiff: University of Wales Press, 1992.

Bruyn, Günter de and Gerhard Wolf, Eds. *Märkischer Dichtergaren*. Berlin: Der Morgan, 1983.

Buller, Charles. 'Letters of a German Prince'. *Foreign Quarterly Review* 9 (1832): 290–312

Burton, J.H. 'Across the Channel'. *Blackwood's Edinburgh Magazine* 92 (1862): 15–39.

Busk, Mary Margaret. 'Horae Germanicae (No. XX): Schiller's *Wilhelm Tell* (Part 1)'. *Blackwood's Edinburgh Magazine* 17 (1825): 299–318 and (Part 2): 417–36.

Busk, Mary Margaret. 'Horae Germanicae (No. XXI): *Sappho* by Franz Grillparzer'. *Blackwood's Edinburgh Magazine* 19 (1826): 404–15.

Busk, Mary Margaret. 'Russell de Albuquerque'. *Foreign Quarterly Review* 12 (1833): 241–5.

Busk, Mary Margaret. 'Madame Dudevant's Novels – *Indiana* – *Valentine, etc*'. *Foreign Quarterly Review* 14 (1834): 271–97.

Busk, Mary Margaret. 'English Literature'. *Foreign Quarterly Review* 15 (1835): 347–60.

Busk, Mary Margaret. 'French and German Belles Lettres'. *Blackwood's Edinburgh Magazine* 37 (1835): 513–22.

Busk, Mary Margaret [?]. 'Raumer's *England in 1835*'. *Foreign Quarterly Review* 17 (1836): 209–16.

Busk, Mary Margaret. 'Lucien Bonaparte and Friedrich Von Raumer'. *Blackwood's Edinburgh Magazine* 41 (1837): 21–31.

Busk, Mary Margaret. 'Sternberg's *Tales and Novels*'. *Foreign Quarterly Review* 18 (1837): 433–54.

Busk, Mary Margaret. 'Mrs. Trollope's Vienna and the Austrians'. *Blackwood's Edinburgh Magazine* 43 (1838): 494–508.

Busk, Mary Margaret. 'Philosophy of Fiction: Balzac, Dumas, Soulie, Etc.'. *London and Westminster Review* 29 (1838): 73–98.

Butler, E.M. 'Introduction'. *A Regency Visitor. The English Tour of Prince Pückler-Muskau Described in his Letters 1826–1828*. Trans. Sarah Austin. Ed. E.M. Butler. London: Collins, 1957.

Buzard, James. *The Beaten Track. European Tourism, Literature, and the Ways to 'Culture' 1800–1918*. Oxford: Clarendon, 1993.

Buzard, James. 'The Grand Tour and after (1660–1840)'. *Cambridge Companion to Travel Writing*. Ed. Peter Hulme and Tim Youngs. Cambridge: Cambridge University Press, 2002.

C., M. [Mary Carpenter]. 'Offerings from the Old World to the New, by Englishwomen'. *Howitt's Journal* 3 (1848): 26.

'Canada'. *Saturday Review* 11 (26 January 1861): 100–101.

Carlyle, Thomas. 'Historic Survey of German Poetry'. 1831. Repr. *Critical and Miscellaneous Essays*. Vol. II. London: Chapman and Hall, 1901.

Carlyle, Thomas. 'Goethe's Works'. *Foreign Quarterly Review* 10 (1832): 1–44.

Carlyle, Thomas and Jane Welsh. *The Collected Letters of Thomas and Jane Welsh Carlyle*. 7 Vols. Ed. Charles Richard Sanders. Durham, NC: Duke University Press, 1977.

Cheney, R.H. 'Italian Tours and Tourists'. *Quarterly Review* 103 (1858): 346–90.

Chorley, H.F. 'Mrs. Jameson's Winter Studies and Summer Rambles'. *British and Foreign Review* 8 (1839): 134–53.

Chorley, H.F. 'Lady Travellers'. *British and Foreign Quarterly* 13 (1842): 486–508.

Christ, Carol T. '"The Hero as Man of Letters": Masculinity and Victorian Nonfiction Prose'. *Victorian Sages and Cultural Discourse. Renegotiating Gender and Power*. Ed. Thaïs Morgan. London: Rutgers University Press, 1990.

'Classical Learning in England'. *North American Review* 54 (1842): 269–82.

Clifford, James. *Routes. Travel and Translation in the late Twentieth Century*. London Harvard University Press, 1997.

Colley, Linda. *Britons. Forging the Nation 1707–1837*. New Haven and London: Yale University Press, 1992.

Cooley, W.D. [?]. 'Meyen's Voyage Round the World'. *Foreign Quarterly Review* 15 (1835): 1–48.

Copley, Stephen and Peter Garside, Eds. 'Introduction'. *The Politics of the Picturesque. Literature, landscape and aesthetics since 1770*. Cambridge: Cambridge University Press, 1994.

Courtney, W.P. rev. Ian Maxted. 'Richard John King'. *Oxford Dictionary of National Biography*. Oxford: Oxford University Press, 2004.

Craik, Dinah Mulock. *Mistress and Maid*. 1862. London: Hurst and Blackett, n.d.

Croker, John Wilson. 'Raumer's *England in 1835*'. *Quarterly Review* 56 (1836): 530–83.

Cronin, Michael. *Across the Lines. Travel, Language, Translation*. Cork: Cork University Press, 2000.

Cubitt, Geoffrey. *Imagining Nations*. Manchester: Manchester University Press, 1998.

Curran, Eileen. 'Holding on by a Pen: the Story of a Lady/Reviewer Mary Margaret Busk (1779–1863)'. *Victorian Periodicals Review* 31/1 (1998): 9–30.

Daly, Nicholas. *Sensation and Modernity in the 1860s*. Cambridge: Cambridge University Press, 2009.

Davies, Ceri. *Welsh Literature and the Classical Tradition*. Cardiff: University of Wales, 1995.

Dearnley, Moira. '"I Came Hither, a Stranger": A View of Wales in the Novels of Anne Beale (1815–1900)'. *New Welsh Review* 1 (1989): 27–32.

'Death of Mr. F. Sinnett'. Adelaide *Register* (29 November 1866): 6.

Di Biase, Carmine G. 'Introduction'. *Travel and Translation in the Early Modern Period*. New York: Rodopi, 2006.

Duncan, James and Derek Gregory, Eds. 'Introduction'. *Writes of Passage. Reading Travel Writing*. London: Routledge, 1999.

Eliot, George. 'Ashford Owen's *A Lost Love* and C.W.S. Brooks's *Aspen Court*'. Repr. *Selected Essays, Poems and Other Writings*. Ed. A.S. Byatt. London: Penguin, 1990.

Eliot, George. 'Dred, Never Too Late to Mend and Hertha'. Repr. *Selected Essays, Poems and Other Writings*, Ed. A.S. Byatt and Nicholas Warren. London, Penguin, 1990.

Eliot, George. *The George Eliot Letters*. Ed. Gordon S. Haight, 9 Vols. New Haven: Yale University Press, 1954–78.

Eliot, George. *Middlemarch*. 1871–2. London: Everyman, 1997.

Eliot, Simon. 'Some Trends in British Book Production 1800–1919'. *Literature in the Marketplace. Nineteenth-Century British Publishing & Reading Practices*. Ed. John O. Jordan and Robert L. Patten. Cambridge: Cambridge University Press, 1995.

Ellis, T.P. and John Lloyd, *The Mabinogion. A New Translation*. Oxford: Clarendon, 1929.

'English on the Continent, The'. *Foreign Quarterly Review* 32 (1843): 90–106.

Enzensberger, Hans Magnus. Trans. Gerd Gemünden and Kenn Johnson. 'A Theory of Tourism'. *New German Critique* 65 (1996): 113–35.

Esterhammer, Angela. 'Review of Antoine Berman's *The Experience of the Foreign: Culture and Translation in Romantic Germany*. Trans. S. Heyvaert'. *Wordsworth Circle* 27 (1996): 232–4.

Euben, Roxanne L. *Journeys to the Other Shore. Muslim and Western Travelers in Search of Knowledge*. Princeton and Oxford: Princeton University Press, 2006.

Faith, Nicholas. *The World the Railways Made*. 1990. London: Pimlico, 1994.

Falk, Johann, Friedrich von Müller, et al. *Characteristics of Goethe. From the German of Falk, von Müller, etc. with Notes, Original and Translated, illustrative of German Literature*. Trans. Sarah Austin. 1833. Philadelphia: Lea & Blanchard, 1841.

Felden, Tamara. 'The Different Faces of Slavery. German-Speaking Women Authors of the 19th Century Discuss Race, Gender, and Culture'. *Schatzkammer der Deutschen Sprache, Dichtung und Geschichte* 23 (1997): 31–48.

Ferris, Ina. 'Mobile Words: Romantic Travel Writing and Print Anxiety'. *Modern Language Quarterly* 60/4 (1999): 451–68.

'Few Words on Tours and Tourists, A'. *Fraser's Magazine* 63 (1861): 340–55.

Finch, Marianne. *An Englishwoman's Experience in America*. London: Richard Bentley, 1853.

Finkelstein, David. '"Long and Intimate Connections": Constructing a Scottish Identity for *Blackwood's Magazine*'. *Nineteenth-Century Media and the Construction of Identities*. Ed. Laurel Brake, Bill Bell and David Finkelstein. Basingstoke: Palgrave, 2000.

Fisher, D.R. 'Thomas Wentworth Beaumont'. *Oxford Dictionary of National Biography*. Oxford: Oxford University Press, 2004.

Ford, Patrick K. *The Mabinogi and other Medieval Welsh Tales*. London: University of Cardiff, 1977.

'Frederika [sic] Bremer's Impressions of America'. *Spectator* 26 (1853): 898–9.

'French Criticism of English Writers'. *Foreign Quarterly Review* 30 (1842): 1–12.

'French Libels on the English'. *New Monthly Magazine* 39 (1833): 401–10.

Fry, Michael. 'John Hill Burton'. *Oxford Dictionary of National Biography*. Oxford: Oxford University Press, 2004.

Fynes, R.C.C. 'Max Müller'. *Oxford Dictionary of National Biography*. Oxford: Oxford University Press, 2004.

Gantz, Jeffrey. *The Mabinogion*. Harmondsworth, Middlesex: Penguin, 1976.

Garland, Henry and Mary, Eds. *Oxford Companion to German Literature*. Oxford: Oxford University Press, 1997.

Gaskell, Elizabeth. 'The Well of Pen-Morfa'. Repr. in *The Moorland Cottage and Other Stories*, Ed. Suzanne Lewis. Oxford: Oxford University Press, 1995.

Gates, Barbara. *Kindred Nature. Victorian and Edwardian Women Embrace the Living World*. Chicago and London: University of Chicago Press, 1998.

Genovese, Eugene D. *Roll, Jordan, Roll. The World the Slaves Made*. London: Andre Deutsch, 1975.

Gentzler, Edwin. *Contemporary Translation Theories*. London: Routledge, 1993.

'German Tourists'. *Westminster Review* 22 (1835): 510–20.

Girton College, University of Cambridge, GCPP Parkes 6/59/1 and 2 and 3.

Goethe, Johann Wolfgang von. *Iphigenia in Tauris. A Play in Five Acts*. Trans. David Luke. *Goethe's Collected Works. Volume 8. Verse Plays and Epic*. Ed. Cyrus Hamlin and Frank Ryder. Princeton, NJ: Princeton University Press, 1987.

Goethe und Schiller Archiv, Weimar, Germany. Anna Jameson, Manuscript Letters, MSS GSA 40/VIII, 9, 1 and GSA 40/VIII, 4.

Guest, Lady Charlotte. *The Mabinogion from the Llyfr Coch o Hergest and other Ancient Welsh Manuscripts, with an English Translation and Notes*. 3 Vols. London: Longman, Brown, Green, and Longmans, 1849.

Guest, Lady Charlotte. *Lady Charlotte Guest. Extracts from her Journal 1833– 1852*. Ed. The Earl of Bessborough. London: John Murray, 1950.

Guest, Revel and Angela V. John. *Lady Charlotte. A Biography of the Nineteenth Century*. London: Weidenfeld & Nicolson, 1989.

Hadgraft, Cecil. 'Introduction'. *The Fiction Fields of Australia* by Frederick Sinnett. St. Lucia: University of Queensland Press, 1966.

Halsted, Caroline. *Investigation; or, Travels in the Boudoir*. London: Smith, Elder, 1846.

Hamburger, Lotte and Joseph. *Troubled Lives: John and Sarah Austin*. Toronto: University of Toronto Press, 1985.

Hamburger, Lotte and Joseph. *Contemplating Adultery. The Secret Life of a Victorian Woman*. New York: Fawcett Columbine, 1991.

Handbook for Travellers in Switzerland. 1837. 16th edn. London: John Murray, 1879.

Hannay, James. 'The Classics in Translations'. *Cornhill Magazine* 16 (1867): 109–28.

Harling, Philip. 'Abraham Hayward'. *Oxford Dictionary of National Biography*. Oxford: Oxford University Press, 2004.

Hayward, Abraham. 'Dr. Meyen's Voyage round the World'. *Quarterly Review* 53 (1835): 313–38.

'Home; or, Family Cares and Family Joys, The'. *Athenaeum* No. 811 (1843): 457–8.

'Homes of the New World, The'. *Athenaeum* No. 1353 (1 October 1853): 1153–4.

'Homes of the New World, The'. *Literary Gazette and Journal of Science and Art* No. 1914 (24 September 1853): 929–33 and No. 1916 (8 October 1853): 973–5.

Houghton, Walter E. *The Wellesley Index to Victorian Periodicals 1824–1900*. Ed. Walter E. Houghton et al. 5 Vols. Toronto and London: University of Toronto Press and Routledge & Kegan Paul, 1987.

Houston, Gail Turley. *Royalties. The Queen and Victorian Writers*. Charlottesville and London: University Press of Virginia, 1999.

Howarth, Janet, Ed. 'Editor's Introduction'. *The Higher Education of Women (1866)* by Emily Davies. London: Hambledon, 1988.

Howe, Julia Ward. *A Trip to Cuba*. Boston: Ticknor and Fields, 1860.

Howitt, Mary. 'Preface'. *New Sketches of Every-Day Life: A Diary*. London: Longman, Brown, Green & Longmans, 1844.

Howitt, Mary. 'Memoir of Frederick Douglass'. *People's Journal* 2 (1847): 302–305.

Howitt, Mary. 'William Lloyd Garrison'. *People's Journal* 2 (1847): 141–4; 166–8; 179–80; and 185–6.

Howitt, Mary. 'To the Editor of the Times'. *The Times* (26 December 1853): 9.

Howitt, Mary. *Mary Howitt. An Autobiography*. Ed. Margaret Howitt. 1889. London, Isbister, n.d.

Howitt, William. *German Experiences: addressed to The English; both Stayers at Home, and Goers Abroad*. London: Longman, Brown, Green, and Longmans, 1844.

Huc, Évariste. *The Chinese Empire: Forming a Sequel to the Work Entitled "Recollections of a Journey through Tartary and Thibet"*. Trans. Jane Sinnett. London: Longman, Brown, Green & Longmans, 1855.

'Huc's Chinese Empire'. *Spectator* 28 (1855): 54–6.

Imlah, Ann G. *Britain and Switzerland 1845–60*. London: Longmans, 1966.

'Improvisatore; or Life in Italy, The'. *Quarterly Review* 75 (1844–5): 497–518.

'Introduction'. *A Handbook for Travellers in South Wales and its Borders including the River Wye. With a travelling map*. London: John Murray, 1860.

Jameson, Anna. *Early Canadian Sketches by Mrs. Jameson*. Intro. G.H. Needler. Toronto: Burns & MacEachern, n.d.

Jameson, Anna. *Visits and Sketches at Home and Abroad*. 1834. 3 Vols. London: Saunders & Otley, 1835.

Jameson, Anna. *Characteristics of Women, Moral, Political and Historical*. 1832. 2 Vols. London: Saunders & Otley, 1836.

Jameson, Anna. *Diary of an Ennuyée*. 1826. London: Saunders & Otley, 1838.

Jameson, Anna. *Social Life in Germany, illustrated in the Acted Dramas of Her Royal Highness the Princess Amelia of Saxony*. London: Saunders & Otley, 1840.

Jameson, Anna. *Winter Studies and Summer Rambles in Canada*. 1838. Toronto: McClelland & Stewart, 1990.

Jameson, Anna. *Letters of Anna Jameson to Ottilie von Goethe*. Ed. G.H. Needler. London: Oxford University Press, 1939.

Jenkyns, Richard. *The Victorians and Ancient Greece*. Oxford: Basil Blackwell, 1980.

Johnston, Judith. *Anna Jameson: Victorian, Feminist, Woman of Letters*. Aldershot: Ashgate, 1997.

Johnston, Judith. 'The Pyramids of Egypt: Monuments to Victorian Desire'. *Australasian Victorian Studies Journal* 7 (2001): 71–88.

Johnston, Judith. 'Victorian Appropriations: Lady Charlotte Guest translates *The Mabinogion*' in *Studies in Medievalism. Appropriating the Middle Ages: Scholarship, Politics, Fraud* XI (2001) published by Boydell and Brewer.

Johnston, Judith. 'Fracturing Perspectives of Italy in Anna Jameson's *Diary of an Ennuyée*'. *Women's Writing* 11 (2004): 11–24.

Johnston, Judith. 'Britain's Intellectual Empire and the Transformation of Culture: The Case of Mary Howitt and Fredrika Bremer'. *Australasian Victorian Studies Journal* 11 (2005): 54–64.

Johnston, Judith. 'Sarah Austin and the Politics of Translation in the 1830s'. *Victorian Review* 34/1 (2008): 101–113.

Johnstone, Christian Isobel. 'Travels in Germany; By Mrs. Trollope, Mrs. Jameson, and Simeon South, Esq.' *Tait's Edinburgh Magazine* 1 (1834): 552–67.

Johnstone, Christian Isobel. 'Raumer's England in 1835'. *Tait's Edinburgh Magazine* 3 (1836): 315–25.

Johnstone, Christian Isobel. 'Mrs. Jameson's Winter Studies and Summer Rambles in Canada'. *Tait's Edinburgh Magazine* 6 (1839): 69–81.

Johnstone, Christian Isobel. 'New Novels. The Neighbours, – Evelyn Howard'. *Tait's Edinburgh Magazine* 13 (1842): 779–99.

Jones, Gwyn and Thomas Jones. *The Mabinogion*. 1948. London: Everyman, 1974.

Kellett, E.E. 'The Press'. *Early Victorian England, 1830–1865*. Ed. G.M. Young. 2 Vols. London: Oxford University Press and Humphrey Milford, 1934.

Kemble, Frances Anne. *Records of a Girlhood*. New York: Henry Holt, 1879.

King, Andrew. 'Sympathy as Subversion? Reading *Lady Audley's Secret* in the Kitchen'. *Journal of Victorian Culture* 7/1 (2002): 60–85.

King, R.J. 'Travellers and Handbooks'. *Edinburgh Review* 138 (1873): 483–510.

Kohl, J.G. *Travels in Canada, and Through the States of New York and Pennsylvania*. Trans. Mrs. Percy Sinnett. Revised by the author. London: George Manwaring, 1861.

Kranidis, Rita. 'Introduction: New Subjects, Familiar Grounds'. *Imperial Objects. Essays on Victorian Women's Emigration and the Unauthorized Imperial Experience*. Ed. Rita Kranidis. New York: Twayne, 1998.

'Lady's Second Journey Round the World, A'. *Literary Gazette* No. 2031 (1855): 810–12.

'Lady's Voyage round the World, A – [Eine Frauenfahrt um die Welt]'. *Athenaeum* No. 1232 (7 June 1851): 602–604.

Laing, Samuel. 'Frederika (sic) Bremer's Novels'. *North British Review* 1 (1844): 168–83.

Langbauer, Laurie. *Novels of Everyday Life: The Series in English Fiction, 1850–1930*. Ithaca, NY: Cornell University Press, 1999.

Latané Jr., D.E. 'Mary Margaret Busk'. *New Oxford Dictionary of National Biography*. Vol. 9. Oxford: Oxford University Press, 2004.

Lefevere, André and Susan Bassnett. 'Introduction: Proust's Grandmother and the Thousand and One Nights: the "Cultural Turn" in Translation Studies'. *Translation, History and Culture*. Ed. Susan Bassnett and André Lefevere. London: Pinter, 1990.

Lefevere, André. 'Translation: Its Genealogy in the West'. *Translation, History and Culture*. Ed. Susan Bassnett and André Lefevere. London: Pinter, 1990.

Lefevere, André, Ed. *Translation/History/Culture. A Sourcebook*. London: Routledge, 1992.

Lefevere, André. *Translation, Rewriting, and the Manipulation of Literary Fame*. London: Routledge, 1992.

Leonard, John. *Lonesome Rangers. Homeless Minds, Promised Lands, Fugitive Cultures*. New York: New Press, 2002.

Lofsvold, Laurel Ann. 'Blaming the Messenger: Mary Howitt's Translation of Fredrika Bremer's *Hemmen i den Nya verlden*'. *Scandinavica* 35 (1996): 213–31.

Lofsvold, Laurel Ann. *Fredrika Bremer and the Writing of America*. Lund, Sweden: Lund University Press, 1999.

Lowe, Emily. *Unprotected Females in Norway; or, the Pleasantest Way of Travelling There, Passing through Denmark and Sweden*. London: George Routledge, 1857.

Lowell, J.R. 'New Translations of the Writings of Miss Bremer'. *North American Review* 58 (1844): 480–508.

'Mabinogion, The'. *Athenaeum* (24 November 1838): 833–5.

'Mabinogion, The, – Early Welsh Legends'. *Spectator* 2 (1838): 1067–8.

'Mabinogion, The, Part II'. *Monthly Review* 150 (1839): 132.

'Mabinogion, The, Part III'. *Monthly Review* 153 (1840): 610.

'Mabinogion, The, Part IV'. *Athenaeum* (30 April 1842): 379.

'Mabinogion, The, Part IV'. *Monthly Review* 158 (1842): 284–7.

Manton, Jo. *Mary Carpenter and the Children of the Streets*. London: Heinemann, 1976.

McCord, Norman. *British History 1815–1906*. Oxford: Oxford University Press, 1991.

Merivale, Herman. 'Mrs. Austin's *Characteristics of Goethe*', 57 (1833): 371–403.

Mill, John Stuart. 'Periodical Literature. Edinburgh Review'. *Westminster Review* 1 (1824): 505–41.

Mill, John Stuart. 'On Liberty'. *On Liberty, Representative Government, The Subjection of Women. Three Essays by John Stuart Mill*. Introduced by Millicent Garrett Fawcett. 1859. London: Oxford University Press, c. 1912.

Mill, John Stuart. *The Subjection of Women*. 1869. New York: Prometheus, 1986.

Miller, J. Hillis. 'Border Crossings, Translating Theory: Ruth'. *The Translatability of Cultures. Figurations of the Space Between*. Ed. Sanford Budick and Wolfgang Iser. Stanford, CA: Stanford University Press, 1996.

Mills, Sara. *Discourses of Difference. An Analysis of Women's Travel Writing and Colonialism*. London: Routledge, 1991.

Mills, Sara. *Discourse*. London: Routledge, 1997.

Milnes, Richard Monkton, 1st Baron Houghton. 'On the Present Social Results of Classical Education'. *Essays on a Liberal Education*, Ed. F.W. Farrar. London: Macmillan, 1868.

Monticelli, Rita. 'In Praise of Art and Literature. Intertextuality, Translations and Migrations of Knowledge in Anna Jameson's Travel Writings'. *Prose Studies. History, Theory, Criticism* 27/3 (2005): 299–312.

'Mrs. Jameson in Canada'. *Monthly Review* 148 (1839): 65–79.

'Mrs. Jameson's Winter Studies and Summer Rambles in Canada'. *Spectator* 11 (1838): 1166–8.

Mügge, Theodore. *Switzerland in 1847: and its Condition, Political, Social, Moral, and Physical, Before the War*. Edited by Mrs. Percy Sinnett. 2 Volumes. London: Richard Bentley, 1848.

Murphy, G. Martin. 'Michael Joseph Quin'. *New Oxford Dictionary of National Biography*. Vol. 45. Oxford: Oxford University Press, 2004.

Mylne, Margaret. 'Woman, and her Social Position'. *Westminster Review* 35 (1841): 24–52.

'Mythology and Legends'. *Monthly Review* 148 (1839): 20–29.

National Library of Scotland, Edinburgh, Blackwood Papers. MS4014, ff. 103–104 and 113–14, MS4029, ff. 99–100; MS4032, f. 73; MS4040, ff. 126–7; MS4046, ff. 90–91 and MS4714, ff. 146–7.

National Library of Scotland, Edinburgh, John Murray Archive. Sarah Austin. Manuscript letters MS40031 dated 25 December 1830 and 22 March 1831.

National Library of Scotland, Edinburgh. MSS. 1774, f. 32, Sarah Austin to Jane Welsh Carlyle.

'National Literature – The Mabinogion: Legends of the Rhine'. *Spectator* 12 (1839): 760–61.

Nelson, J.L. 'A Sense of Humour in Daddy's Presence'. *London Review of Books* 25/11(5 June 2003): 23–4.

[Note of Rectification]. *Athenaeum* No.1365 (24 December 1853): 1557–8.

'Note on *Homes of the New World*'. *Athenaeum* No. 1365 (24 December 1853): 1557–8.

'Notices'. *Monthly Review* 153 (1840): 610.

'Novels'. *Monthly Review* 159 (1842): 507–23.

O'Donnell, Arnout. 'Prince Talleyrand'. *Blackwood's Edinburgh Magazine* 37 (1835): 76–81.

Onslow, Barbara. *Women of the Press in Nineteenth-Century Britain*. Basingstoke: Macmillan, 2000.

'Our Weekly Gossip on Literature and Art'. *Athenaeum* (23 July 1836): 523.

Parker, Charles Stuart. 'On the History of Classical Education'. *Essays on a Liberal Education*. Ed. F.W. Farrar. London: Macmillan, 1868.

Petermann, Augustus. 'Madame Pfeiffer in Africa'. *Athenaeum* No. 1258 (6 December 1851): 1281.

Pfeiffer, Ida. *A Woman's Journey Round the World*. Trans. Anon. London: Office of the National Illustrated Library, 1852.

Pfeiffer, Ida. 'Introduction'. *A Lady's Voyage Round The World: A Selected Translation from the German of Ida Pfeiffer*. London: Longman, Brown, Green, and Longmans, 1852.

Pfeiffer, Ida. 'Author's Preface'. *Visit to Iceland and the Scandinavian North*. 2nd edn. London: Ingram Cooke, 1853.

Pfeiffer, Ida. *A Lady's Second Journey Round The World*. London: Longman, Brown, Green, and Longmans, 1855.

Pfeiffer, Ida. *A Lady's Voyage Round the World: a Selected Translation from the German of Ida Pfeiffer*. Trans. Jane Sinnett. 1851. London: Century, 1988.

Phillips, Rhys D. *Lady Charlotte Guest and the Mabinogion*. Carmarthen: Spurrell, 1921.

Powell, David. *Nationhood and Identity. The British State since 1800*. London: I.B. Tauris, 2002.

Pratt, Mary Louise. *Imperial Eyes. Travel Writing and Transculturation*. London: Routledge, 1992.

'Prince Pückler Muscau and Mrs. Trollope'. *North American Review* 36 (1833): 1–48.

Pückler-Muskau, Hermann. *Tour in England, Ireland, and France, in the Years 1828 and 1829; with remarks on the Manners and Customs of the Inhabitants, and Anecdotes of Distinguished Public Characters. In a Series of Letters*. By a German Prince. Trans. Sarah Austin. 2 Vols (1.2 and 3.4). London: Effingham Wilson, 1832.

Pückler-Muskau, Hermann. *A Regency Visitor. The English Tour of Prince Pückler-Muskau Described in his Letters 1826–1828*. Trans. Sarah Austin. Ed. E.M. Butler. London: Collins, 1957.

Pugh, David V. 'Goethe the Dramatist'. *Cambridge Companion to Goethe*. Ed. Leslie Sharpe. Cambridge: Cambridge University Press, 2002.

Pym, Anthony. *Exploring Translation Theories*. New York: Routledge, 2010.

Quin, M.J. 'Raumer's *England in 1835*'. *Dublin Review* 1 (1836): 131–51.

Raumer, Frederick Von. *England in 1835: Being a Series of Letters written to Friends in Germany, during a Residence in London and Excursions into the Provinces*. Trans. Sarah Austin. 3 Vols. London: John Murray, 1836.

'Red Book of Hergest, The'. *Saint Pauls* 3 (1868): 308–20.

'Reviews'. *Magazine of Domestic Economy* 1 (1836): 305.

Richards, Jeffrey. 'The Role of the Railways'. *Ruskin and Environment. The Storm-Cloud of the Nineteenth Century*. Ed. Michael Wheeler. Manchester: Manchester University Press, 1995.

Rigby, Elizabeth. 'Lady Travellers'. *Quarterly Review* 76 (1845): 98–137.

Robertson, Janet. *Lights and Shades on a Traveller's Path; or, Scenes in Foreign Lands*. London: Hope, 1851.

Rojek, Chris. *Decentering Leisure. Rethinking Leisure Theory*. London: Sage, 1995.

Rojek, Chris and John Urry, Eds. *Touring Cultures. Transformations of Travel and Theory*. London: Routledge, 1997.

Rooth, Signe Alice. *Seeress of the Northland. Fredrika Bremer's American Journey, 1849–1851*. Philadelphia: American Swedish Historical Foundation, 1955.

Ross, Janet. *Three Generations of English Women. Memoirs and Correspondence of Susannah Taylor, Sarah Austin, and Lady Duff Gordon*. London: T. Fisher Unwin, 1893.

Roy, Wendy. *Maps of Difference. Canada, Women, and Travel*. Montreal and Kingston: McGill-Queen's University Press, 2005.

Russell, C.W. 'Huc's Chinese Empire'. *Dublin Review* 38 (1855): 134–69.

Said, Edward. *Orientalism*. London: Routledge and Kegan Paul, 1978.

Said, Edward. 'Reflections on Exile'. *Granta* 13 (1984): 159–72.

Said, Edward. *Culture and Imperialism*. 1993. London: Vintage, 1994.

Saunders, Ian. *Open Texts, Partial Maps. A Literary Theory Handbook*. Nedlands, WA: CASAL, University of Western Australia, 1993.

Scholl, Lesa. *Translation, Authorship and the Victorian Professional Woman*. Farnham: Ashgate, 2011.

Schweitzer, Christoph. 'Sarah Austin's Assessment of Goethe's Character and Works and of Weimar'. *A Reassessment of Weimar Classicism*. Ed. Gerhart Hoffmeister. Lampeter: Edwin Mellen, 1996.

Sedgwick, Catherine. 'Slavery in New England'. *Bentley's Miscellany* 34 (1853): 417–24.

Shattock, Joanne. 'Work for Women: Margaret Oliphant's Journalism'. *Nineteenth-Century Media and the Construction of Identities*. Ed. Laurel Brake, Bill Bell and David Finkelstein. Basingstoke: Palgrave, 2000.

Shelley, Mary. *Rambles in Germany and Italy in 1840, 1842, and 1843* (1844). Repr. in *The Novels and Selected Works of Mary Shelley. Volume 8. Travel Writing*. Ed. Jeanne Moskal. London: William Pickering, 1996.

Simon, Sherry. *Gender in Translation. Cultural Identity and the Politics of Transmission*. London: Routledge, 1996.

Simpson, James. 'The Authority of Culture: Some Reflections on the Reception of a Classic'. *Goethe and the English-Speaking World. Essays from the Cambridge Symposium for his 250th Anniversary*. Ed. Nicholas Boyle and John Guthrie. New York: Camden House, 2002.

Sinnett, Jane. 'Schiller'. *Dublin Review* 11 (1841): 477–505.

Sinnett, Jane. *Byways of History from the Twelfth to the Sixteenth Century*. 2 Vols. London: Longmans, Brown, Green, and Longmans, 1847.

Sinnett, Jane. 'Youthful Life and Rambling Sketches'. *Athenaeum* No. 1016 (17 April 1847): 409–11.

Sinnett, Jane. 'Editor's Preface'. *Switzerland in 1847: and its Condition, Political, Social, Moral, and Physical, Before the War*. By Theodore Mügge. Edited by Mrs. Percy Sinnett. 2 Volumes. London: Richard Bentley, 1848.

Sinnett, Jane. 'Switzerland and its Condition'. *Westminster Review* 48 (1848): 531–52.

Sinnett, Jane. 'Colonization and Emigration'. *Dublin Review* 26 (1849): 316–37.

Sinnett, Jane. 'The Present Time'. *Westminster Review* 50 (1849): 577–83.

Sinnett, Jane. 'Alpine Journeyings'. Parts I and II. *Westminster Review* 51 (1849): 497–512 and 52 (1850): 545–61.

Sinnett, Jane. 'Foreign Literature'. *Westminster Review* 52 (1850): 227–31.

Sinnett, Jane. 'Contemporary Literature of Germany'. *Westminster Review* 57 (1852): 677–97.

Sinnett, Jane. 'Translator's Preface'. *A Lady's Voyage round the World; a Selected Translation from the German of Ida Pfeiffer*. London: Longman, Brown, Green, and Longmans, 1852.

Sinnett, Jane. 'Contemporary Literature of Germany'. *Westminster Review* 59 (1853): 617–34.

Sinnett, Jane. 'Belles Lettres'. Review of Edouard Servan de Sugny's *La Muse Ottomane*. *Westminster Review* 61 (1854): 301–15.

Sinnett, Jane. 'Belles Lettres'. *Westminster Review* 61 (1854): 619–33.

Sinnett, Jane. 'Translator's Preface'. *The Chinese Empire: Forming a Sequel to the Work Entitled "Recollections of a Journey through Tartary and Thibet"*. Evàriste Huc. London: Longman, Brown, Green & Longmans, 1855.

Sinnett, Jane. 'Belles Lettres'. *Westminster Review* 63 (1855): 275–91; 588–604.

Sinnett, Jane. 'Travels in Canada'. *Athenaeum* No. 1711 (11 August 1860): 185–7.

Sinnett, Jane. 'Preface by the Translator'. *Travels in Canada, and Through the States of New York and Pennsylvania* by J.G. Kohl. Trans. Mrs. Percy Sinnett. Revised by the author. London: George Manwaring, 1861.

Southern, Henry. 'Tour of a German Prince'. *Westminster Review* 16 (1832): 225–43.

Spurr, David. *The Rhetoric of Empire. Colonial Discourse in Journalism, Travel Writing, and Imperial Administration*. Durham and London: Duke University Press, 1993.

St. John, Bayle [?] 'A Woman's Voyage round the World'. *Westminster Review* 56 (1851): 249–57.

Staël, Germaine de. 'De L'Esprit des Traductions'. *Oeuvres Complètes de Mme La Baronne de Staël*. 1816. Paris: Treuttel et Würtz, 1821.

Stark, Susanne. *Behind Inverted Commas. Translation and Anglo-German Cultural Relations in the Nineteenth Century*. Clevedon, Somerset: Multilingual Matters, 1999.

Steinmetz, John. 'Modern French Romance'. *Dublin Review* 9 (1840): 353–96.

Stephens, Meic, Ed. *The Oxford Companion to the Literature of Wales*. Oxford: Oxford University Press, 1986.

Sutherland, John. *The Longman Companion to Victorian Fiction*. Harlow, Essex: Longman, 1988.

Swayne, G.C. 'The Art of Travel'. *Blackwood's Edinburgh Magazine* 79 (1856): 593–608.

'Switzerland in 1847'. *Athenaeum* No. 1060 (19 February 1848): 181–3.

Thackeray, William Makepeace. 'The German in England'. *Foreign Quarterly Review* 29 (1842): 370–83.

Thackeray, William Makepeace. 'French Romancers on England'. *Foreign Quarterly Review* 32 (1843): 226–46.

Thackeray, William Makepeace. 'The Kickleburys on the Rhine'. 1850. *Christmas Books, Rebecca and Rowena, and Later Minor Papers, 1849–1861*. Vol. X. London: Henry Froude and Oxford University Press, n.d.

Thomas, Clara. *Love and Work Enough. The Life of Anna Jameson*. London: Macdonald and University of Toronto Press, 1967.

Thomas, J., P.T. Killick, A.A. Mandal and D.J. Skilton. *A Database of Mid-Victorian wood-engraved Illustration*, http://www.dmvi.cf.ac.uk.

Thomson, Thomas. 'Henry Bell'. *Biographical Dictionary of Eminent Scotsmen*. 1870. New York: Georg Olms Verlag, 1971.

Tipping, Marjorie J. 'Frederick Sinnett (1830–1866)'. *Australian Dictionary of Biography*. Ed. Geoffrey Searle and Russel Ward. Vol. 6. Melbourne: Melbourne University Press, 1976.

'Tour of a German Prince'. *Fraser's Magazine* 5 (1832): 533–44.

'Traveller's Library, The'. *Spectator* 24 (28 June 1851), 618.

Trollope, Anthony. 'An Unprotected Female at the Pyramids'. *The Complete Short Stories. Volume Three: Tourists and Colonials*, Ed. Betty Breyer. London: William Pickering, 1991.

Trollope, Frances. *Belgium and Western Germany in 1833*. 2 Vols. London: John Murray, 1835.

Trollope, Frances. *Domestic Manners of the Americans*. 1832. London: Folio Society, 1974.

Trollope, Frances. *Paris and the Parisians in 1835*. 2 Vols. London: Bentley, 1836.

Trollope, Frances. *Vienna and the Austrians*. 2 Vols. London: Richard Bentley, 1838.

Trollope, Frances. *A Visit to Italy*. London: Richard Bentley, 1842.

Turner, Frank M. *The Greek Heritage in Victorian Britain*. New Haven and London: Yale University Press, 1981.

'Two Years in Switzerland and Italy'. *Athenaeum* No. 1728 (8 December 1860), 785–6.

'Two Years in Switzerland and Italy'. *Spectator* 33 (22 December 1860), 1221–2.

University of Nottingham, Manuscripts and Special Collections. Howitt Collection (ACC 1280), Box 1: Mary Howitt to Anna Harrison, Ht/1/1/138/1-2; Ht/1/1/153; and Ht/1/1/168/1, 2 and 3.

Urry, John. *The Tourist Gaze. Leisure and Travel in Contemporary Societies*. London: Sage, 1990.

Vaughan, Adrian. *Isambard Kingdom Brunel. Engineering Knight-Errant*. London: John Murray, 1991.

Vaughan, Robert and Henry Allon. 'Our Epilogue on Books'. *British Quarterly Review* 18 (1853): 569–70.

Venuti, Lawrence. 'Translation as cultural politics: Regimes of domestication in English'. *Textual Practice* 7/2 (1993): 208–23.

Venuti, Lawrence. *The Translator's Invisibility. A History of Translation*. London: Routledge, 1995.

Venuti, Lawrence. *The Scandals of Translation. Towards an Ethics of Difference*. London: Routledge, 1998.

Warren, Samuel. 'Uncle Tom's Cabin'. *Blackwood's Edinburgh Magazine* 74 (1853): 393–423.

'Welsh Fiction'. *Monthly Review* 160 (1843): 431–68.

Wilson, John (Christopher North). 'Noctes Ambrosianae No. LXI'. *Blackwood's Edinburgh Magazine* 31 (1832): 693–720.

Wilson, Mona. 'Travel and Holidays'. *Early Victorian England, 1830–1865*. Ed. G.M. Young. 2 Vols. London: Oxford University Press and Humphrey Milford, 1934.

Wiseman, Nicholas. 'Superficial Travelling – Dickens – Trollope'. *Dublin Review* 14 (1843): 255–68.

Withey, Lynne. *Grand Tours and Cook's Tours*. New York: Aurum Press, 1997.

Wolff, Janet. *Feminine Sentences*. Cambridge: Polity, 1990.

Wolff, Janet. *Resident Alien. Feminist Cultural Criticism*. Cambridge: Polity, 1995.

Wordsworth, William. 'I am not One who much or oft delight'. *William Wordsworth*. Ed. Stephen Gill. Oxford: Oxford University Press, 1984.

Index

For detailed Safety Concerns and Information please contact our
representative GPSR/jurinfo@taylorandfrancis.com Heyne & Huber
Verlag GmbH, Raubgerstadt 24, 80311 München Germany

THE NINETEENTH CENTURY

The Nineteenth Century Series general editors are
Vincent Newey, Professor Emeritus of English,
and Joanne Shattock, Director of the Victorian Studies Centre,
at the University of Leicester.
The series covers the full spectrum of nineteenth-century cultures.
Central to this project are original studies in literature and history, but it
also includes texts of the period.

'... an authoritative study of an important area of women's participation in the profession
of writing, engagingly written and persuasively argued. It makes a timely and effective
intervention in current critical debates about translation and travel literature, and
broadens our understanding of Britain's interactions with other nations and cultures in
the nineteenth century.'
— Hilary Fraser, Birkbeck, University of London, UK

Judith Johnston taught at the University of Western Australia and is now an Honorary
Associate at the University of Sydney.

an **informa** business

Routledge
Taylor & Francis Group
www.routledge.com

ISBN 978-1-138-24583-9

9 781138 245839

Religion in the Neoliberal Age

Political Economy and Modes of Governance

Edited by Tuomas Martikainen and François Gauthier

Ashgate AHRC/ESRC Religion and Society Series